WHY I BELIEVE IN NARNIA

33 Reviews & Essays
on the Life & Work of
C. S. Lewis

JAMES COMO

Why I Believe in Narnia
Copyright © 2008 James Como
Allentown, PA

All rights reserved. Except in the case of quotations embodied in critical articles or reviews, no part of this book may be reproduced or transmitted in any form or by any means, electronic or mechanical, including photocopying, recording, or by any information storage or retrieval system, without written permission of the publisher. For information, contact Zossima Press www.Zossima.com

Zossima Press titles may be purchased for business or promotional use or special sales.

ISBN 0-9723221-8-3

To the members of the

New York C. S. Lewis Society,

then and there, here and now.

"But, for a Christian, there are, strictly speaking, no chances. A secret Master of the Ceremonies has been at work. . . . Let us not reckon without our Host."

— *The Four Loves*

Table of Contents

Whenever the original publication was *CSL: The Bulletin of the New York C. S. Lewis Society* the provenance has been given as such, no matter the venue of its republication, as the *CSL* version would be the more ample and accurately reflect my intention. The only exception is the first item, in which case the *Chesterton Review* version does the latter. Of course, inevitably there are small changes that reflect sounder . . . authorial judgment . . . than prevailed originally.

	Foreword	*i*
	Preface	*v*
I.	**Reviews**	
	1. Spirit in Bondage (1991) *All My Road Before Me: The Diary of C. S. Lewis* *The Chesterton Review*, XXVII.3&4 (August/November, 1991[special issue]), pp. 479-485.	3
	2. Routes of Regression (1982) *Brothers & Friends: The Diary of W. H. Lewis* *CSL*, no. 158, December 1982.	11
	3. Land of Shadows, *and* Even Though . . . (1993, 1994) Lord Attenborough's *Shadowlands* *CSL*, no. 282, April 1993 and *VII: An Anglo-American Literary Review*, 11 (1994), pp. 31-33.	19
	4. Land of Light: Not Quite a Movie Review (2006) *Narnia: The Lion, the Witch and the Wardrobe* *CSL*, no. 411, January-February 2006.	31
	5. *The Magic Never Ends* (2001) A television documentary *VII: An Anglo-American Literary Review*, 18 (2001), pp. 115-16.	35

6. Messages of Hope (2004) 39
   C. S. Lewis at the BBC: Messages of Hope in the Darkness of War.
   VII: An Anglo-American Literary Review, 21 (2004), pp. 109-110.

7. Faith(less) v. Reason(able) (2002) 43
   Armand Nicholi's *The Question of God*
   National Review, May 20, 2002.

8. The People's New Clothes: A Biography, Its Readers, and Its Subject (1975) 47
   C. S. Lewis: A Biography, by Roger Lancelyn Green and Walter Hooper *CSL,* no. 63, January 1975.

9. As Secondary Sources Go ... *Il Libro de Tutti Libri* (1996) ... 53
   C. S. Lewis: A Companion and Guide
   CSL, nos. 323-324, September-October 1996.

10. A Sophisticated Man (2004) 57
    The Collected Letters. Vol. II: Books, Broadcasts and War 1931-1949
    CSL, no. 403, September-October 2004.

11. Arc of Surrender (2007) 61
    The Collected Letters of C. S. Lewis. Three Volumes.
    The New Criterion, 25:7 (March 2007), pp. 60-64.

II. Critical Views

12. Broadening the Lewisian Context (1981) 71
    CSL, no. 134, January 1981.

13. The Prophetic Realist and *The Abolition of Man* (2003) 79
    Broadening the Lewisian Context, Part Two
    Closing address, VII Symposium of the New York
    C. S. Lewis Society, August 10, 2003.

14. Culture and Public Philosophy: Another C. S. Lewis (2007) ... 85
    Broadening the Lewisian Context, Part Three
    Plenary address, October 27, 2007. *C. S. Lewis: The Man and His Work,* October 26-27, 2007, Southeastern College at Wake Forest.

15. Disobedience and Self-discovery (1998)   101
Reflections on Meaning in *Till We Have Faces* [**to Eternity**]
Adapted from a lecture delivered in the Great Hall of Cooper
Union, November 13, 1998 for *C. S. Lewis: The First Hundred
Years*, a Conference of the Wethersfield Institute.

16. *The Screwtape Letters*: of Evil, and Its Antagonists (2008)   117
Plenary address, March 15, 2008, *The Nature of Evil as Depicted in
Christian Literature*, Nassau Community College Center for
Catholic Studies.

17. Belief in *Perelandra*: Myth, Frazer and Jung (1972)   127
CSL, no. 38, December 1972.

18. C.S. Lewis in Milton Criticism (1972)   139
CSL, no. 36, October 1972.

19. The Book Reviewer: An Enjoyment (2008)   143
Delivered to The New York C. S. Lewis Society, April 11, 2008.

20. The Critical Principles of C. S. Lewis (1971)   155
CSL, no. 17, March 1971.

21. *Rhetorica Religii* (1999)   169
Renascence, 51:1 winter, 1999 [lead article, special issue].

22. Lewis, C. S. (2006)   179
American Conservatism: An Encyclopedia, edd. Bruce Frohnen,
Jeremy Beer, and Jeffrey O. Nelson. ISI, 2006.

III. Personal Views

23. A Clerke of Oxenforde (1974)   183
CSL, no. 61, November 1974.

24. A Toast (1979)   187
CSL, no. 121, November 1979.

25. A Man for Our Season (2007)   189
Strictly Right: William F. Buckley, Jr., and the American Conservative Movement
CSL, no. 420, July-August 2007.

26. A Faithful Steward: Walter Hooper (1992)   191
Crisis, February, 1992, pp. 34-37.

27. The Seeing Eye (1994)   199
CSL, nos. 297-299 July-September 1994.

28. Tides of Timelessness (1997)   207
CSL, nos. 337-338, November-December 1997.

29. Why Not in the World? (2005)   215
Preface to the third edition of *C. S. Lewis at the Breakfast Table* (*Remembering C. S. Lewis*), Ignatius Press, 2005.

30. Neo-Narnia? (2001)   223
A Narnia Editorial *and* a *New York Times* Letter
CSL, no. 379-380, May-June 2001.

31. Why I Believe in Narnia (2005)   227
Revisiting Narnia: Fantasy, Myth and Religion in C. S. Lewis's Chronicles, ed. Shanna Caughey. BenBella Books, 2005.

32. Along the Way   239
Forthcoming in a collection of recollections from Baker Books (2009), *Mere Christian* ed. Andrew Lazo and Mary Anne Phemister.

33. Mere Lewis (1994)   243
The Wilson Quarterly, XXVIII.2 (Spring, 1994), pp. 109-117.

Index   255

Foreword

by Clara Sarrocco

In a letter written to Dom Bede Griffiths, OSB on December 21, 1941, C.S. Lewis stated: "Is any pleasure on earth as great as a circle of Christian friends . . . ?" When I was faced with the task of writing a dissertation, I confessed to Jim that I was uncertain how to begin. Being the consummate rhetorician, he outlined in fifteen minutes the procedure which guided me to the completion of the work. Joining him and his wife for dinner, sharing ideas, enjoying their friends and having the pleasure of meeting their children and grandchildren is truly to participate in that "circle of Christian friends," for which one can only express eternal gratitude. That is the light in which I offer the following.

When C.S. Lewis was asked what inspired him to write the *Chronicles of Narnia*, he replied, "all my seven Narnian books . . . began with seeing pictures in my head . . . . Some of these pictures have a common flavour . . . which groups them together. Keep quiet and watch and they will begin joining themselves up . . . ." Well, the New York C.S. Lewis Society began with a letter. Henry Noel, a Christian convert owing largely to Lewis's influence, wrote one to *National Review* inviting, "all those living in or near New York City who are longstanding admirers of Lewis books, or who, for whatever reason, cherish feelings of affection and gratitude toward his memory, to get in touch with me."

The "common flavour" was noticed by twelve people who began joining on November 1, 1969. Among the twelve was a very young teacher and his new bride, James and Alexandra Como. Jim and Xandra, as they are known to those who know and love them, are now proud grandparents as well as godparents of The New York C.S. Lewis Society. One of the questions asked at that first meeting was, "do we hope the Society will become a permanent affair and, if so, what leads us to hope that this will be the case?" Well, not only is the Society soon to celebrate its 40th Anniversary but it has published a bulletin, first monthly and then bi-monthly, for all of those 40 years. The dedication of this book explains the underlying cause of this longevity, as well as its richness. I attended my first meeting of the Society with some trepidation. At that time the meetings were held in the library of the Rudolf Steiner School on 79th Street and Fifth Avenue in Manhattan. I had some negative questions about C.S. Lewis and over coffee I posed them to Jim. To my surprise he agreed with me. I realized then that this was the place to be because Truth takes priority.

Which brings us to this book. These essays and reviews are a good deal of what Jim wrote over the years of his affiliation with the New York Society but also what he wrote and spoke of CSL generally for very many other venues. (The table of contents tells the reader the original light-of-day for each piece.) But my most recurring experience is with him at our Society. Once he invited some of his students from York College to attend a meeting of the Society and to do dramatic readings from Lewis books. The students were wonderful, enjoyed themselves thoroughly, and were obviously quite happy to give credit to their teacher. At the December meeting, the members always read from the cycle of plays *The Man Born to be King* by Dorothy L. Sayers. When he was assigned the role of Judas Iscariot, he performed admirably even though the tenor of the character was so distant from his own – then complained that the role was underwritten! Memories abound.

He interviewed Lord Richard Attenborough, Sir Anthony Hopkins and Debra Winger during the filming of the 1993 film *Shadowlands*. Sir Anthony played C.S. Lewis, Debra Winger Lewis's wife, Joy Davidman. Lord Attenborough directed the film. The interviews became the basis of two presentations at the Society. He also was interviewed by PBS for *The Question of God* with Dr. Armand Nicolai from the Harvard Medical School. The Society's members were quite proud to be able to say, "we know that person. He is one of us." He names among his dearest friends Walter Hooper, the Lewis scholar and foremost editor of Lewis materials. It has been a long and enduring friendship, and Hooper has attended meetings and symposia sponsored by the New York Society at Jim's behest. His love of the thoughts and writings of C.S. Lewis is greatly intertwined with his own life and thought. For example, one sees from the articles and essays in this book the same Christian and humanistic approach that marked his dozens of highly-praised lectures at the Fifth Avenue Presbyterian Church, along with his variously-faceted view of C.S. Lewis: the shape of his life and rhetoric; the lineaments of his thinking; his cultural influence, reputation and personal impact.

❧ Foreword ❧

We will never know how many people have come to discover the writings of C.S. Lewis and have had life-changing experiences as a result. Nor will we ever know how many have come to Lewis through Jim's efforts; and that is the way it should be: known only to God. We do know, however, that this collection of essays shows us C.S. Lewis in a sometimes startling light, reminiscent of the Narnian light of the lamppost, with Lucy and Mr. Tumnus, which began as a picture in the mind of C.S. Lewis so many years ago. I hope that these essays inspire many to read all of Lewis's books. *Why I Believe in Narnia* has been written and brought together by one of Lewis's most ardent admirers, of whom it can be said, as Chaucer said of his Clerk of Oxenford ". . . . And gladly wolde he lerne, and gladly teche."

Gratias tibi ago, Jim.

Preface

A quick look at the Table of Contents and the few details of each article will tell the reader how long this book has been in the making. Actually, the earliest piece, "The Critical Principles of C. S. Lewis," saw the public light-of-day as a presentation to the New York C. S. Lewis Society some time before its publication in *CSL: The Bulletin of the New York C. S. Lewis Society*. That amplified the first piece of writing I had ever done on CSL: a senior paper for a literary criticism course taught by the redoubtable Dorothy Jones at Queens College of the City University of New York, from which I was graduated in 1967. In those days, serious teachers of literature read Lewis' professional work assiduously, but Professor Jones, a devoted member of the Episcopal Church, had read more than that. Her stern intellectual sympathy was palpable, refreshing and welcome. Then there is Forbes Iverson Hill. Intellectual and personal elegance are rare enough, rarer still when in the company of enormous imaginative sympathy: thus it was (and remains) with the man who directed my master's thesis on *Perelandra*, my first rhetoric teacher and first boss, the least obtrusive and most understanding of mentors, and, more than forty years later, still the best of all of these.

The most vivid writing memory, still the most painful, remains that of "A Clerke of Oxenforde," part of the Society fifth anniversary celebration. I was on a sabbatical from York College during the fall of 1974. My wife, very young son, Walter Hooper, and I were just arriving for the first time into family quarters in the upper floor of 286 Iffley Road. Barely had I dropped the suitcases when the phone rang: my brother Joe would tell me that our father had just, abruptly and unexpectedly, died. This devastation was mitigated by one fact: returning briefly to America for the wake and funeral I was leaving my wife and son in the care, not only of Walter, but of his wonderful mother Madge (Mrs. "Hooper-Hooper") and her sister, Aunt Twiggy, who were visiting Walter from North Carolina. There are no coincidences. When I returned very little work would get done, but writing that essay was a great comfort.

My presentations to the New York Society are always very enjoyable, but here I record what seems to me an odd response of my own. Though I am a teacher of rhetoric and a practiced public speaker, and have addressed large audiences often filled with strangers, I am always slightly nervous when addressing the Society, in a room with a few dozen people most of whom I know and who know me, some for decades. Certainly my being a founding member of the Society (the first such in the world, dispositive in re-establishing Lewis' popularity and reputation when it was waning in the late Sixties and early Seventies, and now nearing its fortieth year) has something to do with that – as well as how concentratedly knowledgeable are our members. I am deeply grateful to the Holy Spirit for allowing the Society to abide, and to do so with such zest, joy, and high intellection; and I am grateful for all the opportunities I've been afforded by my friends and colleagues to think aloud, to take some chances, and to polish an idea or two. (Although some I've left unpolished. I notice that I've *proven* Lewis based *Perelandra* on a combination of Frazer's *The Golden Bough* and the psychology of C. G. Jung, even though I did not set out to do so. Precisely here, as in so much scholarship, a Lewis letter is helpful; to Merril Rogers, January 20, 1963, Lewis writes: "Speculations about the Grail have a strange way of causing people who have found something to claim that they have found *everything*.")

Among my most enjoyable addresses was one of the most recent, "Culture and Philosophy" at Southeastern Baptist Seminary and College in Wake Forest, North Carolina. Professor Michael Travers, with his colleagues at the L. Russ Bush Center for Faith and Culture, mounted an extraordinary conference: rich, varied, authoritative – and exceedingly congenial. The venue of the address was a local, most beautiful, Baptist church. I worked very hard on the piece, my intention being to suggest that there is a relatively untrodden path in Lewis' thought and that Lewis scholars might follow it. The immediate response was, I happily report, more than a speaker could hope for; but a private comment immediately thereafter seemed to top that. An officer (I think) of the church approached me to say that "today you have made history." "Made history?" I asked. "Surely," I demurred, "my suggestions were not of *that* magnitude"; and I demurred *humbly*, or as humbly as I had it in me to be. "Oh no. History. You made *history* here today." "Well," I muttered, "thank you. Thank you very much." (Too much Elvis there?) "Yes," he continued, "today is the first time in history the word *orgasm* has been uttered in a Baptist church!" He gave my shoulder a squeeze, turned, and walked away chuckling, doubtless not hearing my lamely muttered, "but I was quoting Lewis . . . " It took me a few seconds to realize that the gentleman had merely been funnin' a Yankee – and a good job he had made of it, too.

My very favorite presentation is one I assisted in but did not conduct. At the May 2001 meeting my wife, Alexandra, spoke of Warnie Lewis, for whom she has a deep-rooted affection, at first owing to their mutual love of French history and society, especially during the reign of the Sun King, then to the man as revealed in his diary. The Major's books on France prompted Alexandra to write a fan letter to him, allowing that she believed him a better writer than his brother Jack. "Well," Hooper reports Warnie as having said, "now you see Walter? That makes two of us!" My job that evening, sitting next to Alexandra, was simply to read quotations and to fill in any CSL matter that was required. I spoke very little. The Society has never better understood or appreciated Warnie Lewis than we did that evening, or since.

I have repeated myself (e.g. a number of applications of the thinking of the critic Wayne Booth) – or is that consistency? Rhetoric has mattered greatly to me, as it did to Lewis, though ambivalently. The discipline has been at the heart of Western education and literary practice, and its explanatory power ought to be understood and applied, not least to the work of a man who understood it so well, applied it so assiduously (in fact, unrelentingly), and feared it so greatly. Often (too often?) vexed by the fact that a certain aspect of Lewis takes up most of the reputation oxygen, I've tried to suggest a re-focusing of our attention on Other Lewises by way of fresh avenues of study. For example, we should place Lewis among constellations of writers other than the Inklings, argue more frequently with the great man, and note, examine, and assess parts of his work and life (there were nine of them, along with four selves, all pivotally influenced by five key deaths) that he . . . guarded. There is much guarding in Lewis: the full story of what he overcame – what he converted from (and it was not atheism) – is yet to be told. (The reader here will find my own efforts relatively early on and in my *Branches to Heaven: The Geniuses of C. S. Lewis*.)

We need more tough work on *Pilgrim's Regress* (especially as a template of nearly all Lewis would write), on his anti-Catholicism (Tolkien seems to have thought him a bigot, and Lewis came close to admitting as much – and I would aver that, if true, it is remarkably unimportant, remarkably, because how such a trait comes *not* to matter, which it does not, must be fascinating), on why *Till We Have Faces* is one of the two greatest first-person modern novels in the language, the other being *Lolita*. (How is Orual like Humbert Humbert?) Lewis' reputations and the influences upon them, too, warrant our attention. Different original venues for some works, as well as different styles of presentation, surely would have altered both popular and critical views of his person: metaphorically and literally, one cannot tell any book (see the front of the first American paperback version of *Perelandra*) by its cover.

Not long after writing that paper for Prof. Jones I visited Wheaton College for the first time and met Prof. Kilby. He gave me his personal notes on *Perelandra*, and his letter would introduce me to Walter Hooper in Oxford, where (within a very few years) I would dive into a treasure trove of Lewis papers and lose myself in the Bodleian Library. These four elements – Walter Hooper and Oxford, Clyde Kilby, The Wade Center (as it is now designated: it wasn't even close to that when the gracious and omni-capable Ruth Cording presided over the single aisle and two file cabinets that were the "Lewis Collection" in 1967) – these four elements have been like the vertebrae of a very strong spine that supports nearly the whole body of C. S. Lewis scholarship.

In addition to thanking these two men I am enormously happy to have an opportunity to thank all my friends from the New York C. S. Lewis Society. Among these are many no longer with us: Phyllis and Byron Lambert, Hope and John Kirkpatrick, Jack Boies, Bill Linden, Richard Hodgens . . . so many. And of the many who, every month and in between the months, continue to make the Society tick, I thank particularly Mary Gehringer, Bob Merchant, Bob Trexler, Gene McGovern, Gordon Weston, Maggie Goodman, Bev Van Rooy: drawing the line is as arbitrary an act as any act could be. But especially I thank Clara Sarrocco (here, the title Corresponding Secretary is like designating Joe DiMaggio an "outfielder"), who without knowing it planted the mental seed of this book. And thanks to my wonderful uncle Lou (the "unc") who long ago marveled at what fruit that first term paper would bear.

In the near future I hope to argue what I posit now, that above all, Hope is the essence of Lewis' achievement and that the single most applicable verse of Sacred Scripture to Lewis is from Romans: "May the God of hope fill you with all joy and peace in believing, so that by the power of the Holy Spirit you may abound in hope" (15:13).

Bronxville, New York
Memorial Day, 2008

Part 1

REVIEWS

1

Spirit in Bondage

Our knowledge of C.S. Lewis is marked by a very great gap, that "one huge and complex episode" he omits from *Surprised by Joy* and which he doubts "has much to do with the subject of the book," his conversion and its spiritual and intellectual antecedents. He is not disingenuous. Between the ages of twenty-three and twenty-eight Lewis – home from the Great War, supported at Oxford by a patient and devoted father, possessed of staggering and already well-finished intellectual gifts – should have been done with adolescent dues-paying and been well on his way to the man he would become. In fact, he was curiously out-of-sync, his life backyards. He was a householder who, entirely unprepared to hold a house, worked hard to make a go of it, at once busy, anxious, responsible, self-indulgent and profoundly dishonest. Only thereafter would he become the bachelor don known to the world as one of the greatest Christian apologists of the century.

The household is, of course, the one presided over by Mrs. Moore, the mother of Lewis' slain army buddy Paddy Moore and about whom Walter Hooper writes (in a fine Introduction) that "the notion of sexual intimacy between [Mrs. Moore and Lewis] must be regarded as likely." Referred to as "D" throughout, she was the person who both urged that the diary be kept and served as its primary audience: Lewis regularly read it aloud to her. When the diary begins Lewis, Mrs. Moore, and her young daughter Maureen have been a ménage for some three years; not until four years after the last entry would Lewis become Christian. So Mrs. Moore is axiomatic to the story. This household is Lewis' settled life: where D and Maureen are, there is home.

Thus the "huge and complex episode" is a great deception. Albert Lewis, his long-widowered father, knew nothing about his younger son's household. And though he faithfully supported his son throughout the undergraduate years – generously and naively, for Lewis sometimes lied, then rationalized the lie, in order to get more money from Albert – he is subjected to abuse in several entries.

On Christmas Day, 1922, Lewis records that, while walking to church, Albert and the brothers were discussing the time of sunrise. "My father [said] rather absurdly that it must have risen already, or else it wouldn't be light." Later, Albert admonishes Warnie for wanting to keep his coat on while taking Communion. Lewis could not "help wondering why" it would be "most disrespectful." At that point he remembers that Mrs. Moore would be turning out for Maureen's "first communion, and this somehow emphasized the dreariness of this most Uncomfortable [sic] sacrament." Earlier that year Lewis, during a visit, had a "curious feeling" that his father had "given [him] up . . . this time one felt – rather pathetically – that the effort was over for good on his side. I can truly say I am sorry I have contributed so little to his happiness: whether he deserves it or not is another matter." He complains of needing more money or of not being able to receive Mrs. Moore's letters in Ireland when the clandestine route (Arthur Greeves or, later, Mrs. Greeves) breaks down; wonders how in the world he could have spent more than the expenses he falsely reported to Albert; and protests at the suggestion that to save money he spend more time at home, which would be "nerves, loneliness and mental stagnation." This, upon Lewis' receiving a letter in which Albert offers to raise his son's allowance. Taken together these are the most distasteful words Lewis ever wrote. Worse, they contrast maddeningly with what Lewis had to say on Mrs. Moore, whose kindness and generosity are regularly extolled. The irony peaks when Lewis praises her for being "so anxious not to influence" him and later when he says of her that she "hates a lie of all things."

Withal, we see a contingent life, one approaching a frontier. Lewis is brilliant, persistent, capacious, and except with (and to) Albert, tolerant, honest and loyal; there is enough to suggest that this young man will achieve greatness, but not a hint that he would do so as he did. When he writes that Maureen's confirmation is like the slaughtering of a pig, or insists that in combat he had "never sunk so low" as to pray, we are reminded of just what he was converted *from* and must appreciate the depth of that conversion. Like some forests, this book is almost always thick and heavily shaded (though with unexpected clearings and welcome patches of sunlight) and scored by interesting, promising footpaths. And dangerous, for it is a Wood of Error. In it the young man who would become a great Knight of the Cross has lost his way.

But that way is varied indeed and often surprising to the reader who already knows much of Lewis. He was, for example, a great player of games: chess, croquet, bridge, ping-pong, and (most assiduously) badminton, complaining after a loss that he "was off [his] game." He frequently attends concerts and (often with Maureen, who usually seems the prototypically annoying little sister) the theatre. Once he visits the National Gallery. Routinely, though, he is walking and talking. When he is not meeting with the Martlets, the Philosophical Society, or (later) the Kolbitars to speak or to listen (he is a very good listener), he is with friends, especially A.K. Hamilton-Jenkin, Leo Baker, and Owen Barfield, who Lewis regards as the most gifted person he knows (himself included) and who is, simply, one of the best and best-balanced people anyone could know. (Mrs. Barfield, by the way, likes Lewis dearly because he will have nothing to do with Anthroposophy and thus brings Barfield some relief from what she regards as obsessive nonsense.) Arthur Greeves (here sometimes a comic figure) and Lewis' beloved brother, Warnie, are prominent.

He records several dreams, some dramatic and highly suggestive. He and his friends comment on everything, but psychoanalysis (he has read Freud), women, marriage and sex (he reads Havelock Ellis) appear frequently enough to qualify as recurring motifs. There is cynicism about marriage but not about women, if you allow that they are really "not worth knowing till they have passed forty." The diary includes episodes, long and short, that are exciting, even terrifying. Mrs. Moore's brother, the Doc, is the man to whom Lewis referred in his autobiography as having lost his mind. Here we get the entire two-week, harrowing tale of horror. More exciting, though less terrible, is the tale of Maisie, a young women abused by her parents and, in effect, rescued by Lewis. There are Lewis' academic achievements, and throughout we encounter foreshadowings of his later thinking and writing: on Milton, Chaucer, and the personal heresy, for example. (Surely a description of the pathetic Doc anticipates the Unman of *Perelandra*?)

We are struck overwhelmingly by Lewis' appetite for work of all sorts. On almost every page he prepares lunch, picks berries, washes up, takes down wallpaper, cleans rugs, runs errands, buys groceries, and brings hot-water bottles to Mrs. Moore. Along the way he wins a triple first, writes a dissertation on "The Hegemony of Moral Values," seriously inquires into the Civil Service (the test is harder than the Schools exams at Oxford), applies for three different academic positions (losing all three), and finally – finally! – publishes *Dymer*. Seldom does Lewis sleep more than five or six hours a night; once, at one in the morning and really tired, he can do no more than read Book Two of the *Republic*. Thus, although he continually notes the appearance, especially the faces, of others, he pays scant attention to himself. Once he goes to town to buy trousers because the one pair he already owns borders upon immodesty; on another visit to town he buys one razor blade. He is no Boswell or Pepys, his tone almost always aloof and his entries short; but he is a superb portraitist and raconteur, with an eye for detail and a ready wit. Even "two years ago," he notes after a swim, "every second man had a wound mark"; these undergraduates, though, are not veterans. And near the end of the diary, now himself a don, he recounts a discussion of the question "'Whether God can understand his own necessity': whereupon Hardie got down St. Thomas' *Summa* and after ferreting in the index suddenly pronounced, without any intention of being funny, 'He doesn't understand anything.'"

A straightforward account: always interesting, frequently provocative, sometimes gripping, and often amusing, even if – as diaries are wont to be – not uniformly engaging. But this is a Wood of Error and therefore not what it seems. Albert was the object only of the most egregious deception. A longer perspective than that afforded by the diary *per se* reveals yet deeper levels of falsehood. Lewis' life was not only backwards, but inside-out as well.

In *Surprised by Joy* Lewis described the two lives he led from his mother's death until his conversion: the Inner, of painful longing (that desire he famously called Joy, or *Sehnsucht*); and the Outer, of the intellect. The diary, however, presents a third life, or at least a major variant of the second – the Official. It was "self-regarding," as the Outer is described in the autobiography; and Joy hardly makes an appearance. The intellection is at least adumbrated (though not the influential Great War, a prominent feature of the autobiographical landscape and an omission noted with surprise by Owen Barfield). Yet, notwithstanding its many causes for complaint, Lewis' life during this period was not the Outer Life of the autobiography: it simply does not seem, either to the reader *or to the diarist*, especially "grim and meaningless", as the autobiographer would call it some thirty years later. Thus, as the later book is essentially true, then the diary, like most Official Stories, must be false. The deception of Albert envelopes a deception of Mrs. Moore who, although the primary audience of the diary, *learns nothing of the crucial Inner Life*. It is utterly impossible that Lewis was unaware of it. Could he have been merely inattentive to it? Or repressed it? Hardly: the Inner Life simply did not fit the Story nor suit its overseer, just as the menage itself required a cover story – residential undergraduate life – to deceive Albert.

True to this dishonesty is the diarist's failure even to mention the book that was among the most influential upon his Inner Life. G.K. Chesterton is praised in *Surprised by Joy* as having "more sense than all the other moderns put together; bating, of course, his Christianity." There Lewis ascribes a pivotal role to Chesterson's *The Everlasting Man*, which showed that Christianity itself was very sensible 'apart from its Christianity'." In the diary there is no reference to *The Everlasting Man*, and we can note that among the several references to Chesterton the most suggestive is one he fails to make. And it is no surprise that George MacDonald is referred to even fewer times than Chesterton.

A chart of this psychological redoubt would be fascinating. It includes the interplay of the death of Lewis' mother when he was not yet ten years old; his resentment of his father, who not only could be insufferable but who failed – with God the Father – to save his mother; Mrs. Moore, a mother-surrogate, and instrument of punishment, even of revenge, upon his father, and a willing partner in the *Weiberherrschaft* he alludes to in his correspondence with Arthur Greeves; and *Dymer*, wherein "a man ... on some mysterious bride, begets a monster: which monster, as soon as it has killed its father, becomes a god," as Lewis himself put it. Not only did he admit the psychoanalysts would have a field day with the poem, but in 1926, when it was complete, he would write, ironically, "Of course *I'm not Dymer.*" Perhaps not. But he was what we would today call "unintegrated": an Inner Life apart from the Outer, two related but separate Official Stories apart from the first two lives, and a Deeper Life, that of the dormant Christian.

Not-too-roughly speaking, Lewis' liaison with Mrs. Moore began as he was preparing for publication (1919) his cycle of lyrics, *Spirits in Bondage*, and ended with his conversion, shortly after the publication of *Dymer*. (The menage would continue until Mrs. Moore's death in January 1951.) Part I of the cycle is entitled "The Prison House" and includes "Dungeon Gates":

> So piteously the lonely soul of man
> Shudders before this universal plan,
> So grievous is the burden and the pain,
> So heavy weighs the long, material chain
> From cause to cause, too merciless for hate,
>
>   *   *   *
>
> O! but we shall keep
> Our vision still, One moment was enough,
> We know we are not made of mortal stuff.
> And we can bear all trials that come after,
> The hate of men and the fool's loud bestial laughter

And Nature's rule and cruelties unclean,
For we have seen the Glory – we have seen.

Symptomatically, the "atheist" sought escape in Mrs. Moore. But the would-be-fugitive, still a witness to Joy/Glory, remains a poet – an imaginative man – and "imagination," as Lewis would later write, "is the organ of meaning." So he devotes himself to the writing of *Dymer*; and its very last stanza epitomizes the purgative, therapeutic and catalytic effect the writing must have had on him:

> And from the distant corner of day's birth
> He heard clear trumpets blowing and bells ring,
> A noise of great good coming into earth
> And such a music as the dumb would sing
> If Balder had led back the blameless spring
> With victory, with the voice of charging spears,
> And in white land long-lost Saturnian years.

The poet in him knew that he was ready to leave all Official Stories behind. Shortly after the publication of *Dymer*, Lewis virtually reconciled with his father, who shortly thereafter died. And very soon after that Lewis professed belief, though not yet Christian belief, and prayed. So Lewis' acceptance of Christianity was less a conversion than a recovery, "no sudden plunge into a new life," as Warren Lewis has written, "but rather a slow steady convalescence from a deep-seated spiritual illness of long standing."

The last line of the diary reads, "Is there never to be any peace or comfort?" The apologist who years later would write "We Have No 'Right to Happiness'" is here gestating; and the choice of title, taken from *Dymer*, I.1, seems just right: "You stranger, long before your glance can light / Upon these words, time will have washed away / The moment when I first took pen to write / With all my road before me." And we are grateful to God that he finally traveled that road, "round the whole world till [he] came back to the same place." Whereunto, and how, did the reconverted fugitive arrive, after escaping (like Prince Rilian loosed from the Silver Chair) his bondage? One of the books most beloved by Lewis was James Stephens's *The Crock of Gold*. It ends with an answer:

> "They swept through the goat tracks and the little boreens and the curving roads. Down the city they went dancing and singing; among the streets and the shops telling their sunny tale; not heeding the malignant eyes and the cold brows as the sons of Balor looked sidewards. And they took the philosopher from his prison, even the

intellect of man they took from the hands of the doctors and lawyers, from the sly priests, from the professors whose mouths are gorged with sawdust, and the merchants who sell blades of grass … and then they returned again, dancing and singing, to the country of the gods."

2

Routes of Regression

"But, for a Christian, there are, strictly speaking, no chances. A secret Master of the Ceremonies has been at work. Christ, who said to the disciples 'Ye have not chosen me, but I have chosen you,' can truly say to every group of Christian friends 'You have not chosen one another but I have chosen you for one another.' . . . At this feast it is He who has spread the board and it is He who has chosen the guests. . . . Let us not reckon without our Host."

— *The Four Loves*

Kilby and Mead's edition of the Major's diaries reveals a Lewisian character so deep and rich, a brotherhood and friendship of such devotion and sheer magnitude, that only this quotation (and its context) could apprehend them. I may as well say now as in conclusion: C. S. Lewis was providentially served, indeed, to have had such a brother — such an elder brother — and friend; and we are immensely fortunate to have this book, a praiseworthy achievement.

We have known Warnie as Jack's "greatest friend" because the latter has told us so, many times; and we have known him as Jack's secretary, as the compiler of their family papers, as memoirist, editor, and as well-regarded historian; we have even known him as a troubled man, an alcoholic. (We seem always to have known him as an ex-soldier, the Major.) But until now we had never met him. We have known, for example, that he was an Inkling; but we have never known how — and how much — it mattered to him that he *was* one. We have known that he complemented CSL; but we did not know that he was very much the Ground (in this world) of his brother's life. And if we know him to have been a gentleman, and a courtly man, we could not have suspected how profoundly and simply *good* a man he was. He was as solid as they come.

Two worlds — Britain and Logres, shall we say? — seem to be with us always. Edmund Wilson, F.R. Leavis, and the early Eliot, Auden, and Muggeridge populate the former; the later Eliot, Auden, and Muggeridge — along with the Inklings, Chesterton, and, say, de la Mare — the latter. Logres is the home (not heaven on earth but heaven in earth) to which we must regress. (A happy word with which to prick psychologism!) For the Lewis brothers, home, or at least its front porch, was Little Lea and Mammy, Boxen and county Down, each other, and joy. Eviction occurred early, with the death of Mammy, the banishment of God, and a prolonged antagonism towards Pappy. Thereafter the brothers wandered for a while; but after Pappy's death they became Christians, and wandering turned into pilgrimage. It is at this point, following a short and useful preamble, that Kilby and Mead pick up the diary in earnest.

1.

At the very first and last, and though in the company of others, Warren was without Jack and thus was virtually alone. In between he travels a route divisible, it seems to me, into four sections, though Kilby and Mead divide it in three: part I, 1912 -1929; Part II, 1930 -1939; Part III, 1939 -1973. The last, however, strongly invites further division at the death of Mrs. Moore in January of 1951. The final nine-and-a-half years form a coda: Jack's absence is poignantly felt, and Warren is a saddening, perhaps himself a sad, figure.

First he is a soldier. In February of 1914 he enters Sandhurst; by November he is fighting in France, and within two years he is promoted to the rank of captain, at which he retires in December of 1932. Along the way he graduates first in his class from Mechanical Transport School (1918), attends an economics course at London University (1926), and serves in Sierra Leone and (twice) in China. He had commanded large supply units and was present during the Japanese attack on Shanghai. (In May of 1940 he would be at Dunkirk.) It is during this period that he travels around the world: an uproarious journey especially noteworthy for his impressions of Los Angeles and of New York. On May 9, 1931, he returns to Christianity.

Thereupon follow the golden years. He is happily and productively at work compiling the Lewis Family Papers; and he is planning, carrying out, and recalling eight annual walking tours with Jack (1931, 1933 - 39). They loved valleys, especially the Wye Valley, to which we are treated by way of some of the most fetching passages in the entire diary. We learn, too, from one harrowing description why they hate snow so tenaciously and enduringly. The tours, and this second stage, end with the onset of World War II. There was alcohol but not alcoholism, and Mrs. Moore had not yet descended to a sort of self-centered insanity. He was not Home, but he once again had one that mattered greatly to him.

By October of 1939 he is at Le Havre and in January of the following year he is promoted to the rank of major. The third stage, marked by contrasts, is underway. After Dunkirk, his participation in, and dependence upon, the Inklings grows steadily. He works, desultorily but happily, at his special interest, the France of Louis XIV. Long a motorcyclist, he becomes a boatsman as well, sailing inland waters in a boat specially built to his liking. But he is drinking more than ever; Jack – with no explicit reference to Warnie – begins to diminish the amount of alcohol available at the Inklings. Each of these elements might have emerged no matter what the state of domestic affairs; yet they do smack of escapism, and if that requires a jailer from whom to escape then there is Mrs. Moore: Minto.

Warren had always noted his spells of depression (and, frequently, his spells of Joy, though he did not call it by that name). Now depression becomes anger and even desperation, on his own and Jack's behalf. The cause is always Minto. The entries describing both her routine insufferableness and her fits of maniacal selfishness, along with Warren's response to them, are vivid and painful – the more so because of his awareness of his own susceptibility to an encroaching uncharity. With respect to Mrs. Moore, the reader of these entries is sorely pressed to judge not.

Thus are both we and the brothers released by her death, which initiates the fourth stage: busy, even exciting, touched by love and sadness, not essentially unsettling, finally contented. *The Splendid Century* (written in 1942) is finally published in 1953, to be followed by seven other books, of which two (including CSL's *Letters*) are edited works. (Although these two appeared after Jack's death, which brings this stage to a close, they were in preparation during the period proper.) Yet these are as much the years of Joy Davidman as they are the years of authorship. At first wary of her, Warren came to respect, then admire, and finally to love Joy. Meetings of the Inklings remain important, but extra-Inkling contacts (with Tolkien, for example) decline in frequency. (He kept steadily and warmly in touch with Parkin, his old army buddy, until that man's death in 1958.) He becomes increasingly aware of his alcoholism and earnestly fights it, not unsuccessfully. When Joy dies, Warren suffers a double blow, for not only did he love her and delight in her presence but Jack's grief burdens Warren even further. And the elder brother is – not for the first time – up to the task. Having been cared for by Jack, Warnie now cares for him: his mere presence, loving and steady, must have been profoundly consoling. Then the brothers were alone together as they had been in the distant past, and they were with each other as they had been always.

2.

Kilby and Mead have achieved a rhythm consonant with the pace and temper of the Major's inner and outer lives. Large gaps between the two are usually unobtrusive, for the prevailing tone of a given sequence is rarely broken abruptly and never simply abandoned. An alert reader (especially one knowledgeable of C. S. Lewis' life and works) begins to anticipate certain episodes and changes of temper and is often satisfied. The surprises are never capricious or facile. It is gratifying to see Warnie live up to the many claims made for him by Jack and testified to by others (Sayers, Tolkien, and Wain, for example), but the unity in this book – its lambent faithfulness – is Warren's own. At the Wade Collection, Wheaton College, I have had great difficulty in gaining access to the entire diary and so cannot judge the representativeness of what is, after all, a mere ten percent of the original, and Kilby and Mead provide a too-brief statement of editorial policy; and the man we meet is possessed of as much integrity and sanity as his more brilliant brother. He is the person we expect him to be – only more so. The few reviews (Kirkus, *The Library Journal, Publisher's Weekly, The National Catholic Register*, as examples) have noticed this and other qualities in terms ranging from objective and mild, to unabashedly partisan, praise.

Preceding the diary *per se* are an introduction (short but insightful and probably by Kilby, who has a gift in this regard: see the invaluable introduction to his CSL anthology *A Mind Awake*), a long, informative, yet choppy and (it seems) erratic, chronology, *two* genealogies, and the editorial note. Part I, sixteen pages long, is marred by typographical ambiguities; the distinction between Lewis and editorial interpolation is obscure. Part II, entries from the thirties, covers 160 pages. Part III, ending on page 302, is followed by the index (perfunctory). Not at all perfunctory, ambiguous or erratic are the photographs (two sets), which are both illustrative and documentary. An attentive reader must be puzzled, though, by the reference (p. 115) to Green and Hooper as editors of *C.S. Lewis: A Biography*, and all readers will be angry if their copies (like mine and, I am told, others') break apart after a sixteen dollar cost and careful handling.

Two important weaknesses deserve special attention. The first of these is the footnotes, persistently annoying. Most of the 293 notes are interesting and helpful but not strictly necessary. A large minority are downright distracting: we ought not to have our enjoyment dispelled in order to be reminded that Tolstoi was Russian. A few, though assertive, are unconvincing. On what grounds am I to believe that "Minto" (Mrs. Moore's nickname) derives from a favored brand of chocolates rather than from an overbearing, late-eighteenth-century viceroy of India (which country lent its name to Warren's juvenilia)? On the other hand, why is the reader not told *that*, besides the Whipsnade bear, there are two Mr. Bultitudes, the bear in That *Hideous Strength* and – almost certainly Lewis' source for the name – the father in F. Anstey's *Vice Versa*? Finally, would the ordinary reader know what a "soaking machine" is? (A guess would be disastrous, for it involves neither a soaking nor a machine.)

The second weakness – of which there is a single instance – is substantive and important. An editorial note on page 227 reads, "an absence of entries in Warren's diary from June 17 until August 14 allows only speculation as to the reason for Jack's foregoing of his promised holiday in deference to Warren's long-anticipated Irish vacation." In fact, speculation is unnecessary. On June 23 (1949), Jack wrote to Arthur Greeves (*They Stand Together*, no. 221) about the forthcoming trip in detail and with enthusiasm; in the next letter (July 2), Jack explains his inability to travel; "W's trouble is to be called 'nervous insomnia' in speaking to Janie and others; but in reality (this for yr. private ear) it is Drink. This bout started about ten days ago." Whence, then, the mystery? Kilby and Mead must know the Lewis-Greeves correspondence, I suppose, as well as anyone, and as early as the Introduction they had adumbrated (emphatically) Warren's alcoholism. Thus the only puzzle is the inconsistency itself.

Withal, there is much more in this book than even the most demanding reader has a right to expect. The commonplaces abound. (Although Jack Lewis' career and books seem slighted, actually the reader, while welcoming Warren's few telling remarks, does not miss the Learned Editorial Analysis.) Often enough the commonplace, too, is revealed in an uncommon light: Warren's comments on Paddy and on Mr. Moore are trenchant. Best of all, and far above all else, the commonplaces are transmuted, somewhere along the way, by the character and perceptiveness of Warren Lewis himself – by the sheer *quiddity* of the man – into incandescent motifs, beacons that illuminate this extraordinary man's route of regression.

Always and frequently depression challenged, just as Joy nourished perseveringly: "Whilst waiting . . . I had one of those blinding flashes of exquisite happiness which come and go like lightning. Always a mysterious thing, and must I think be a direct and individual intimation of heavenly bliss – and a strong hint to strive for it." (October 31, 1948). His imagination was lively and receptive; after all, it was the numinosity of the Buddha of

Kamakura that was instrumental in his conversion, and he loved *The Prelude* all of his life. His intellect was quick, alert, and penetrating. Few questions escaped his curiosity. (Is the best poetry that which is understandable at first reading? How is it that woodpeckers do not bang out their own brains?) I leave it for the reader to say whether or not the entry for November 7, 1933 – in its acuity, concision, and analytical rigor – could not just as well have been written by C. S. Lewis. (The comparison applies equally to narration, description, and the portrayal of character as to exposition and argument; to paraphrase what a critic wrote of Jack upon reviewing *Perelandra*, Warnie could write.)

He had his prejudices, to be sure. Catholicism (never Catholics), Americans (hardly ever America), and Shakespeare's tragedies were puzzling, exasperating, and confoundedly bad, respectively. American women, in particular, he thought the plainest in the world; and though some might think this ironic coming from an Englishman, it comes also from a man who was tolerably fond of women, attractive ones in particular, to whose charms he was not insusceptible: "I also met Shanghai Mary, looking the same as ever, who neatly took advantage of my reminiscent mood to tease me into buying her a bottle of champagne." Perhaps if he had seen *Hamlet* in the company of an attractive woman he would have thought differently of it:

> There is one admirable character in this, Polonius. . . . but alas all too soon he was killed. . . . As for *Hamlet* [sic] I have rarely conceived such a sudden antipathy to any character, and there was an intolerable deal of him . . . this snivelling, attitudinizing, platitudinizing arch bore. I could have screamed.

Yet throughout no prejudice seems to have gone unexamined, let alone unleashed. He was, to the contrary, attentive, even vigilant, and reflective; fortitudinous, prayerful, and always appreciative. He was out of himself, into talk and good fellowship (his presence made a concrete difference to others, who regarded him highly), nature and walking, books and music, and joy. At some level he knew, as we all do, where that "road right out of the Self" ought to lead.

3.

Home – the desire to have one, to hold membership in a family – was at the center of Warren Lewis. The commonplaces were waystations. His own books often bespeak his fondness of domestic solidity and his appreciation of its importance. Many of the most appealing entries in the diary are those which describe his involvement with music when at home; it was the cause of harmony in others. He grew from disliking Maureen Moore a good deal to loving her greatly when he saw the patience and charity in her willingness to teach him to play the piano. Thereafter the household listened together, not only to his gramophone records, but to his piano recitals and to the melodies he had composed. This household, however, was a surrogate; Mr. Papworth, the beloved and temperamental dog; Paxford, the pragmatically skeptical gardener and majordomo; Maureen, and Minto, the second focal point of this family ellipse (Jack, of course, was the first): these could never replace what was at the center of Warren. Although years after having made the decision (based explicitly upon his desire for a solid home life) to enter into the Kilns arrangement he pronounced himself happy with the results, Warren never failed continually to return to his own genuine core: Little Lea: Jack, Mammy, and Pappy.

There is too little space here to do justice to this theme; I can only assert this strong impression: except in the physical sense, the four were never apart. At the center of the book, with Warren, is Jack, and even the tidbits about him are savory. I had not known that CSL's favorite English translation of the *Odyssey* was William Morris's, or that his opinion of *The Three Musketeers* was (according to Jack) copied from Warren's (an opinion, by the way, which Warren forgot ever having held), or that it could be "highly characteristic" of Jack "that during the period in which he is recording walks with Arthur, visits to Glenmachen, etc., I have reliable evidence that he was in England." Nor did I know how much the elder brother endured for the younger, from Minto's bullying (her dogs had to be walked several time a day, every day), through the pain and confusion he felt at seeing Jack endure that bullying, to the sadness he felt when wondering why Jack was absolutely silent on the whole affair.

If Jack is at the center of the book, Mammy and Pappy were at the center of the home. Warren's recollections of the former are few but very touching, especially the one which pre-dates Jack but includes Albert. In these Warren not only recollects but analyzes as well, and the reader is relieved along with

Warren as he gains comfort from his insights. As they accumulate, it becomes clear to the reader that the brightest revelation is to the true character of Albert Lewis, Pappy. He was not actually cruel to his own father, as the boys believed, but tempered his response to a man who was in fact himself horrible and cruel. Was he thoughtless in not having had erected a stained glass window in memory of his wife? Warren learns otherwise, and scales of disapprobation built up over the years instantly fall away. Warren contended with him, rebuked him, wondered about him, laughed with him and at him, and always loved him, more at the end – when Warren had a substantial Face of his own – than at the beginning. If Albert was always something of a Polonius, he was also always the man who was solemnly praised by the Great Knock (on the occasion of Mammy's death) for being true to himself, "no slight achievement," he wrote, "in the estimate of all who know the facts."

After pondering hard, Warren chose "Man goeth to his long home" as Albert's epitaph, complementing "Men must endure their going hence," which Albert reserved for Mammy and which Warren selected for his brother and himself. At the very end, the coda, Warren endured a sort of purgation: bouts of alcoholism, an edition of his brother's letters which he thought "botched", and television. But, as Warren said of Jack, what lingers most vividly is the early, not the late, impression. He looked back at Little Lea one last time, after Albert died, and then set out for Home.

This good man, as fine a Christian model as his brother, wended his way back to Jack, Mammy, and Pappy. Of course he would have walked all the way, eschewing the bus ride imagined by his brother in *The Great Divorce*. And when they received him, then surely, as we read at the very end of *The Last Battle*, "they found themselves all walking together – and a great, bright procession it was – up towards mountains higher than you could see in this world even if they were there to be seen. But there was no snow on those mountains: there were forests and green slopes and sweet orchards and flashing waterfalls, one above the other, going up forever. And the land they were walking on grew narrower all the time, with a deep valley on each side: and across that valley the land which was the real England grew nearer and nearer."

3

Land of Shadows
Shadowlands
Dir. Richard Attenborough, 1993

Whoever in the world could have guessed that when C. S. Lewis made a Comeback – his return to popcult star, nearly forty-seven years after the appearance of his picture on the cover of *Time* magazine – that It would be in, of all things, a movie, and one which tells "one of the greatest love stories of the twentieth century?" Near this thirtieth anniversary of C. S. Lewis' death on November 22, 1963, what Hollywood calls a "based upon" constitutes a major commemoration. First a fine, small-scale BBC *film* (shown here on PBS), then a book, and thereafter a (modest) hit on the London and Broadway stages (and a triumph for Nigel Hawthorne as Lewis), the "fact-based" (not nearly the same as "true") story of a monotony-loving Oxbridge don and his liaison with a middle-aged American seems an unlikely object of mass-audience interest. But as a love match – and that is what it genuinely became – it was itself no less unlikely. So near Christmas and thereafter we will have had *Shadowlands* again, a Major Motion Picture. Please forgive the impertinence, but fifteen years ago I predicted "we may soon expect that C. S. Lewis will become an established figure ... so that people who know little will assume much." He has become that, indeed, and more: "someone who is famous," wrote Daniel Boorstien, "for being well-known" – a Celebrity.

I knew that a theatrical movie was being made some time before I received a call, last spring, from a chap in New Jersey asking for advice on marketing the film, especially to schools. The call was brief, and I have not heard from him since. I did, though, hear from the American publicist for Savoy Pictures, the American distributor that would have some success with *A Bronx Tale*, Robert De Niro's directorial debut. She, too, asked for marketing tips and knew very little about Lewis. I told her I would be writing about Lewis and the film. But my biographical information (notwithstanding her questions about Lewis) seemed of little interest, and I useless, to her. She said she would call back with other questions, reminding me along the way that *Shadowlands* was "not an autobiography (sic)." And in a third call, when I asked her to help me gain access to the Magdalen College set, she proved unwilling. Later she did include me in a "press junket" during which I viewed a private screening of the film and was able to interview (by now Lord) Richard Attenborough, Sir Anthony Hopkins, Debra Winger, and Joey Mazzello, the little boy who captures the audience as the young Douglas Gresham.

During the summer my son and I (thanks to the influence of *National Review*) did travel to Magdalen for a one-day visit. Alison Webb, an associate producer who was both an indefatigable and omniscient host, arranged my first interview with Attenborough – a transcendently courteous, good-humored and generous man who not only asked my son to stay for the interview but included him in it and who later, in New York, would ask me to be sure to give young Jim his regards! Miss Webb also invited us to lunch with the movie folk. (The same outfit that catered *Batman*. The roast breast of duckling, richly creamed desserts, and fresh fruit were deadly fine: movie folk eat very well.) I was allowed to witness the filming of the penultimate ("Chadwick") scene of the movie: four hours of work for some forty seconds of screen time. Their workday *(not* ours!) would extend from 7 a.m. to nearly midnight.

Clear and intelligible beyond almost any writer our language has ever produced, Lewis was, amidst much hopeful argument and glorious imagery, severe and unsentimental. So when on June 30th I arrived on the set I wondered if this was to be a movie about redemptive suffering, the pilgrimage of (as I see her) a manipulative and determined woman who, over the course of seven years, is converted quite thoroughly into what at first she longed to become, and "shadowlands," Lewis' word for this world as an insubstantial copy of the ultimately real *and* concrete next one.

The BBC film and the stage play (which I have read but not seen) both posited a psychic link between the death of Flora Lewis, the illness (but eventual recovery) of Digory's mother in *The Magician's Nephew,* and the illness, inexplicable recovery, and inevitably agonizing death of Joy – as seen through both Lewis' eyes and (a lovely and affecting touch) those of pre-adolescent Douglas Gresham: our losses here can be not only unbearably painful but crippling to both faith and reason. And yet they are as shadows, no match for the promise of the Light to come.

The movie, though, is relentlessly simplified: the most startling improbability of Lewis' life. In movieland, of course, the central crisis of that life – a soul-scouring conversion to Christianity – necessarily would be alluded to. DeMille is dead and *The Song of Bernadette* is no longer bankable; and his friendships (no actual friends are depicted at all), love of animals, seminal intellectual and artistic achievements, academic trials and triumphs, and almost everything else that thickens a life must be flattened and shrunk if not eliminated altogether. But one realizes that the screenplay (containing three times the number of words as the stage play) remains but a single element among hundreds that go into the making of a movie, the final cause of which is, after all, the healthiest possible bottom line. Attenborough would tell me that he never considered Hawthorne, a very fine actor but lacking a "cinematic name," the lead. (Hawthorne, by the way, wrote a kind letter to Attenborough letting him off the hook.) People, a lot of people, have to come, and they have to "get it," and they must tell other people about it; and so the "it" can be only so demanding.

Arguably the most effective and inspiring Christian apologist, the greatest writer of children's tales, and the foremost authority on medieval and renaissance English literature of this century (and poet, preacher, lecturer, teacher, novelist and journalist besides) Lewis has received much, but very narrowly-focused and largely conventional, attention. His apparently-settled life was in fact a highly improbable one, the stuff of movieland indeed – from his brilliant and dear mother's tragic death when he was not yet ten years old and an Ulster upbringing by a generous, but over-bearing and garrulous, father, to the taking of German prisoners while seeing action in World War I, to his taking of a mother-mistress figure and subsequent thirty-year indentureship to her shortly after the war, through caring for his increasingly alcoholic older brother, the publication of best-selling books, a career as a BBC broadcaster, his picture on the cover of *Time* magazine, the proffer of a knighthood (declined), and his late-life marriage. Now consider the *wife* of those autumn years, Joy Davidman Gresham Lewis: a Jewish divorcee from the Grand Concourse, the Bronx, New York, an atheist, a card-carrying Communist (trebly devoted after the Hitler-Stalin pact), a prizewinning poet, a novelist, editor and journalist, a self-confessed intellectual prostitute, a foul-mouthed and (by some accounts) loose-living wife of the equally-brilliant, erratic, occasionally violent, alcoholic novelist William Gresham *(Nightmare Alley)*, then a devoted mother of two sons, a convert to Christianity, an expatriate, and finally, when married to C. S. Lewis, a tormented victim of cancer, dying at forty-five. Here are two solid people, notwithstanding my own omissions of nuance, irony, and at least one possible miracle, Joy's early remission. But the all-important context, without which there can be no reliable meaning, is richer still.

Flora Lewis (1862-1908) must have been a remarkable woman; she witnessed what may have been a miracle at age twelve while visiting a Catholic church in Florence and later earned a B.A. from Queens College, Belfast, in mathematics and logic. In *Surprised by Joy,* his spiritual autobiography, Lewis likened his mother's death to a continent sinking into the sea. After came some harrowing schooling, much youthful writing, superb private tutoring, life-long bonding with his brother Warren (1895-1973), alienation from his father Albert (1863-1927), a solicitor, and the loss of his Christian faith. These years represent a great gap in what was the published autobiographical record; but the recently-issued diary, *All My Road Before Me,* shows a young man out-of-sync. He worked to hold a house – that is, to "husband" it – yet too young and immature to head it, or even to know what he had gotten himself into. Albert and Warren, however, knew nothing of the menage, at least early on. When he did convert, was he, as his lifelong friend Owen Barfield has suggested, "emerging from the husk of his previous Immaturity"? Or was the change "no sudden plunge into a new life," as Warren wrote of his brother's conversion, "but rather a slow steady convalescence from a deep-seated spiritual illness of long-standing," what we might call neurotic atheism? Instrumental in his conversion were two Roman Catholic friends, Alan Bede Griffiths and J. R. R. Tolkien, who would remain puzzled by the fact that he would not join the Church. And he always remained uneasy with his own verbal spells, since they symptomized to him an inability to let go of his old, needful, theatrical ego. John Wain, the writer and Professor of Poetry at Oxford who was Lewis' pupil in the 'forties, saw Lewis somewhat differently:

> All these people I admired . . . were dramatic personalities, making a strong impact.. . . I do not mean that they posed. . . . They are always giving a performance in the role for which they have cast themselves. . . . Such people are in fact fulfilling a moral duty. The Creator . . . has equipped them with a certain identity, and they are all the time delightfully aware of this identity and out to get, and to give, as much fun as possible with it.

But the new film relies upon what Lewis himself called his "trumpery" at the expense of much else. During my visit to the set, I spoke with but one person, the author William Nicholson, who did not either confess or proclaim a near-total ignorance of Lewis' life; but he did not want to distract from the "intensified love story" in any way. The stage and film producer Brian Eastman told me it was this motif and its attendant emotional wallop that most attracted and inspired him to bring the script to Attenborough's attention. Hopkins himself called the script relentless, and so it must be, since (Nicholson told me) Lewis was a man who, until Joy came along, was "afraid of commitments" and thus quite unable to make any until late middle-age. In truth, I believe that those of us who pay attention to C. S. Lewis may be all Joyed out, and there is now a lack of proportion. There was, after all, that context in which the liaison occurred. Lewis, freed from Mrs. Moore, pouring forth Narnia, producing the Oxford University history of sixteenth century English literature, talking with friends, walking with Warnie, and basking in the honor of the professorship bestowed upon him by Cambridge University (much of this and more before he met, let alone fell in love with and married, Joy) – this Lewis could hardly be described as morose, melancholy or otherwise especially unhappy. And during this seven (not two) years with Joy (a damaging concision) he certainly did more than wander about like a love-struck sentimentalist undergoing a mid-life crisis. That Joy and her loss jolted Jack and deepened some aspect of his soul is, I believe, beyond all doubt; but after her death productive life went on. Indeed, one could argue that, notwithstanding the many changes that marked the lives of the Lewis brothers, they were nearly restored (the Gresham boys were in their care, though often away at school) to the sort of "mutual solitude" that marked their brotherhood after their mother's death. This coda recapitulated that earlier, defining part of their lives, just as Jack's marriage had enabled Jack to become the husband he could not be in his twenties, and brought these two pilgrims, as Warnie's diary suggests, closer not only to Mammy and Pappy but to the Home they were made for.

Brian Sibley's book (1985), "too documentary" for the BBC and so rejected in favor of Nicholson's version (which was first offered to Columbia pictures and the director Sidney Pollack, only to languish), seems to me excessively sanitized, uninquiringly taking Joy's point-of-view. The play and film do the same (even though, in both, Joy's part is woefully underwritten). But the film, though avowedly a "based upon," the sort of adaptation to which audiences have become accustomed, gratuitously misleads its audience by including the legend "this is a true story" along the bottom of the screen. So Joy really did think that Jack would befriend only those whom he could control, as she righteously and angrily sneers during one scene placed in his College rooms? And Jack really burst out impatiently and uncharitably in the Senior Common Room when his friends offered consolation? I pass over the obvious liberties (there were two sons not one, for example; when they married Jack was at Cambridge, not Oxford; Joy's first trip was alone, a "scouting expedition" without children, among others) and instead lament the more serious distortions. That Jack is a Christian is evident. But would he have uttered the name of Jesus only once? Would he have referred to his need to pray but actually have prayed only once? The Lewis who fed his dog Papworth ("man with dog closes a gap in the universe") by throwing food over his own shoulder because the dog would not eat if watched; who could not, after three tries, spell 'rivet' when writing *Screwtape* so changed it to 'fix'; who needed to record telephone and other numbers of long-standing because he was *always forgetting them*; who turned down both that knighthood and an appointment as Commander of the British Empire; and who gave away most of his income – that Lewis is in the movie.

A person I regret not having spoken to is Edward Hardwicke, son of the great Sir Cedric, and Watson to Jeremy Brett's Holmes. His Warnie is, well, Warnie, an adroitly written role: I hope he gets the recognition he so richly deserves. The relationship of the two brothers is depicted as deftly and as accurately as any of us could wish. Witness one of the best scenes this indefatigable movie-goer has seen over his last, say, two dozen movies: Jack and Warnie "deciding" that Warnie will in fact not move out now that Joy is coming to the Kilns. But be alert: it lasts some twenty seconds only and, as heavily dependent upon timing as it is, required, remarkably, only one take. Upon hearing this praise Hopkins was especially delighted, for it was he who suggested for the role his old friend from their days together at The Royal National Theatre. I would give a good deal to have heard their signature imitations of Guinness, Olivier and others as though in conversation.

We do get a Lewis who, we are given to understand, may have given "easy answers to difficult questions," as his cynical friend Christopher charges. Attenborough told me he did not believe that: rather, he sees Lewis as a man who, having converted millions of people notwithstanding his semi-cloistered existence, would now himself be "converted," a stretch, perhaps, but no less telling an insight for its hyperbole. Hopkins is manifestly sympathetic to Lewis. In fact, his impatience bordered on anger when I read out to him an ugly quotation attributed to him in print. I will not repeat it: he not only denied it but expressed the opposite. "Jack," he said, "was no more repressed than any other man." Hopkins's one gift to his young co-actor, Joey Mazzello, was *The Four Loves*. "He told me," Mazzello said, "'don't read this now, but read it when you get older.'" By the way, the ten-year-old Mazzello could not understand a word he read at all until his fourth-grade teacher suggested that he read the first paragraph of *The Lion, the Witch and the Wardrobe*, which he did understand, and has continued to understand and love a good deal. Winger did much research, a considerable amount of reading and a two-day trip to the Wade Collection, at the end of which she prayed with Lyle Dorsett (though she is not herself a Christian). She got some facts wrong, and when I corrected one she did give me the Winger Death Stare – a happy moment of fixed attention for this long-time admirer. But she got much more right than wrong, including at least two very important insights. The first is that the film tells us far too little about Joy, fascinating in her own right, and not only for the mix of motives that brought her to Lewis. The second was about Lewis. She was unmistakably direct in her denial of Christopher's charge, and her answer is worth quoting in its entirety:

> He may make difficult *questions* accessible. I don't think he makes the answers easy. I don't think he answers questions. I think he discusses them. He's in that school of discourse where his statements are not like books that are written by experts. He's saying "think about this." That's why I think he opened [Christianity] to so many people. He wasn't dogmatic.

Would that the script took that same position more consistently than it does. Instead, we see, recurrently, a lecturing Lewis who repeats, from one platform to another, that "pain is God's megaphone." His docile and eager listeners (mostly middle-aged women thrilled to have him among them) lap up a phrase which to the viewer becomes increasingly facile, especially after Joy is stricken by cancer and Lewis by irony. The phrase is from chapter six of The *Problem of Pain*: "But pain insists upon being attended. God whispers to us in our pleasure, speaks in our conscience, but shouts in our pains: It is His megaphone to rouse a *deaf* world. . . ." So far so good, notwithstanding the absence of immediate context and the falsehood of Lewis' tiresome reiteration of the theme. But twelve pages later in the chapter he writes:

> You would like to know how l behave when I am experiencing pain, not writing books about it. You need not guess, for I will tell you; I am a great coward. When I think of pain . . . it "quite o'ercrows my spirit". . . . I am not arguing that pain is not painful. Pain hurts. That is what the word means. I am only trying to show that the old Christian doctrine of being made "perfect through suffering" is not incredible. To prove it palatable is beyond my design.

This proclamation is perfectly consistent with Lewis' prefatory declaration: "I must add, too, that the only purpose of the book is to solve the intellectual problem raised by suffering; for the higher task of teaching fortitude and patience I was never fool enough to suppose myself qualified, nor do I have anything to offer my readers except my conviction that when pain is to be borne, a little courage helps more than much knowledge, a little human sympathy more than much courage, and the least tincture of the love of God more than all."

But in movieland, Lewis must be lessoned, experientially. Miss Winger, where were you when William Nicholson needed you? Now, with the movie already over two hours long, it is fair to ask how I might achieve even a portion of my own agenda.

Simple: I would eliminate altogether the tendentious, gratuitous, fictitious *and* false Whistler subplot. Though not without its dramatic use in context, it is a net loss and seems to have dropped in from another movie.

Yet we who cannot count our debt to Lewis, let alone repay it, should be very happy to have *this* film. *Shadowlands* is quite beautiful and, as movies that deal with religious themes and characters go, refreshingly and wholly sympathetic. Not the slightest tinge here of a smirk at some "radical religious right." Perhaps in not sufficiently advertising Lewis' Christianity (one interviewer asked Attenborough if it were risky to make a movie in which the words 'God' and 'religion' were mentioned frequently!) it sneaks "past those watchful dragons" (to use a Lewis phrase). It will encourage people who never read him surely to do so; those who only knew *of* him will now have some Inkling of why he is worth knowing about; and those who know well his life and work will realize that his marriage was not a mere codicil to that life but an episode that leavened it fundamentally during its final three years, when Lewis, though still busy, was himself ill.

Nicholson, Attenborough, Hopkins and Winger bring concretely to life this influence in one splendid scene, Jack and Joy's first night together: written with a poignant understatement, directed with elegant simplicity, and played with an unaffected grace (and humor) that is both utterly disarming and absolutely convincing. On this note *Shadowlands* rings quite true. But when, at the very end of the film, we *hear* that twice Lewis had been offered a choice (at the deaths of Flora and Joy) and that the boy chose safety but the man suffering, we are reminded that something unnecessarily false is afoot. Thus Walter Hooper is probably right when he says, "there is now a wide gap between the Mythology of C. S. Lewis and the Facts of his life. *Shadowlands* is a beautiful addition to the mythology but it should be taken as a dessert – it must be combined with the meat and potato *facts.*" I merely wish that this movie, now, came closer than it does to being as demanding – as complex and challenging – as Lewis was, an iconoclast in his own unassuming way.

"The only reason to believe in Christianity is that it is true," he wrote, not because it is comforting, or builds self-esteem, since "all that is not eternal is eternally out of date." And he defended that Faith like a frontiersman, as though, wrote his friend Austin Farrer, "every ditch was his last dike." Finally, he was a surprising man, Joy being only one of the last surprises. If you have read much Lewis, are you sure you know his opinion on people living together before marriage? Or on obscenity and sodomy laws? Or on the discovery and conquest of the New World? Or that he spelled very poorly but could not *forget* anything he read? Like his great lion-Creator Aslan, he was not quite tame. He knew better. After all, that is why a man, even one who has thought, seen and felt things through "to the ruddy end," keeps his own spiritual advisor to the very end of his life.

So after you have seen the movie, read the books. Like the rest of us he is eternal: We are all "possible gods and goddesses. . . . There are no *ordinary* people. You have never talked to a mere mortal. Nations, cultures, arts, civilizations – these are mortal, and their life is to ours as the life of a gnat"; but unlike most of our works, and thirty years after his death, Lewis left a legacy of living and of thinking and of expression that is perpetually fresh. Surely he would loathe the idea of a film biography with himself as its subject. Not being among those who welcome any recognition by popular culture of Lewis, I could almost agree: no film about Lewis could fully satisfy most of us, and this one could have been better even on its own terms. *Almost* agree, but not quite. For this film is better than I had hoped for. And in five years we will not commemorate his death and our loss, but celebrate the centenary of his birth. "Our need for such a guide," as Eugene McGovern has argued, will not have diminished; and I, for one, cannot wait for the jubilation, including the cinematic prequels.

Lewis' former pupil Peter Bayley was among the few to attend his funeral. He has since written that "there was one candle on the coffin as it was carried out into the churchyard. It seemed not only appropriate but almost a symbol of the man and his integrity and his absoluteness and his faith that the flame burned so steadily, even in the open air, and seemed so bright, even in the bright sun."

"Even though": *Shadowlands*, briefly

I remain happy to have this film; happy that it is not, though it easily could have been, very much worse, and happier than if it had not been made in the first place. Happy, even though. . . .

Rocky Balboa is more religious than C. S. Lewis. He prayed more often and more submissively. He sought out blessings when at risk. *He* went to church to petition Jesus to save *his* stricken wife. *Desiree*, a biography with Jean Simmons and Marlon Brando, bankable stars (to say the least) and with high, money-making production values, is more loyal to fact than is William Nicholson's script. *The Godfather*, as the *roman a clef* Lord Attenborough's film *ought* to have been, is more fundamentally truthful than *Shadowlands*. And the Jesus of the notorious Abel Ferrara's *Bad Lieutenant* is more redemptive, convincing and theologically compelling than the off-stage demi-presence of *Shadowlands*, just as the lieutenant's epiphany is more important by far than Lewis'.

Even on its own soap-operatic terms the film could have been "thicker" – and far, far less condescending than it was. And why, then, was it not? The production notes have it that Lewis was appointed a fellow of Magdalen College in 1935 and that, in the 1950s, "had only recently been appointed one of the youngest Dons." Are these factual errors symptomatic of simple carelessness only? If so, then what are we to make of, "Lewis also gave highly-successful radio talks regarding morality and behavior, which were later published under various titles . . ."? No mention here of Lewis' Christian commitment. In fact, Nicholson told me that (like Nicholson himself until *he* met *his* wife) Lewis was incapable of making *any* commitments, until he met Joy. Attenborough and Nicholson were not going to allow the intrusion of anything that would, according to Nicholson, "dilute the intensified love story." Note: not the *actual* love story but the *intensified* love story. We must not, then, be surprised that what we got was a high-tone . . . *Love Story*.

But how is it condescending?

First, by exploiting Lewis' name at the expense of his reputation, which is certainly distorted, if not demeaned. The (true) assertion that it has helped sell thousands of Lewis books (to which I add that it put the second edition of my book into a second printing) is beside the point. Does *Narnia* need the help? Will *Surprised by Joy* requite the reader's eager anticipation or, when it turns out *not* to be Lewis' memoir of Mrs. Gresham, disappoint and, perhaps, even discourage further reading? And, second, could not a different sort of film – or even this one with a more adroit script – have done Lewis the greater service, whether measured in sales of his book or otherwise?

Adroitness. I could proliferate the examples; here are two: After Joy recites her war poem, she herself calls its verisimilitude into question. Lewis demurs and at that point *could have said*, "... and I should know. I saw men blown to bits in the trenches. My shrapnel up here still twinges occasionally." You see? *Lewis was a combat veteran*, and one who had seen and felt great pain, physical and otherwise, long before he had written of it or had "learned" of it from Joy. Or we could have seen Lewis feeding his dog by throwing food over his shoulder, as he in fact did with Mr. Papworth. I remember that the dog was dead by the time of Joy's arrival, but even I know that we are not filming a documentary; rather, we would be depicting the absolute revelry that animals could occasion in Lewis. These two examples together, by the way, would consume ... what? Twenty seconds? There are fifty other such details that could be added. But they, unlike historically accurate bras or coats, might have "diluted the intensified love story."

And how might it –indeed, how should it – have been a different film, and therefore a better story? Elsewhere I have suggested answers; here I will mention three, in rising order of importance. Get rid of the Whistler subplot. Not only does he seem to have dropped in from another film, but if Lewis is going to be someone *else's* foil better that he be lessoned (if he be lessoned at all) by a Tolkien or the like. Next, depict the actual seven years that Lewis and Joy had, not an absurd two. Joy could then change, as she must have, Douglas could be a much more affecting adolescent when his mother dies, instead of a sentimentalized juvenile, and Jack could evidence his *multi-faceted* intensity, including his humor, rather than some perpetual waiting-room resignation. After all, George Sayer, in the second edition of his biography of Lewis, allows that Lewis might have married Ruth Pitter, in whose company he "seemed unusually quiet and peaceful," *after* Joy died, had only his health been better. (Pitter's friend Mary Thomas said that Jack "came back to" Pitter after Joy's death, since they had always been "very happy together.") Lewis did far more than mope about during the final three years of his life.

And last, excise the nonsensically reiterated "pain-megaphone" line: not only did Lewis both know and say better, but he prospectively refuted the very "dilemma" posited in the film. At least then he might be worthy of going a few rounds with Rocky.

4

Land of Light:
Not Quite a Movie Review

All my life I've loved movies, but only at age twenty did *The Chronicles* find me. I've spent much mental energy paying close attention to both, and now that they have met and that I've witnessed that meeting I am thrilled. We could get picky, but we would be picky indeed seriously to fault this book-to-movie.

Like most people I've more often suffered over than been delighted by this sort of transmutation. In moving from printed page to my mind, the book becomes my own; and I know that you, another reader, have your own book too. Certainly our mental books overlap, but the differences between them are a big part of what keeps us talking. In moving from the printed page to the screen, however, the book must first hit my eyeballs and my ears. Two senses are assaulted, and that is no small thing. Twenty-five hundred years ago, Aristotle wrote in his *Rhetoric* that to be persuasive one should "set it before their [the audience's] eyes." (He didn't say "ears," but he didn't have amplifiers.) He was right then and he's still right, which is why movies are so irresistible: heavy-handed or not, spectacle up there on that big screen makes all the difference. (And note well: in his *Poetics* Aristotle included spectacle as one of the five major features of dramatic poetry.)

As I watch the book-to-movie I may be (in truth, I usually am) swept away – but not, as with my mental book, when the movie is done. Moreover, you and I and all of us will have seen more or less (though never exactly) the same spectacle, so our talk changes. We no longer discuss author X's book but director Y's movie; we no longer talk about our own mental books – the one we've taken solitary walks within and lived through – but about our shared spectacular experience.

The point: if we cherish the book, if we regard our mental book as what the author closely intended, and if the director gets that wrong – or worse, betrays it – well, then, we want to throttle the director, who is undoing not only the author's cherished world but our very own mental book as well. Worse: now with the director's betrayal out and about, anyone who had not read the book but has seen the movie *will get it all wrong*. These . . . these turnips . . . will *not* know that director Y is the knucklehead, or worse.

Why, then, has the Narnia movie thrilled me? Faithful both to the substance and, more, to the spirit of the book, it overdoes nothing. This matters enormously, for the great danger of lavish spending on the production of a movie with epic promise is *excess*. In this case, though, from deep meaning to sheer spectacle, with the effect of talking and exotic beasts somewhere in between, we behold *ordinateness*: this movie is fitting.

That is a lot not to have to worry about: a great relief, given my not-inordinate worry. How unlikely an accomplishment is this absence of excess – in how very many ways the movie should have been seriously overwrought, given all the temptations of greed, proselytizing, and vanity, and all the risks of writing, casting, formal complexity, and technical innovation – how unlikely an accomplishment this ordinateness is I leave for each of us who love the books to marvel over and to give thanks for. I do thank God, and all the people who labored. And – without quite knowing exactly what he did or how he functioned, what he contributed or (more importantly) what he prevented – we should thank Lewis' stepson and a co-producer of the movie, Douglas Gresham, and I do.

All of which is not to say there has been (or is) nothing at all to worry about. Along with Lewis' Narnia (with our mental correlative) and the movie, there is the Twilight Zone Narnia – the Narnia of publicity, marketing and media chatter which bears little relation to either of the first two.

Over here we have a schizophrenic sales pitch: on the one hand an Evangelical Narnia, with its study guides designed to awaken every sleeping dragon that Lewis had sneaked past, and on the other hand a perfectly non-Christian Narnia that, according to a version of one Gresham interview, couldn't offend the most devout secularist because there is nothing Christian about it. Over there we have venomous conflict and willfully wrong-headed criticism: the opportunistic Philip K. Pullman (the Christophobe of *His Dark Materials* fame) and a few smart-aleck New York pundits with really loud megaphones. And a bit further away – barely discernible but no longer merely on the horizon – we have a tarted up Narnia, including a new Narnia tale "inspired" by C. S. Lewis, a simplified version of *The Lion, the Witch and the Wardrobe*, and a growing pile of trivializing merchandise. In short, the books and the movie have become both a goldmine (and we really must ask of C. S. Lewis Pte Ltd, the copyright holder, How much is enough?) and a battleground.

In truth, however, although Lewis had an indisputably Protestant cast of mind, he did not have an Evangelical one. He limited his religious thinking, writing, speaking, and witnessing strictly to those venues he thought appropriate; he had many Catholic beliefs and practices; and it is doubtful he ever would have referred to himself as having been "born again." Furthermore, we know that he did not set out to write Christian propaganda when he wrote *The Chronicles*. In other words, unless you are of Pullman's febrile ilk, you really don't have much to worry about; and if you don't believe that then just ask the many thousands of people who love Narnia and who aren't Christians and who don't see its Christianity and who don't care that others do. If Lewis was a commando, "behind enemy lines" as he put it, surely his battlefield was less the culture-at-large than the heart of each of his readers.

In that light, I note finally Lewis' great accomplishment with Narnia. We recall his famous late-night talk with Tolkien and Dyson in 1931, the one that resulted in Lewis realizing that a myth could remain a myth and still be a fact. What Lewis has done in *The Chronicles* is to *re-mythologize* Christianity, re-locating our response from the intellect to the imagination. That is, with his fairy tales – and we do well to recall that, according to Lewis, "sometimes fairy stories may say best what's to be said" – Lewis has restored that stage just before facticity, or its potential, breaks through, that stretch of time when the *longing* evoked by the myth as such still beckons pure. Let everyone who sees this movie feel *that*, and then let each of them stand in wonder.

5

The Magic Never Ends:
The Life & Work of C. S. Lewis

Of the handful of recent C. S. Lewis documentaries that are planned or actually begun, this is the only one so far to make it into the can, and my involvement with two of the zygotes makes me wonder: surely the simplicity, conventionality and leanness of *The Magic Never Ends* have something to do with its completion? Not only do these features help solve the Big Problem of documentary-making, finance, but they conduce to a "product" appealing enough for a television station (WTTW, Chicago) to roll the dice with an hour of precious airtime.

And the station would be right to do so. To introduce someone to CSL – someone who has read only a bit or nothing, or who has heard a great deal or nothing, or who knows only the inadequate Attenborough *Shadowlands* – we would do considerable good by screening this film. Not only are the stages of Lewis' life noted but the big events as well; not only his career, but its surprises (for example, the move to Cambridge); not only the shape of his faith but of his conversion (especially the centrality to it of the nature of myth); not only the scope of his work, but its dazzling successes (Screwtape, Narnia); and not only the touchstones of his spirit, but its resting places, too (nature, friendship). Moreover, we do hear what, oh, twenty years ago we would not have heard but which has since become convention: that CSL probably had a sexual liaison with Mrs. Moore, that Warnie was alcoholic, that Jack's marriage with Joy resulted from her desire to die (when death was near indeed) wedded in the Church. Only Lewis' ideas (especially *Sehnsucht*, which in the final cut was barely alluded to) are short-changed, but given the documentary intent in this particular film, that must count as a quibble.

The varied pace afforded by a nimbly-edited mixture of still-photo montage (how *very* beautiful is the restored Kilns), of contemporaneous film (e.g. of WWI combat), and of on-camera commentary adroitly sustains forward movement; the impressively economical script is a wonder of canny exposition. The mood, however, owing to a sappy score, to one-too-many Hallmark images, and to a pervasive *genteelness*, is excessively elegiac. Would a few strokes of exuberance – we are talking about C. S. Lewis, after all – have been too . . . untoward? Even the great Kingsley falls prey: I wouldn't want the maniac of his riveting *Sexy Beast*, but an Anglified Ghandi?

On screen, Christopher Mitchell, Walter Hooper, and Debra Winger best suggest what such documentaries struggle to achieve: the impression of ongoing conversation. Furthermore, Mitchell's command is palpable; Winger's thinking consistently fresh; and Hooper's understanding of Lewis' achievement definitive. Other critics are always solidly helpful (especially Lyle Dorsett providing a welcome reminder of Lewis' early problem of pain, and, acutely, Colin Manlove cutting to the quick of *The Chronicles* with very few strokes), sometimes provocative (was CSL's favorite reading really medieval romance, or Mere Christianity "his" religion?), but only once jejune (a reference to "denominational rubbish"). *Actual* conversation (among younger scholars, say, at a pub) and man-in-the-street responses would have cost little and contributed an attractive angularity.

As Pope John Paul II has said (and Hooper reminds us, though the papal reference was surely and lamentably cut) Lewis "knew his apostolate and did it." The result is as Mitchell argues: Christianity is plausible; the effect is as Dorsett asserts: "lives are utterly changed"; and the achievement is as Hooper describes: "With Lewis the curtains just open up wide and extend to the sides of the theatre, and you see everything that's in front of you . . . more than you've ever seen before. To see through Lewis' eyes is to see the universe, I think, almost as God sees it."

Reliable, affecting and inviting, this film serves its subject well – a first for television, and no small thing.

6

Messages of Hope

C. S. Lewis at the BBC: Messages of Hope in the Darkness of War
Justin Phillips, London: HarperCollins: London, 2003

How startling to learn that the master polished his touchstone idea, composed the masterpiece that conveys it, *and* perfected his lean, direct apologetic style under what can only be regarded as the *very* tight rein of the BBC. Walter Hooper especially has ably adumbrated the broadcast history of *Mere Christianity*; but only adumbrated. The full – and often dramatic – tale of that seminal conception coming to life has not been told till now.

On the one hand a devoted admirer of Lewis, on the other a lifelong and loyal BBC-man, Justin Phillips' own sense of enthusiastic struggle is infectious. Here are CSL's reservations, vexations, and labor; his utterly unlikely achievement and its impact; and finally the burdensome aftermath. And here are the BBC's persistent pursuit, its scalpel-like severity of judgment, and finally its nagging. (Whatever nag you've known, you've not known nagging if it wasn't by the BBC.) Phillips' adroit quoting from correspondence, memoranda, and other contemporaneous sources, and his emphasis upon the telling personal recollection, elicit a human interest that strikes off one surprising delight after another. (My own was to find myself rooting for the nag, though only barely.)

The late Mr. Phillips (who died before completing his book; the manuscript was edited and brought to publication by his daughter Laura Treneer) deftly sets the stage with a sketch of the BBC. Then amidst images of what must have been great confusion – Poland invaded and broadcasts interrupted with that news (as secret orders are opened), nearby London buildings blown to bits and Broadcasting House itself bombed and flooded (its work virtually uninterrupted), one million children evacuated as Resistance broadcasts are begun and early television broadcasts halted – *then* we meet men who were not at all confused: Val Gielgud, Director of Drama and

Features and the brother of John (the actor already famous and influential, a connection that would prove pivotal); James Welch, Director of Religious Broadcasting; and the indefatigable, unembarrassable, single-minded Eric Fenn, Welch's assistant.

This patient scene-setting is dynamic: as a result we understand that these Three Wise Men – pioneers, really – re-invented the BBC. The Corporation's remarkably constrained religious broadcasting protocols did not allow for talks such as Lewis'. These were contingent and blessedly *Providential*. How else to explain Fenn's fortitude in inviting Lewis (again and again); his cajoling, sometimes confusing (then scolding, though barely), patronizing, and editing (almost always cutting, sometimes expanding, but also, to great effect, *revising*), of the great man; and finally his astonishment before CSL's prodigious gifts?

After courtship the marriage was fruitful and multiplied. Not only were millions of sorely-tested wartime listeners piqued, enlightened, assured, and comforted, but the BBC's religious broadcasting was secured. Lewis himself, of course, did not profit; he gave away the paltry fee. Instead he was mostly put out. We get a concrete feel for his almost comically inconvenient travel arrangements (Mrs. Moore would not endure an evening alone), toil, trials of composition (the vast correspondence engendered by the broadcasts did bring about penetrating revisions), and penitential home-life. Not altogether new, the narrative is always robust; contributions by Jill Freud, for example, are particularly vivid. The reader comes away impressed, not only by the extravagant standards of the BBC, but with the ability of its officers and employees to sustain them and to get others to do so. Fenn's exacting equanimity under dire circumstances (including Lewis' occasional impatience) is admirable. A critique of the talks is astute and restrained; the lip-smacking chapter on Dorothy L. Sayers and the BBC is rollicking: the corporation was sorely overmatched! We can easily forgive occasional, but really quite palpable, syntactical rocks and hard places.

Phillips and Treneer allow us to *enjoy* rather than merely to *contemplate* C. S. Lewis during this central period of his life and its seminal event; so as biography their book is a fresh and important contribution to the secondary canon. But as a personal (and encomiastic) history it is more. The magnitude of the achievement that CSL has bequeathed is greater than we had thought: wider, now that we behold the full cast of characters, and much deeper, given our understanding of the heroic professionalism that overcame harrowing, even diabolical, obstacles impeding the Word. Finally we know this authoritatively: Richard Baxter + CSL = *Mere Christianity* is henceforth Baxter + Lewis *x* the BBC = *Mere Christianity plus* a good deal of the master's pellucid style.

7

Faith(less) v. Reason(able)

A month's pay says this title was not chosen by the author. Not only must high-concept projects (Heroes battling over The Universe) end with a bang, but other pleasures along the way usually shrink to insignificance, and no serious author wants *that*. So, first, forget the silly sub-title; second: you can do this easily *and* establish the right state of mind by remembering that the book began as an undergraduate course, which I hasten to add is not at all a slight.

In fact that reminder becomes a compliment if the course has a long and luminous pedigree. This one has been going for twenty-five years at Harvard College and the Medical School and is both demanding and rewarding besides. I believe this for three reasons. 1/ I have been the neighbor of a young friend who took the course, who described it in considerable detail, and whose life it changed, for the better and forever; 2/ I am an "advisor" on an attempt to film this idea and so necessarily have learned of its instructor's reputation for rigor (although I do not know Armand Nicholi); 3/ Dr. Nicholi is a psychiatrist, a professor at Harvard Medical School and Massachusetts General Hospital, a clinician in private practice, and clearly a teacher of no mean intellectual range, professional commitment, and predilection for live, sustained and disinterested argument (a predilection lamentably rare in ivied halls).

His design is simple. In nine chapters between prologue and epilogue he allows his protagonists to treat, more or less alternately and for themselves, what we should believe (Part One) and how (Part Two); in doing so they address the Creator, Conscience, Happiness, Sex, Love, Pain and Death. Now this method, title aside, does arouse a thirst for the real thing – say, Lewis v. Freud at the Oxford Socratic Club, where CSL prominently took on all comers on precisely these questions; and that thirst goes unquenched. There is no Bang. But if you follow my instructions and put yourself back in the classroom then neither will you hear a Whimper, for along the way there are *very* many pleasures; not lesser pleasures, either, but different from the thrill of a knockout and at least as important.

Perhaps some readers who know one champion better than the other will be a bit uneasy with the treatment afforded their favorite. Certainly I will pick a bone or two respecting Nicholi's discussion of Lewis. But, knowing Freud hardly at all, I must wonder if a *Freudliebhader* might not have the bigger gripe. In a nutshell, in this War of the *Weltanschauungen* it is Lewis who emerges as the reasonable advocate achieving plausibility and Freud who is the Fundamentalist whose utter faith in the non-existence of God elicits assertion after assertion, one paradigm after another, all designed to uphold the one true church of disbelief.

What seemed a contrivance – Why these two from among so many candidates? And why just two? – turns out to be a more effective intellectual scalpel than any the doctor could have chosen. Hardly anyone would read (though those who did would surely profit from) Lewis *versus* Russell, or Russell v. Chesterton. But Lewis v. Stephen Jay Gould? or *Sagan*? No. Freud's and Lewis' lives overlapped, Lewis had read Freud, and even if Freud begs as many questions as he actually argues he was forthrightly *engagé*. His and Lewis' compelling directness, conviction and clarity (could *any* other two write this well?), put forth with Nicholi's adroit and lean command, offer the significant, ample, and telling intellectual delights. This is *the* Great Debate, these *are* its central issues, these two figures are their *most* prominent and accessible advocates, and these are *their* prevailing arguments.

Finally – and for this I am particularly grateful to the doctor – the reader will be happy even for that not-quite-quenched thirst for live argument, realizing just how right my young friend (who by the way graduated *magna cum laude* and since has gone on to both a divinity degree and a life of Christian devotion) really was.

8

The People's New Clothes:
A Biography, its Readers and its Subject

In England one hears that Collins, when at long last presented with a final version of *C.S. Lewis: A Biography*, actually considered not publishing the book. The American publisher, Harcourt Brace Jovanovich, has seen fit to advertise the book in no more than six organs, the best known being *Commonweal* and *The Christian Science Monitor* – no *Saturday Review*, no *Atlantic*, no *New York Times*. Admittedly, composition of the work was not untroubled; technical difficulties of collaboration and an editorial policy that required considerable cutting delayed completion of the typescript beyond several tentative deadlines, and the final product reasonably might have been viewed as unmarketable: a constrained perspective on the life of an academic who jealousy guarded his privacy and who claimed to *like* monotony. In fact, though, the book met with immediate (if limited) success. The first edition, 3000 copies, sold out before publication, and the authors were invited to be interviewed on radio and television. Then the book was widely reviewed, and a peculiar pattern began to emerge. Though the tone was generally favorable, a lengthy description of shortcomings invariably followed praise for a yeomanlike job; indeed, the shortcomings were so portrayed as to make the book seem a failure, yet not more than a handful of reviews actually *called* it a failure (with just as many calling it an unqualified success). In America the response is especially puzzling: except for a smattering of minor reviews there has been no recognition.

Whence the anomaly? Why is the book perceived as somehow, yet not thoroughly, unsatisfying? Are Green and Hooper to blame for simply doing a bad job? Has Lewis himself so intimidated us (and his biographer-friends) concerning the hazards of "the personal heresy" and of invasions of privacy that he has frightened off ally and foe alike? Or are reviewers looking for fern-seeds, as CSL might have said, when they cannot see the elephant before them?

The last question, I think, is the most useful, and to it we must answer a resounding "yes." At the sixty-third meeting of the Society it was noted that "the authors are very clear that this is *a* biography and not *the* biography and they are very willing to agree that much remains to be done by other students of Lewis." Now, this (accurate) observation merits two comments: 1) every single review has made precisely that same observation, and 2) no review has described, or taken into account, its meaning. As honestly as possible the authors tell us that they are *not* going to interpret, analyze, or evaluate, but that they *will* "tell his story as best" they can, laying before the reader "as clear a picture as we could capture of his everyday life, of his friendships and interests, and of how he came to write his books." The important question, then, is: How clear and complete a picture do Green and Hooper provide of CSL's everyday life, friendships, interests, and the writing of his books? And it is precisely at this point that the confusion begins, for while pretending to answer that question, most reviewers actually begin to evaluate (not an illegitimate exercise *per se*) the purpose itself. Thereafter – and here is the rub – purpose after purpose pours forth, until the reviewer has offered his own biographical perspective, has in fact criticized Green and Hooper for not having taken that perspective, has in fact gone so far as to make it appear as though Green and Hooper have done a bad job even on their *own* terms. Well, we are free to complain if a dog barks badly; we are even free not to like dogs at all. But we are not free to complain that a dog does not meow, and still less legitimate is it for us to insist that a bark is a meow and then to criticize if for being dog-like.

Consider the review in *Eternity* (December, 1974) by Faith Sand Pidcoke, an ardent and knowledgeable Lewis admirer. The piece is straightforward, generally consistent, and unfavorable; but note the bases of evaluation: 1) "C.S. Lewis himself would have discountenanced this biography since he felt it was a waste of time to read *about* a writer instead of just reading what he *wrote*!" 2) "The rest of the book" – after "the first part" – "is really only a biography of Lewis' college life. . . . In the absence of more data from his non-scholastic world, the authors turn to brief literary critiques of his writings . . . . Green and Hooper seem to be too deeply concerned with how the literary world reacts *to* C.S. Lewis – hardly pertinent to a biographical study." And 3) the last paragraph of Mrs. Pidcoke's review,

> "Although Green and Hooper have ably accomplished their goal of providing a biographical framework of C.S. Lewis' life, they have painted for us a rather prosaic, dull man who somehow doesn't fit the soaring imagery or intense feeling we find in his books. The reader is left hoping that one day someone who can integrate all the worlds of C.S. Lewis will write a biography that paints him three-dimensionally."

Doubtless these objections seem reasonable and telling, yet their appearance shows errors of fact, judgment and reasoning. Where, for example, does CSL claim it is a waste of time to read about a writer? Surely not in *The Personal Heresy*, where he strongly denounces biographical methodology *when used as an interpretative instrument.* And if Lewis did think it a waste of time to read about a writer, would he not discountenance *any* biography, even one "that paints him three-dimensionally"? The argument over CSL's approbation is, I suspect, of questionable relevance; but for the record I would suggest that Lewis might be pleased by this biography, which scrupulously avoids "the personal heresy." Not without some insight of his own did he call Green his biographer and provide Hooper with many of the necessary resources. The second point is more puzzling and, because more relevant, more seriously in error than the first. The most obvious question is: why are literary responses to a literary man impertinent in a biographical study? And surely when a biographer is "in the absence of more data" from one source he necessarily turns to another? But Pidcoke's worst error is to disparage ("only a biography of Lewis' college life") the attention paid to CSL the author-academician; as Malcolm Muggeridge put it in his review ("Donnish Evangelist," *Observer,* July 7, 1974), Lewis' "teaching and his writing were his *opus dei.*" Finally, with regard to the third point, one can only wonder why "the reader is left hoping" if (in fact) Green and Hooper "have ably accomplished their goal." Or would Pidcoke have us look to "the soaring imagery or intense feeling we find in his books" in order to draw biographical inferences – that is, to indulge a form of "the personal heresy"?

Perhaps we will be Freudians in spite of ourselves, irremediably bound to the psychological method of Ernest Jones or of Irving Stone, or to the melodramatics of Lady Antonia Fraser or of André Maurois. All the more reason to recall that some six years ago Chad Walsh – who twenty years before had written one of the first and (still) one of the best books on Lewis' thought – chose as his topic "C.S. Lewis: The Man and the Mystery" (in *Shadows of Imagination,* ed. by M.R. Hillegas) and concluded that, really, there is no mystery, except insofar as Lewis reacted against modish modernism, or possessed a sensibility that was not "sick of everything," or made loving use of the word 'sane'."

English reviews, for the most part, have avoided this psychological pitfall – have, in fact, avoided all such pitfalls by (in effect) avoiding the book. Certainly the pattern of praise followed by a description of shortcomings holds true, and it is well worth noting that praise far outweighs blame. But any attention to the book *per se* occupies only a small portion of most reviews, which when describing shortcomings address themselves to shortcomings *in Lewis* or in "his world." John Carey, for example, cites the absence of any mention of I. A. Richards and of F. R. Leavis in Lewis' tutorials, concluding that Lewis was possessed of "blindness, prejudice, and sheer bull-necked stupidity" ("Captured by the Giant," *New Statesman*). John Raymond ("To Be a Pilgrim," *Sunday Times*) tends to support "those who also thought . . . that his theology stank of logic." And Martin Jarret-Ker gathers a variety of responses which add up to a Lewis who was loathful, arrogant, and condescending; as one philosopher put it, he was "merely a Greats man who never got beyond Plato" ("All Right, Jack," *Guardian*). Manifestations of a frustrated, jealous, impotent rage? Perhaps. The point is: where is the book? Surely not in the sympathetic reviews. Muggeridge talks much of the "sheer goodness and personal sanctity" in Lewis' "innermost being." Norman St. John-Stevas occupies most of his space with a discussion of Lewis the "born communicator" ("The Varnished Truth," *The Spectator*). H. D. Ziman praises, in elaborate detail, CSL's intellect, calling him "a splendid philosophy tutor" ("How the Don Became the Guru," *Daily Telegraph*). Finally, John Bayley revels in Lewis' personality – its innocence and quiddity – but seems to dismiss it as part of "a world gone by" ("A Passionate Pilgrim," *Times Literary Supplement*).

The point, I think, is evident: the English reviewers do not offer a counter-method but, being more intimately acquainted with the man than their American colleagues, do offer a counter-specimen, fulfilling in only a perfunctory way the primary function of a book review. (Two exceptions strike me as being the best reviews written so far: Father Gervase Mathew's in the *New Blackfriars* (November 1974), and – a surprising choice but one which I would be willing to defend – Christopher Derrick's "A Life Observed" in *Triumph* (January 1975). (I do wish, by the way, that journalists would either refrain from using, or justify their use of, the word 'cultist' as applied to a member of a Lewis society.) The questions, then, persist: how good, or bad, a book is *C.S. Lewis: A Biography*, and why?

Of course anyone interested in C.S. Lewis should read this book; but that could be said about any first biography, even a mediocre one. In fact, I believe that this particular book, offered as a first biography, has been ideally conceived. Note the circumstances. No one could have done a more authoritative job than Green, the "appointed" biographer, and Hooper, the man most thoroughly steeped, and expert, in the *oeuvre*. But, one might respond, they are too sympathetic, even sycophantic. Then, I would ask, what *better* type of biography than that which manifestly does *not* seek to interpret, to analyze, or to evaluate? There may be no such thing as a metaphysic of biography, but insofar as a *first* biography is likely to establish public expectations for years to come, I will opt for raw-boned authoritativeness every time. So we cannot complain over the scrupulous fulfillment of a scrupulously chosen purpose. We can, though, complain over faulty execution. Here are my complaints.

A handful of minor flaws distract the reader or, worse, annoy him. American readers and, I would wager, many English readers do not necessarily know what 'Mods', 'Greats', 'Responsions', or 'Univ.' are; and Mrs. Pidcoke hits the mark when she observes that "early in the book . . . the reader must worry about O.U.D.S., but 80 pages later we have it spelled out: Oxford University Dramatic Society." Now, given the emotional proximity of authors and subject the reader tends to attribute to Lewis the superciliousness inherent in those locutions. It seems, as well, that imperfect collaboration has resulted in a) repetition, as in the overlapping of chapters VI and VII, and b) a sort of bifocal perspective, a tensiveness which the reader senses but never quite discerns explicitly. I suspect the difference is attitudinal rather than just stylistic, yet after three readings I cannot quite put my finger on it. The last of the minor flaws is the most telling and probably goes a long way towards explaining the charge of shallowness often leveled against the book: Green and Hooper have provided little, painfully little, atmosphere. What were Belfast, Oxford, and Cambridge like? And the houses, and the College rooms? We never really find out, intellectually or imaginatively.

Such are minor flaws; the reader encounters them, psychically resolves them, and then moves on in more or less the same groove as he was in before the encounter. They never distort the picture of Lewis. But with regard to the recounting of two episodes there is distortion, troublesome and confusing: and therein lies the single major flaw in the book.

Notwithstanding the authors' love for their subject, they do not write (as some reviewers have claimed) devotionally; the book is manifestly not hagiography. But this discipline breaks down when Mrs. Moore, and then Joy Davidman, enter the narrative. The authors seem to want to minimize the wrinkles, and in so doing prompt the reader to see a few where in fact there may be none. Was Mrs. Moore or was she not Lewis' lover? She is referred to as the object of "the only really overwhelming 'love-affair' of" Lewis' early life, and we are told that the relationship took so surprising a turn "that it can hardly be classified with the ordinary 'lusts of the flesh'" – presumably that sort provoked by the dancing mistress at Cherbourg. Was it, then, an *extraordinary* lust of the flesh? Does the fact that Lewis' passion "very soon turned from the desire for a mistress into the creation of a mother-substitute" mean that the desire was never satisfied *before* the transformation? On this point I think Christopher Derrick's words are the wisest; he suggests that if the sexual relationship existed at all, "it was small stuff by the standards of that time, and *very* small stuff by the standards of this later day." So why not be out with it? But even *that* is not the point. Presumably, there might be some very good reasons for not being out with it. Then – and here *is* the point – why bring it up at all? Why not take advantage of Lewis' own reticence, absolutely expressed in *Surprised by Joy*? As it stands, the account is innuendo, exactly that sort (though tonally, of course, far different) which a slanderer would indulge if he lacked the evidence to support the conclusion.

The account of Lewis' courtship and marriage is just as puzzling, though not nearly as dangerous. Presumably, no single element in the account is itself false, but somehow they do not add up to the mellow, middle-aged bliss claimed for the relationship. The reader suspects that there is more to the story; and that is the one suspicion which – this side of Agatha Christie – is not allowed.

Those, then, are my complaints, minor and major. How debilitating are they? For over ten years I have been reading everything by and about Lewis that I have been able to lay my hands on, yet no single work (including *Surprised by Joy*) has told me more about the whole Lewis than this biography. Doubtless there is more we would like to know. What was the extent of Green's collaboration on *The Chronicles of Narnia*? What is the full significance of Tolkien's remark that Lewis was easily taken in by people? What was Warren Lewis like? How did Lewis assess his own position as a Public Man? (John Wain says he valued it highly and reveled in it.) How seriously did Lewis consider the impact of his tutorials and lectures? (Father Gervase Matthew insists that he considered this question very seriously indeed.) What was the precise nature of the "war" between Owen Barfield and Lewis? And what exactly was the "selfless" choice which, according to Barfield, CSL made shortly after his conversion?

Well then, there *is* room for more to be done; but that is what Green and Hooper tell us to begin with. Who among us would not have had a six-hundred-and-eight-page biography, instead of the three hundred and eight pages we have been given? Yet who would yield a single one of those pages (excepting the half-dozen or so which obfuscate the Mrs. Moore episode)? For it is a simple matter of fact that, in taking the stance they do toward their subject, Green and Hooper have touched every important base and shown us some new ones. The achievement of Green and Hooper is that, without sycophancy, they have not – in spite of the innumerable fern-seeds – lost sight of this elephant before them. It is owing to that achievement that he stands before us as well.

As Secondary Sources Go . . .
Il Libro de Tutti Libri

Twenty years ago we could wait for the Uniform Edition of Lewis and for the inevitable Companion to the Works of; after all, there was much Lewis still to come and much yet to learn about him. His reputation is constantly evolving as he is re-discovered, but re-discovered partially and incompletely, often being misconstrued. Instead of a re-discovery, then, what is needed most (especially in light of the impending centenary of his birth), is a *restoration*. In *C. S. Lewis: A Companion & Guide* we have exactly that. Notwithstanding his modest ambition to fulfill the duties of Dryasdust – to "find out what the author wrote," as Lewis puts it "and what the hard words meant and what the allusions were to" – Hooper in fact has given us a Lewis whole and rich, with all the variegated texture of his life and work. Indeed, such is Hooper's achievement that if he were British it would merit him a knighthood.

The features of this achievement are: a/ a deft mix of the familiar and the novel, thus making for a freshness of the whole; b/ an array of sometimes startling, often quite subtle, information that, again, makes the work penetrating both in part and in whole; c/ a thoroughness of scope and detail that evinces great authority; d/ a fluency that invites reading *seriatim*, a rare quality for a reference work; and e/ a reach that should invite interest even from those not directly nor especially interested in Lewis. Astonishingly, Hooper manages this restoration without abandoning his "Dryasdust" ambition.

In addition to its index (57pp. and exhaustive even by Hooper's usual standard of inclusion) and primary bibliography (83pp.), the *Companion and Guide* has six main sections:

1/ A "Life of C. S. Lewis" (120pp.) containing 39 sub-sections, most self-evident (Childhood in Belfast, Tutor and Lecturer), many not (Warnie in Ireland, Discovered by America, An Entangled Man). The latter reveal much, but so do the former, as with the Cambridge section and its telling treatment of Tolkien's devoted role in Lewis accepting his Professorship.

2/ A "Chronology of C. S. Lewis' Life," (6pp.) with 59 entries.

3/ "Writings," 417pp. and the heart of the book. Thirty-two books are treated, including *Narrative Poems, Poems* and *The Dark Tower* but excluding collections (the contents of which appear in a succeeding section, "Key Ideas"). For each of the thirty-two, Hooper provides Background, Summary, and a sampling of contemporaneous Reviews. The first amounts, in each case, to no less than a biography (always enlightening, sometimes riveting) of the work in question, the second as close to the real thing as possible, and the last often amazing.

4/ "Key Ideas" (63pp.), containing 37 different entries. If the Writings section is the heart of the book, this is its pulse. Many entries would seem familiar (Allegory, Joy, Chronological Snobbery, Bulverism), but very many others are not (The Law of Inattention and Thrills, A Distrust of). Here we both witness and partake of Lewis' astonishing integrity (the entry on Imagination is a mini-landmark), as we benefit from the depth, range, and specificity of Hooper's command.

5/ "Who's Who" (126pp.). with 58 entries ranging from Aldwinckle, Anscombe, and Baynes, through Capron, MacNeil, and the Moores, to Paxford, Penelope, Pitter, and three Tolkiens. Hooper's ambition (as Thackeray has it) to "visit unvisited tombs" is fulfilled and then some, and with a balance and affection (as with the Harwood entry) that puts people who seemed Fifth Business (to use Robertson Davies' phrase) First, entirely in their own right.

6/ "What's What" (50pp). These 67 entries – from Addison's Walk, the Cowley Fathers, *Literae Humaniores*, and Little Lea, to the *Lamp-Post*, the New York C. S. Lewis Society, Translations and (the utterly charming) Dedicatees – put an end to much puzzlement and satisfy more nagging curiosity than all the secondary works on Lewis combined.

All told, the 162 entries of parts four, five and six, are in fact 162 essays, each reminding the reader, even the devoted reader, of all that he did not, but ought to, know, and assuring him now that he does. Everywhere there is greater clarity than before, yet no nuance, shading, or subtlety of Lewis is ever compromised, let alone betrayed.

Samplings from the several sections illustrate the qualities already mentioned and others as well. "Warnie in Ireland" is at once wrenching and wonderful, revealing especially for its depiction of Warnie's life apart from Jack – he was much more an independent man-of-the-world than his brother. "Cambridge" tells the story of Lewis' Professorship and demonstrates Hooper's relentless scholarship with the citation of quite obscure sources, quoting (for example) Joy's previously unpublished and thoroughly penetrating comment on *"De Descriptione Temporum."* In Who's Who, the madman Capron comes frighteningly alive, from sources other than *Surprised by Joy*, as do The Great Knock (who was something of a legend even before Lewis made him one) and Ruth Pitter, whose account of her exchange with Lewis is headlined, "Ruth Pitter defeats C. S. Lewis in Argument." We learn of David Gresham's enormous learning. And we meet, as never before – not even in Lewis' own work – the remarkable Flora Lewis (my single favorite entry).

In What's What Oxford's terms are given their dates and Mods and Greats are finally explained, soon after which we learn that Lewis is translated into Icelandic, Slovene, Welsh and Hawaiian. All of Lewis' pseudonyms are identified and explained, and his own most Influential Books list is re-printed. (It omits Alexander' *Space, Time and Deity*.) In Key Ideas, "Imagination" gets 10 pages, with nine sub-divisions and references to more than a dozen works by Lewis and others. In Writings there is treasure abounding, the entry on *Till We Have Faces* (20pp.) being among the most valuable. (Here note especially Lewis' exchange with Christian Hardie, wife of Colin.)

Hooper's own learning, apart from his command of Lewis, is impressive, his references never remotely adventitious. (Throughout there is much that is previously unpublished.) There are some anomalies. The draft of the entry on *A Grief Observed* (which I was, as with other entries and along with other people, asked to comment upon) bears virtually no serious resemblance to the published version, surely owing to the influence of Douglas Gresham (who apparently would deny all antecedents to a work which simply must be regarded as an entirely spontaneous and ingenuous response to his mother's death only). Hooper had to cut 100 pages for length; he himself cut another 50. How many did Mr. Gresham dictate be cut and wherefore those omissions? The reviewer wishes that there were an entry on C. S. Lewis Pte Ltd, including a description of the roles and authority possessed by Hooper, Curtis Brown (the literary agent), HarperCollins (as well as other publishers), and by Gresham in the issuance of works by and about CSL.

There seem to be no notable errors. We would have liked entries on Lewis' spirituality; and a section on Influential Authors (Hooker, Traherne, Law; MacDonald is included) should be part of a second edition, if not published separately. But withal the restoration is complete, and it is the best we are ever likely to have – unless Hooper has another 1000 pages up his sleeve and the freedom to publish them. This is *the* Lewis book to have, whether it be the only one or one of fifty, for we who did not know this Lewis, who could not have known him (that is, *connaitre,* as he would say, not *savoir*), now have come closer than ever to the man to whom we owe so much and for whom so many of us pray. Among other things Hooper's *Companion & Guide* is a very great act of *Philia*.

10

A Sophisticated Man

Proof-reading and fact-checking have their places in most reviews but not here; after a short spell this book absorbed me beyond my remembering to lend that sort of attention. I can say that I recall too few errors to justify an accounting; so for these and other snippets of open-clawed cattiness I refer you to A. N. Wilson's review in the *TLS* of June 6 (but also to the letters of Michael Ward, Andrew Cuneo and Barbara Reynolds that followed, and to Raymond Edwards' review in *The Tablet* of the U.K., a model of the reviewing art).

Alas, I have one complaint, provoked by my wife. When Lewis reports (November 22, 1931) that he was brought his morning tea, Hooper fails to identify who did so. When I queried Hooper he responded with the disappointing (to my wife) news that the tea-bearer was in fact *not* Mrs. Moore but Lewis' scout, adding "I should have named him." Now, you either prefer compulsive footnoters or you don't. I do; for every note I do not need – and that I wonder if *anyone* would need – there are ten that I and (I suppose) many others heartily welcome.

In that light the time is long past to declare the obvious. Decades ago many devoted readers of CSL wondered about all sorts of people and things related to him and did not wonder about many we knew nothing of. Then along came Walter Hooper. Not alone, of course, but pre-eminently, for forty years now, with neither university support (think of Frederick Pottle working on Boswell's papers, at Yale) nor much assistance other than the *ad hoc* typist, he has labored away, resisting the siren call of Leading Critic, filling in the blanks, giving us not only more Lewis but the *de facto* annotated Lewis. Any sober and serious surveyor of the scene must marvel at his achievement: ample, reliable, steadfast, consistent and, as the reader sees from this middle volume of the three that will constitute the Collected Letters, utterly indispensable.

Indispensable, that is, not only to the student but to the fan, and not just to the fan but to letter-lovers whomever the writer. Certainly when Collections follow Selections redundancy is inevitable. Here the little we do encounter is welcome. The many ellipses in Warren Lewis' selection are filled (and his many obscure conventions clarified: do *not* skip Hooper's preface) and we see, for example, the Greeves letters and so many others as features of a rich, varied and complex life and mind. Here is the heart of the matter, *the very* life and mind the fruits of which blazed so dazzlingly into the firmament of intellectual and literary celebrity and rooted so deeply and so supplely into the souls of men. *That* Lewis. . . .

On October 25th, 1934, Lewis writes to the eminent critic Paul Elmer More. He is appreciating More's new *The Sceptical Approach to Religion,* especially for making him "understand for the first time why most of the representatives of the present Christian renaissance so hate Idealism." But Lewis, who marks Idealism as one the great influences on his conversion, defends Idealism, reminding More of the nature of doors. "I do not think I should be disrespectful in urging you ... to remember that in shutting the door to keep the faithful in.. . you are inevitably, by the same act, shutting out those who might return."

But more, and a more important, matter follows. Lewis asserts that he cannot "relinquish the Absolutist view of God." In fact, he says, his "wish-belief" system demands the eternal and necessary, "while also not wanting the immobile, the unanswering. In fine, I want to have it both ways: and this would be the flimsiest of self-indulgence, but for the huge historic fact of the doctrine of the Trinity. For surely that doctrine is just the doctrine that we are to give up *neither* of those conceptions of God of which you accept one and . . . reject the other." Then the characteristic *coup de* rhetorical *grace:* "Is the Christian belief not precisely this; that the same being which is eternally . . . already at the End etc. etc., yet also, in some incomprehensible way, [a] purposing, feeling, and finally crucified Man in a particular place and time? So that somehow or other, we have it both ways?"

"*We have* it *both ways."* This jolt of intellectual wattage *and* quenching spiritual gulp, so dispositive, gratifying, vindicating - and yet in Lewis' hands so easy and apt that it seems a mere gloss - this letter we have never before seen in print. Alone it is worth the price of the book.

And there is no end of it. If Lewis societies spend their hours at nothing other than browsing over what they have not previously seen, then they would welcome in the dawn. Start with these: Hooper's notes for September 19th,

1935; to Leo Baker on June 24th, 1936; to Warren, the *whole* of the July 20th, 1940, wherein Jack adumbrates the idea for *Screwtape* (and at which, owing to the notes, we find out what Hitler said that Jack found so seductive); to Lyman Stebbins on May 8th, 1945 (and do follow up footnote 33!); and - but there is no end of it.

Some years ago I argued that there were many aspects to the master. He had told us of his Outer and Inner selves; yet on the evidence of Lewis' diary Mrs. Moore knew nothing of the latter, and Albert knew only of an Official (and substantially false) undergraduate self. Moreover, underlying them all was a Deeper (especially but not solely a pre-conversion) self, God's very stone being caned and breathed to life. Lewis was variously open with, blind to, and to some degree secretive about these selves. Now in *Collected Letters II* we meet them all and, in substantial context, know them as never before. The *putative* misogynist, bully, pastiche-meister, along with many another, including the quotidian and the familiar, Lewis, are all here. It is our pleasure - often thrilling - both to contemplate and to enjoy them.

So do take care. As with a book so with a sophisticated man: How one reads either (Mr. Wilson) may tell us more about the reader than the subject.

Arc of Surrender

The Collected Letters of C. S. Lewis, Ed. Walter Hooper, London; HarperCollins. Vol. 1, Family Letters 1905-1931, 2000; Vol. 2, Books, Broadcasts and War 1931-1949, 2004; Vol. 3, Narnia, Cambridge and Joy, 2006.

Forty years ago the *Letters of C. S. Lewis* appeared, with a memoir and edited by Lewis' brother Warren, we were told, but in fact shaped by Lewis' former pupil Christopher Derrick, who stepped in when Warren's alcoholism became an insuperable obstacle to his completing the book. For all its inadequacies the selection revealed much more about Lewis than we knew at the time. Now we have the final volume of the *Collected Letters of C. S. Lewis*. Between the original selection and this final collection, five other volumes of letters (and a handful published separately) have appeared: the slim *Letters To an American Lady* (1967), the revealing *They Stand Together* (1979, to Arthur Greeves), *Lewis' Letters to Children* (1985), a second, much ampler and more reliable version of the original selection, this time edited by Walter Hooper (1988), and *The Latin Letters of C. S. Lewis* (1988, to an Italian priest, now Saint Giovanni Calabria). The *Collected Letters* places these *in situ*, with all deletions fully restored (including sections obliterated by Greeves, restored by Hooper with the use of infra-red photography). Yet together these previously-published letters (the preponderance of them now out of print) make up less than half of this massive collection which, as an appendix in volume 3, even includes Lewis' "Great War" letters written to his "second friend" Owen Barfield (and never before readily available) dealing with the Gnostic beliefs of Rudolph Steiner's Anthroposophy and ramifying to the natures of reality, epistemology and the imagination.

In all, the 3228 letters (fewer than ten late-arrivals are omitted) tell, both outwardly upon Lewis' ambit and inwardly upon his enormously engaging psyche, with strokes that are mundane, reflective, intimate, tender, philosophical, brusque, theological, witty, literary and quirky (e.g. Lewis was a capable and witty cartoonist and sometimes accompanied his letter with a drawing, all of which Hooper always reproduces). This plenitude is supported by nearly one hundred biographical sketches on 211 pages, over eight thousand footnotes (not endnotes), and probably a hundred pages of interspersed, italicized narrative and descriptive links. The effect is that of an annotated autobiography, a primary rendering of one of the richest, most variegated and influential writers in the history of the language. Walter Hooper has served his old friend and us splendidly.

Except for its first segment from Lewis' birth in 1898 to a family move to a grand new house in 1905 (during which he experiences *Sehnsucht*, or "Joy," a longing for Heaven, for the first time), the reader travels the entire curve of Lewis' life. After the first, the segments are these: 2/ to the death of his mother, Flora, in 1908; 3/ to the advent in 1919 of Mrs. Moore ("Minto") with whom he would establish a household after seeing combat in WWI; 4/ to the death of his father Albert (1929), a stage including both his military service and his Oxford career; then a transition: his conversion to Christianity and the composition – in two weeks – of *The Pilgrim's Regress* (Christmas day, 1933), his first Christian work and a paradigmatic one; 5/ to *The Problem of Pain* (1940), during which stage the Kilns is established as the homestead, his scholarly reputation is established (*The Allegory of Love*, 1936), and his brother Warren retires from the army to the Kilns, bringing with him a strong distaste for the mysterious (and often insufferable) Mrs. Moore and his growing alcoholism; 6/ to his own "dark night of the soul": his most prolific stage, establishing his reputation as a religious thinker and Christian apologist, owing largely to the publication of *The Screwtape Letters* and to his wartime BBC broadcasts on Christianity; then a second transition from the late forties to the very early fifties, marked by the death of Mrs. Moore and his recovery from the dark night; 7/ to the arrival of Joy Davidman (1953), nearly a three-year period of liberation, tranquility, hard work (especially on *English Literature in the Sixteenth Century, Excluding Drama*), and a metastasizing correspondence (at its height, two thousand letters a week); 8/ to Joy's death (1960, which occasions Lewis' most poignant work, *A Grief Observed*), including his move to Cambridge (1955) as Professor of Medieval and Renaissance English literature and, of course, his bedside marriage to a dying Joy (April 23, 1956); 9/ to his own death on November 22, 1963.

When not quite seven years old, in November of 1905, Lewis writes to his ten-year-old brother Warren, mentioning Peter the canary, a big black cat ready to pounce on the bird, and Tim, the family dog, who has "the head staggers" as he watches. Then (without capital letters), "I am doing french as well as Latin now, and I think I like the Latin better. Tomorrow I decline that old" – that old! – "'Bonus, Bona, Bonum' thing." Not quite twelve years later, on January 31, 1917, he writes sneeringly to his "first friend" Arthur Greeves, "I wish to goodness (or to Jeshua shall we say?) that you could get out of the office." At the time Lewis is barely eighteen, not yet at Oxford nor in the army (for which would volunteer). The letter is among a short series to Arthur signed "Philomastix," or "lover of the whip," in which he makes occasional reference to his fondness for mild domination of the female, especially if bent over his knee. When not quite thirty-three he writes (again to Arthur) the now-famous description of his epiphany. During a late-night stroll with Hugo Dyson and J.R.R. Tolkien, fellow lovers of myth, he comes to understand that, "the story of Christ is simply a true myth: a myth working on us in the same way as the others, but with this tremendous difference *that it really happened*." He is a combat veteran, an Oxford don, an orphan, and a householder supporting the mother of a fallen comrade-in-arms, one Mrs. Moore, who has been variously a mother-surrogate and some sort of mistress; within a few months of the epiphany, when he is thirty-three, he is a Christian. By his own reckoning he had been "a blaspheming atheist" a self-indulgent, amoral "prig," and a mendacious son to a loving, generous and emotionally battered (albeit difficult) father. Now that very worst period of his life is behind him.

As the arc of Lewis' life ascends, the number of his correspondents increases, the average length of his letters drastically declines, and religious content (theological, apologetic, and pastoral) grows in direct proportion to his growing fame: during the WWII and for some years thereafter he would rise at four a.m. to answer mail, which he never failed to do (thanks to Warren's assistance). Always there is friendship, literature, nature (it is the lost age of long walking tours, not "hiking," which Lewis later is amused to find he has been doing all his life), family, home and its occupants (including children evacuated during the Blitz), conversation, encounters with prominent personages (Yeats, Roy Campbell, and T. S. Eliot stand out, among many others), and personal introspection, especially after Lewis assumes a spiritual director and confessor in the mid-forties, Fr. Walter Adams, and begins his Latin correspondence in the late forties with Fr. Calabria (for which we are provided both the originals and their translation). Fifteen years thereafter he writes to Mary Willis Shelburne (the "American Lady"), "What in Heaven's name is 'distressing' about an old man saying to an old woman that they haven't much more to do here? I wasn't in the least expressing resentment or despondency. I was referring to an obvious fact and one which I don't find either distressing or embarrassing." He would die seven months later.

He was as intellectually sophisticated as any man of his age; his few dozen book reviews (uncollected) and cultural commentary (see, for example, *Present Concerns*, ed. Hooper) are elegant, wide-ranging, and dispositive. During the war years, however, and thereafter Lewis would spend most of his writing time as a Christian apologist for those far less sophisticated than he – a vocation that consumed most of the oxygen of his reputation. Perhaps this naturally argumentative man couldn't help himself, as we see even in his private correspondence. On October 25th, 1934, he appreciates Paul Elmer More's new *The Sceptical Approach to Religion* for making him "understand for the first time why most of the representatives of the present Christian renaissance so hate Idealism." But Lewis, who marks Idealism as one the great influences on his conversion, reminds More that locked doors keep people out as well as in. Moreover, he asserts that he cannot "relinquish the Absolutist view of God." His "wish-belief" system demands the eternal and necessary "while also not wanting the immobile, the unanswering. In fine, I want to have it both ways: and this would be the flimsiest of self-indulgence, but for the huge historic fact of the doctrine of the Trinity. For surely that doctrine is just the doctrine that we are to give up *neither* of those conceptions of God of which you accept one and . . . reject the other." Then the characteristic *coup de* rhetorical *grace*: "Is the Christian belief not precisely this; that the same being which is eternally perfect . . . already at the End etc etc, yet also, in some incomprehensible way, is a purposing, feeling, and finally crucified Man in a particular place and time? So that somehow or other, we have it both ways?" Of course: *We have it both ways*! This high wattage intellectual jolt *and* quenching spiritual gulp seems definitive and is not to be found either conceptually or rhetorically in Lewis' published work.

At least once that argument gene compels Lewis to do what he never did in his published work: discuss a sectarian matter. Between April and June of 1945, Lyman Stebbins, the founder-to-be of Catholics United for the Faith, wrote two letters to Lewis. The first asked for reasons *not* to convert to Catholicism. Lewis (May 8, 1945) invoked, "universal tradition and especially Apostolic Christianity," the inability of Catholic theology to trace some of its doctrines to "within 1000 years of [Christ's] time," and especially the importance of fidelity to Scripture; yet he also allowed for "endless progress." Hooper cites Stebbins's second letter, an astounding refutation, but fails to summarize it in a footnote, where it surely belongs. (I know Hooper was up against considerable gate keeping, but surely we would have welcomed this note over, say, his risible one on, of all things, the Korean Conflict.) Stebbins would attribute his conversion to this exchange, and we know many other

Catholic converts began their journeys by reading Lewis. In that light, how interesting to read Lewis affirm a version of the Catholic doctrine of the Communion of Saints. On April 1, 1952 he writes of his late and very dear friend, the novelist Charles Williams, "I do miss him. But what strikes me even more is the sense that he is already helping me more from where he is than he would do on earth."

The ambiguously rhetorical Lewis is patently evident in the letter of July 20, 1940. Not often is the reading public privy to an idea for a book in its conception, yet there is the zygotic *Screwtape Letters*, at church no less. "Before the service was over – one cd. wish these things came more seasonable – I was struck by an idea for a book wh. I think might be both useful and entertaining. It wd. be called 'As One Devil to Another' and would consist of letters from an elderly retired devil to a young devil who has just started work on his first 'patient'." More revealing, though, is an earlier reference in the letter to a BBC broadcast of one of Hitler's speeches (simultaneously translated). Lewis has been listening with his friend and physician Robert Havard, commonly knows as Humphrey. (Havard is a puzzling omission from the biographical sketches, whereas an exceedingly minor scholar like Kathryn Lindskoog is included.) Hitler is making "a final appeal to common sense," insisting that it has never been nor ever will be his intention to trouble England. To his own distress, Lewis writes, "I don't know if I'm weaker than other people: but it is a positive revelation to me how *while the speech lasts* it is impossible not to waver just a little. I should be useless as a schoolmaster or a policeman. Statements which I *know* to be untrue all but convince me, at any rate for the moment. . . ." Surely he recognized Plato's complaint about the injudicious persuasiveness rhetoric at the core of his own complaint? And just as surely he recalled Socrates' own rhetorical mastery even (as in the *Gorgias*, for example) while condemning rhetoric? Ironically, as a religious thinker Lewis actually profited from his role as apologist; his ideas were polished, their muscularity developed, and their applications sharpened (not least by the stringencies of the BBC). But his unease is no mere temperamental tick. Lewis was always ambivalent towards the ancient art and would be abidingly unsettled by his own rhetorical mastery.

This disjunction is symptomatic of a deep-seated trouble in Lewis' soul which rumbled to the surface in the late forties. On January 14, 1949 he writes to Fr. Calabria that his "house is unquiet and devastated by women's quarrels," referring to Mrs. Moore as his "aged mother" who "is worn out by long infirmity," in fact, mental infirmity. He claims to have nothing left to say, that his public has tired of him, and that such literary emptiness is all to the best, since he might otherwise "fall into that evil disease, vainglory." On September 10th of the same year he confesses to the priest "a certain Accidia, an evil disease and, I believe, of the Seven Deadly Sins that one which is in me the strongest – though few believe this of me." And then, nearly two years later, on December 26, 1951, suddenly this: "As for myself, during the past year a great joy has befallen me. Difficult though it is, I shall try to explain this in words. . . . For a long time I believed in the forgiveness of sins. But suddenly (on St. Mark's day [April 25th]) this truth appeared in my mind in so clear a light that I perceived that never before (and that after many confessions and absolutions) had I believed it with my whole heart." This from a man who some five years earlier had written an essay "On Forgiveness" in which he writes that Jesus *commands* us to accept His forgiveness.

What had happened? Lewis' devoted and beloved mother Flora died just before he turned ten; he was undone, and atheism – or some simulacrum – ensued very quickly. His father died when the young man was twenty-seven, and theism ensued. But just as during his twenties the Holy Spirit (he tells us in his autobiography *Surprised by Joy*) was beckoning his deepest self even during his declensions, just so was there a foreshadowing during the dark night of the late forties of the grace that lay ahead: he began having vivid dreams of lions and decided to have a go at what would become *The Lion, the Witch and the Wardrobe*. Presently Mrs. Moore – the great guilt-inducing burden of Lewis' life, about which he refused to speak, even with his dearest friend Warren – died on January 12, 1951, and thereupon closely followed the grace of Christ's certain forgiveness.

Joy Davidman, jealous, possessive, intelligent and loving, enters the arc at its height, in 1953. Lewis is no match for her, saying of himself that he never expected to find in his fifties the romance that had passed him by in his teens. They marry in 1956, at what seemed to be Joy's deathbed. Throughout this period he maintains a correspondence with a dozen different people: Americans who send him hams and jellies, the American Lady who badgered, Dorothy L. Sayers, Ruth Pitter, the poet who, but for his own ill health, he might have married after Joy's death. He takes the professorship at Cambridge and sees less and less of his friends, virtually abandoning Tolkien, who had engineered the professorship. He writes much, completing *The Chronicles of Narnia*, and produces his one real novel, the masterpiece *Till We Have Faces*, a first-person complaint from a queen. Here Joy's influence was apparently decisive. For those who regard this book as one of our two greatest first-person modern novels (with *Lolita*), these letters are priceless. Lewis seeks guidance from women readers (his women pen-friendships, especially those long-standing ones with Nan Dunbar, Mary Neylan, and Sister Penelope, were sustained and even proliferated, these not including the badgerers and the enamored), who immediately see what he is up to and how well he's pulled it off. His male editor, Jocelyn Gibb, however, is another story: he, apparently, got to a key scene without realizing Queen Orual was, Lewis writes impatiently, "in a most perfectly ordinary, jealous, ravenous, biological fashion, in love with Bardia." He then proceeds to cite every piece of evidence in the book for that love, concluding, "every woman reader so far has [gotten it]." He also comments on the jacket artwork and on the need for secretaries to be sure to mail *all* the chapters in proof. In short, no detail was beyond him. No wonder he discouraged some correspondents – even as he supported many financially – by saying he was "with book" while writing this masterpiece.

But he never discourages children, who continue to write letters to him. Lewis' answers are among the most affecting in the collection, and to see them within the context of all his other correspondence, which work was a small portion of all his other work, is chastening. To one child, who had mentioned a one-way street, Lewis answers that a one-way street seems strange, since in England streets run in *both* directions at once. To another, who thanked God that He had made dogs for us, Lewis answers that the boy shouldn't be so sure God didn't make us for dogs. He gives advice (e.g. on writing), asks questions, discusses his fondness for mice (which he refuses to trap), defends his dislike for the word 'kids', and in one case asks for forgiveness. The mother of one Laurence had written with the news that her son was disturbed that he might love Aslan more than Jesus. After explaining how that simply could not be, he suggests a prayer Laurence might say which would end, "and if Mr. Lewis has worried any other children by his books or done them any harm, then please forgive him and help him never to do it again."

Oscar Wilde had his Hart-Davis, Evelyn Waugh his Mark Amory, Sigmund Freud his Ernest Freud. These collections are solid and frequently brilliant, but none approaches the authority, wholeness, and suggestiveness of this one, which reveals a Lewis not as transparent as his rhetoric and the thinking it conveys. Consider this omission: he scarcely mentions Flora's death, though it haunts all his years. According to the research literature of early parental loss, such a death is something a young boy comes to terms with but never quite gets over; it complicates him. "Philomastix" indentures himself, first to Mrs. Moore, then to Joy Davidman who, like Flora Lewis, would die a painful, cancer-ridden death. Here is the heart of the matter. However obliquely, these letters present the very mind and heart the fruits of which blazed so dazzlingly into the firmament of intellectual and literary celebrity and became rooted so deeply and so supplely into the souls of men. Always eschewing schools and even broad historical periods (he denied the occurrence of the Renaissance), Lewis was essentially a realist. On August 7, 1963, he writes the last letter of this collection. Having been serving as a member of the commission to revise *The Book of Common Prayer*, Lewis now finds that "a prolonged coma" a few weeks earlier has decisively wrecked him. "This is my final and official resignation from the Commission," he writes, "please make my farewells and . . . add my cordial thanks for the great kindness . . . always shown me." A touching, final irony this, at the end of the arc: Lewis thanking others.

Part 2

CRITICAL VIEWS

Broadening the Lewisian Context

> "Let us try to discover how far it might be plausible to define a good book as a book which is read in one way, and a bad book as a book which is read in another... As a natural result of their different behaviour in reading, what they have read is constantly and prominently present to the mind of the few, but not to that of the many. The former mouth over their favourite lines and stanzas in solitude. Scenes and characters from books provide them with a sort of iconography by which they interpret or sum up their own experience. They talk to one another about books, often at length. The latter seldom think or talk about their reading. ... We are so busy doing things with the work that we meet only ourselves. ... If we find that a book is usually read on one way, still more if we never find that it is read in the other, we have a *prima facie* case for thinking it bad."
>
> *Experiment in Criticism*

With regard to our (collective) reading of C.S. Lewis, we generally are The Few. We talk to each other about him, not merely often, but almost always, at length; and by way of that talk we discover that, yes, he sums up our experience both inner and outer. Others see him not only as the provider of our iconography but as the icon itself. It is a false charge, essentially, and a facile one. Simply to deny it is a drudgery. We know that we are attracted to a quality – to the quiddity of the man and of his world of discourse – we know that we are attracted to the quality more than we are to the statuary. Should it be otherwise? If it is to our perpetual nourishment and delight that we "enjoy" him (to use the term as Lewis adopted it from Samuel Alexander), that is because his world is more capacious than the shadowland through which we daily navigate. Like the real stable in *The Last Battle*, Lewis is bigger on the inside than on the outside.

There could be no Few, though, without a Many, including several who should know better. Samuel Hynes, for example. He reviewed Chad Walsh's *The Literary Legacy of C.S. Lewis* and *"C.S. Lewis at the Breakfast Table" and Other Reminiscences* for the *New York Times*, making erroneous and otherwise foolish statements: the sort a reasonable man would be embarrassed to be reminded of. So on the thousand-to-one chance that Hynes is both reasonable and a reader of our Bulletin, I am going to embarrass him. "Lewis' books have not been read by anyone not either a child or a Christian. These two audiences share one quality of imagination – a common willingness to extend reality beyond the visible, and to accept myths of that other reality as a form of truth-telling. . . . he was, all his writing life, both a child and a Christian." Invincibly condescending, this. (And possibly ignorant, as well. Lewis "hated" children? *Breakfast Table* offers more than one instance of eyewitness testimony to the contrary.)

It is not my purpose tonight even to state a case, let alone to make one; rather, I would suggest – it is impossible to overdo the reservations, limitations, and caveats – what the proposition might be were we to acknowledge the need for debate (with all its hazards). Samuel Hynes and others are, I think, like the dwarfs of *The Last Battle* who remain in the old stable and simply refuse to see the glorious meadow bathed in sunlight before them. Yet not everyone who criticizes Lewis or who is impatient with the likes of us is in this category; many are disinterested, generous, but skeptical people who have little regard for Lewis and for the business we are about. They are the Rational Opposition of Goodwill, serious and (as half of the dedication to *Breakfast Table* implies) indispensable. I believe we should trouble ourselves with them much more than we have. Their numbers and vehemence ought to disturb us, for they may be symptoms. Specifically: we – the admiring community of amateur and professional Lewis scholars – too frequently fail Lewis' own criterion for pronouncing a book good. We too frequently "use" rather than "receive"; too frequently fail to read "in the same spirit as the author writ." Thus we represent a Lewis who "merits, invites or compels" rejection.

Recently, at a meeting of a division of the Modern Language Association, an editor from Eerdmans Publishing rose and shouted, "No more books on Lewis, please, no more books on Lewis!" After noting that Lewis and books on Lewis have had no more sincere and industrious friend than Eerdmans, even we must concede that there may be too many; and the only kind of book of which there may be too many is bad books, or at least mediocre or unnecessary books. (Coin of the realm is not the only currency subject to inflation.) Breaking with tradition, I would like to specify some of the books which I believe are weak (some currency, especially of the frenzied periodical type, is not only cheap but counterfeit and not now within our scope) and to say why I think them so. And if there be healthy dispute, it can only be an antidote to the malady noted above.

The nature and scope of Martha C. Sammons's *A Guide Through Narnia*, for example, are too insubstantial for a book. Her analyses are little more than descriptions, those little more than synopses, thus repeating the synopses which constitute the whole of Chapter Three. In six other chapters we learn nearly nothing which is not already obvious or explicit in *The Chronicles* themselves: in *The Last Battle*, "the wonderful world come(s) to an end"; "the one person who makes Narnia worth visiting is Aslan himself"; "the mouse's size deceptively hides his abundant, often impulsive courage." In the final chapter we learn much that is not explicit; every sleeping dragon that would be watchful against a disinterested and attentive response to the literary object is (dutifully, it seems) aroused. "Christian Concepts in the Narnia Tales" takes us through "Creation", "The Tree and the Garden", "Sacrifice and Resurrection", and so on.

All of this comes after a brief introduction in which Sammons quotes Lewis on the need for stealing past those dragons, and after Sammons's own reminder that the tales are not allegorical. Along the way, she does provide a new and useful perspective by citing George MacDonald's essay "The Fantastic Imagination," a provocative rationale for Lewis' work. But the link is quickly dropped; an opportunity lost. Attempting to compensate for that loss, Sammons provides, in two short paragraphs, an inventory of Lewis' "techniques": supposition, transportation, illustration, description, and imagery. In the appendices we get even less; there we are told, for example, that "Charn" is "a form of 'churn' which means to agitate (here the *OED* is trotted out). Surely this book could not have been intended for serious students of the language and its literature; as it would be ruinous for children, so it is patronizing of adults.

A second book which is one of Too Many – I am trepidatious, having heard some praise for this book here tonight – is Leanne Payne's *Real Presence*, the purpose of which is to help us "to marvel at the Holy Spirit's use of Lewis' talent." And so we should, and we do. The weakness is not in the purpose of the book but in the narrowness of the author's context: the presumption, not only of premises shared with the reader across-the-board, but of a temperament, including some biases, common to all reasonable people. Note the number of undefended (and perhaps unexamined?) assumptions in this astonishingly broad and categorical – yet casually posited – judgment: "As the Church, principally through St. Thomas Aquinas, came to accept the Aristotelian epistemology and incorporated it into its theology, the Judeo-Christian understanding of the deep heart (the unconscious mind and its way of knowing) simply dropped from sight." But Jacques Maritain's *Creative Intuition in Art and Poetry* demonstrates exactly the opposite. Again, according to Payne (in a footnote), Lewis is joined only by Alexander Solzhenitsyn in opposing the attempt to combine good and evil; she does not tell us on what grounds Chesterton, say, is excluded from that company.

(Lewis certainly includes him.) Similarly, her reductionist dismissals of Blake, Jung, and B.F. Skinner (all in footnotes) cannot be taken seriously. We need have a special brief with none of these writers to note, along with Lewis, that a small company of like-thinking people – in the absence of a Rational Opposition – can sneak by almost anything.

These two books are striking examples of Bad Reading. Others not so strikingly evidence the same syndrome. I know I am not alone in thinking Professor Kilby's *Images of Salvation* an anomaly; and even Tom Howard's elegantly written and thought-out *The Achievement of C.S. Lewis* possesses the feature common to the category: the rhetoric of the already-converted. In over-doing "enjoyment" we can under-do "contemplation"; and as we continue to talk too much to ourselves, the disinterested public is ignored; group-think takes hold. Thence there develops an image of C.S. Lewis for public inspection. But the positive narrowness of the intellectual and rhetorical boundaries that de-limit the Too Many Lewis books is not the only shortcoming to distinguish the category. This closeness, an error of commission, is accompanied by (glaring) errors of omission. (And these are especially embarrassing, given the perhaps too self-conscious application by Lewis writers of the words "scholar" and "scholarship" to the Lewisian literature and to those who produce it.)

Much has been made, for example, of the abounding presence of archetypes in Lewis' fiction; inevitably, the name of Carl Jung is invoked and some transcendent "influence" implied. Certainly there is one, but it is not of Jung on Lewis; rather it is of Rudolf Otto's *The Idea of the Holy* on both. They emphatically tell us so. Yet there is no major treatment of that book or description of its influence in any work on C.S. Lewis. We also know of the great importance to Lewis – he tells us it taught him one of the great lessons of his life – of Alexander's *Space, Time and Deity*. The author, his book, and its famous lesson are constantly and usefully alluded to. But the influence conveys much more than one lesson. Alexander's major premise is that things are not true and false of themselves but real regarding their own coherence, a premise without which Lewis could not have written as he did on Imagination and could not, for example, have remarked that he believed in Christianity as he believed that the sun is in the sky: not because he could see it clearly – he couldn't – but because by it he could see everything else. And not only could Lewis have written the following quotation from Alexander, but again and again he seems to have re-written it and, of course, to have lived it: "The religious emotion is as unique . . . as hungry appetite or love . . . There is in fact no duty to be religious any more than there is a duty to be hungry. . . . It is in our constitution."

The absence of any serious treatment of these and similar issues becomes conspicuous when it obtains in precisely the sort of book – for example, Walsh's *Literary Legacy* or Gilbert Meilaender's *The Taste for the Other* – which are legitimate scholarship. The list of similar issues, by the way, ought to include discussions (with respect to Lewis) of Jacob Boehme, of St. Athanasius (both a source and a striking influence!), and even of Chesterton ("Morality and Philosophy" says much about Chronological Snobbery, and when Lewis wrote his essay on Kipling he might have had Chesterton's right at hand). Published works scarcely deal with Lewis as essayist, preacher, or theorist of practical communication. Worst of all, there is nary an allusion to Lewis the reviewer-critic (in which role he had a formidable reputation). Of the reviews listed in Hooper's bibliography, about three dozen are in hard-to-come by specialists' journals. (His review of George Steiner's *The Death of Tragedy* is typically revealing; it is both reassuring to greet the same intellectually consistent Lewis to whom we are accustomed and exciting to meet a Lewis slightly differing in temperament from one we know – an urbanely self-assured critic quite ready to be in the world.)

If we do not agree on which books merit criticism, or on the substance of that criticism, or even on a list of omissions (which, of course, I recommend as an agenda of sorts), then perhaps we can agree on this (and thence on its implications): "concentricity" is at work. With Lewis at the center, our reading of him (in the sense proposed in *An Experiment in Criticism*) constitutes a first circle which, in its turning, generates a wider, second circle: a disinterested public (both popular and professional) perception of Lewis himself. Given this paradigm, we simply must embrace Lewis' own tradition (demonstrated at the Socratic Club, for example) of attending to the Rational Opposition, and we would sophisticate our talk. I know – having looked the word up in the *OED* – that the ground is shaky, for the word can mean to render impure, to adulterate, to mix with some foreign or inferior substance; but it might also mean to alter by education or experience so as to be wordly-wise, not naive.

Unlike any other writer, Lewis often seems to me to be the only author I need to ever read; as "icons" go he is not only first, he is alone; in fact, he sums up an astonishing amount of my experience often before it has occurred. Yet in spite of this centrality, he is profitably and properly viewed as a member of a constellation with other members.

In 1948 there appeared a book which did great harm to the social sciences (so-called), exposing their linguistic abuses, their logical fallacies, and their hazards to the common welfare; *That Hideous Strength* we know, fictionally depicts this exposition. This book, though, is not *The Abolition of Man* but Richard Weaver's *Ideas Have Consequences*. And this passage, reminiscent of another that begins "You have never talked to a mere mortal", will sound familiar: " . . . everybody knows in their bones that something is eternal, and that something has to do with human beings. All the greatest people who ever lived have been telling us that for five thousand years. . . . There's something way down deep that's eternal about every human being." That is the Preface to *The Angel That Troubled the Waters*, by Thornton Wilder, who in the late 'twenties wrote of our need for books " . . . religious in a dilute fashion that is a believer's concession to a contemporary standard of good manners. The revival of religion is almost a matter of rhetoric." Do recall Lewis to Sister Penelope: "any amount of Christianity can now be smuggled in under the guise of fiction." Wilder and Lewis, nearly exact contemporaries, seem to have gotten the same ideas, roughly at the same time. In 1955 the first production of Wilder's *The Alcestiad* took place in Scotland; it is, *mutatis mutandis*, a twin to *Till We Have Faces*. And though Lewis takes us "further up and further in" than Wilder does, the latter's inconsolably moving statement of supernatural meaning-in-history which concludes *The Eighth Day* is eminently comparable to the end of Narnia. (The interested reader will want to read *Thornton Wilder and his Public* where, in accounting for his brother's lack of popularity among critics, Amos Wilder could very well be answering Samuel Hynes.)

This broadened perspective discovers allies – Robert Jastrow (*God and the Astronomers*), Bruno Bettelheim (*The Uses of Enchantment*), Karl Menninger (*Whatever Happened to Sin?*) – where previously we suspected there were none. Not only do we delight in seeing Lewis' ideas vindicated, but we gain reinforcements against the likes of, say, Wayne Dyer (who wants us to pull our own strings) and of Carl Sagan ("in the beginning was the cosmos", which is all there is, now and forever). On the popular battlefield, we must make the same use (yes, here "use") of Lewis that he made of himself. And once we begin to look, there is no telling whom Providence will turn up on our behalf. Would Lewis have us attend to the concrete quiddity of the world, to take joy in the homely? "She clapped her hands for joy. What a discovery! . . . the trick lay in leading the most ordinary life imaginable, get an ordinary job, in itself a joy in its very ordinariness, and then be as extraordinary or as ordinary as one pleased." That is the heroine of Walker Percy's *The*

Second Coming, according to which, writes Anatole Broyard in the *New York Times*, "happiness is serious." Will Barret, Percy's hero, recalls the medical diagnosis of his affliction, which he knows to be spiritual and not exactly an affliction: "'. . . Dr. Hausmann listed such items as depression, fugues, certain delusions, sexual dysfunction'" – which Will could do without – "'. . . and what he called *wahnsinnige Sehnsucht* – I rather like that. It means inappropriate longing.'" (Lewis, having used it so frequently as a metaphor, would have liked Percy's choice of a *toothache* as the catalyst that prompts Will to regress to a rediscovery of God.)

As for Lewis himself: the time finally may have come to raise questions not previously posed or, if posed, done so almost clandestinely. I have in mind particularly the sort of hypotheses suggested by Christopher Derrick in "A Life Observed," his review of the Green-Hooper biography for *Triumph* magazine (January 1975): " . . . I think it must be conceded that certain elements in Lewis' mind and life were distinctly odd, and indeed capable of psycho-analytical interpretation. . . . I beg to offer this tentative diagnosis. Lewis had been deeply hurt in childhood, and he grew up with a profound distrust of the world and of the things that were likely to happen in the world. Grace made him into a Christian in due course. . . . My own tentative suggestion is that the stresses of his early days, especially at the hands of an overpoweringly dominant father, had generated within him a somewhat unhealthy and ambivalent concern with patterns of dominance and submission: I suggest also that this included a sexual element, could possibly be interpreted in Freudian terms, and had some kind of connection with his highly aggressive manner in teaching and in controversy." Elsewhere, Derrick has applied the term *Weiberherrschaft* (female-dominance) to Lewis, and *They Stand Together* has vindicated that usage. But I would not misrepresent Derrick, whose article, and whose talk to this Society in December 1971, are at once thought-provoking and wide-ranging, intellectually daring, yet rhetorically cautious; they could be considered seminal. The point is this: Derrick is the only professional writer among avowed Lewis-admirers to have written such an article.

Insofar as Lewis' story is a story of regression, we ought to know that from which the regression issues: neurotic atheism brought on by a mother's death, "failed" prayer, father-resentment, loneliness, adolescent posturing, and an abnormally unhealthy dose of intellectual pride. The Mrs. Moore liaison, *Dymer* (Lewis' own remark in his Preface to the 1950 edition is revealing: "Every one may . . . psychoanalyse it as he pleases"), and the accelerated pace of Lewis' conversion following closely upon the death of his father are some symptoms. His regression to sanity, then, may be regarded as a much greater achievement than even we have suspected.

By now, I know, I have argued at least one case and I have probably stated several others. But I would like to close on some different note from that sounded by "neurotic", "Freudian", "symptom", and *"Weiberherrschaft"*! The Lewis whom I would suggest be represented to the Rational Opposition would not be merely the Theologian, for though he wrote apologetics, a branch of Theology, he was not, he insisted, essentially a theologian. Nor was he essentially an apologist, since only three of his books – *The Problem of Pain*, *Miracles*, and *Mere Christianity* – are sustained, full-fledged works of Christian apologetics. I guess I may as well crawl out to the very end of the limb: there is not a single instance in all of Lewis where he seeks explicitly to demonstrate the veracity of a Christian doctrine *per se*. Even in *Miracles* he does not defend the proposition that Jesus of Nazareth is God Incarnate; rather, he provides a rationale for our belief in it. Perhaps above all, Lewis makes the Creed plausible; there is a road, it leads to the place we were made to occupy, and it is marked by trustworthy signs to which we have access – if only we will pay attention.

He is a guide: to one degree or another always popular (though never a "mere popularizer"), and in one guise or another always polemical. As an interpreter of texts, he is a literary critic; when he makes experience his text, he is a philosopher; his particular text makes him a Christian philosopher. Thus his natural company consists of such writers as Chesterton (to be sure), Samuel Johnson, Hooker, Traherne, and even (perhaps Professor Paul Holmer would say especially) Kierkegaard, for Lewis is (this denomination once provoked considerable heat) an existentialist . . . of sorts. But that is, for now, one case too many.

Lewis saw himself as a translator; we should be no less. But you do not translate a language to those who already speak it. To enjoy Lewis we should regard no one but ourselves. Who would want to diminish the "you too?!" syndrome, whereby one Lewis admirer discovers another? But to contemplate him we must regard those who, after all, deserve our attention. By our Good Reading of Lewis, we might "merit, invite, or compel" their high evaluation of him; they might even become members of The Few. And who knows? Perhaps we might even bring some of those dopey dwarfs out of their stable, if only without being of the world we are more in it. For – like Wilder, like Lewis – we too have an ulterior motive, and it is the only one that really, ultimately, matters.

A Prophetic Realist and *The Abolition of Man* or, Broadening the Lewisian Context (Part Two)

Prophetic Realist?

Imagine the following. You wake up in Boston on the morning of January 4, 1920, and you read "Red Sox Impresario Sells Ruth to Yankees." You, the Prophet, would screech something like, "there will be decades of woe unto Boston! A curse will guide some batted balls through open legs and others up over the left field wall. More good men will be traded for incompetents and strife shall descend upon the clubhouse. Defeat will ever be snatched from the jaws of victory and punishment will endure unto seven times seventy generations." Woe-*cum*-detail – and accurate: the famous Curse of the Bambino (or the Babe's Blessing, as some Yankee fans know it). On the other hand, you the mere Realist would murmur, "how stupid can Harry Frazee be? Selling the Bambino to finance *No No, Nanette*? Somebody's gonna pay!" Woe-*sans*-detail – accurately emotive, but not very specific.

Of course, we do not know CSL's *actual* words upon learning of the sale, but as a Prophetic Realist he would be somewhere between the two, predicting a future along the lines of, "the worst personnel decision in the history of baseball will haunt the game for a long, long time. Ruth is already the greatest player in its short history, he is just what the Yankees need in order to dominate, with growing momentum, the largest market in the game, and the Red Sox will become habituated to the quick fix as a solution to problems both on the field and off." Woe, to be sure, but broadly diagnostic rather than specifically predictive and condemnatory, and reasoned; in other words, Philosophical.

Thus the Prophetic Realist: **1/** *broadly moral*; **2/** *keenly, even intuitively, attentive*; **3/** *intellectually fresh, penetrating, and analytical*; **4/** *anticipatory*; and **5/** *typically admonitory*. And once we discern this class do not other, obvious, members spring to mind? GKC, Orwell, Huxley, Eliot (of "The Wasteland," though CSL could not see it as such), Walker Percy, and lesser lights, too, such as the sadly disregarded Christopher Lasch (*The Culture* of *Narcissism*). Now, *Abolition of Man* is a classic of Prophetic Realism: a dispositive, even a seminal, statement on human nature and natural law, and on the working of these in the realm of practical events (ethics) and on aspects of the broader culture (education), and on several (though subsidiary) conceptions. Or so one – or we few – would think and surely have so spoken this Weekend.

But we are mistaken. In fact, in the greater *current* conversation regarding CSL's subjects in *Abolition* he is AWOL, and the question is Why? Why is Lewis so undispositive and marginal, so utterly and conspicuously MIA, in the debate of which *The Abolition of Man* partakes? And, not so by-the-way, what might we do about it?

The Abolition of Man ought to be dispositive and seminal . . .

After all, it anticipates (though not in detail, of course; remember that Prophetic Realists leave matter, method and dates to the Prophet) cloning, legalized and epidemic abortion, legalized euthanasia, genetic engineering, and the rampant redefinition of fundamental, axiomatic premises (e.g. 'family'). Moreover, it re-vivifies, explores and applies old concepts, such as ordinacy, Natural Law, Reason and "Men without Chests"; reminds us that Values are premises not conclusions; introduces new, telling concepts, such as the Innovator and the Conditioner; and instructs us of what, exactly, is at stake in the debate – freedom and dignity, the *Tao* itself, and the very abolition of Man. In short, it perfectly satisfies the five criteria above.

. . . in spite of its limitations both intrinsic and extrinsic.

The Abolition of Man does indeed present a solid argument respecting an issue of overwhelming importance. But the book is – there is no way around it – rhetorically weak. Lewis' vaunted and telling brevity is here overdone, especially in its lack of expository road signs, and the book lacks his usual rhetorical concessions (for example, abstractness relieved by analogy), allowing too much of the argument to speak for itself. It is *too* economically argued and is thus more the *stating* of a case than the *making* of one.

Furthermore, the book is "nicheless," insufficiently contextualized. It surely worked as the address it was originally, but it does not work as a philosophical statement, for it fails to take other philosophers and their implications into account. This is typical of CSL who, in *An Experiment in Criticism* for example, does not bother to describe the larger current (F. R. Leavis's) against which he is swimming. And of course Lewis eschewed all Schools, which may partly explain his brilliant ability to discern and name his own concepts (e.g. Drab in his Oxford history volume). So *The Abolition of*

Man has the feel of a "make-your-own-book," it *seems* out-of-context, it *looks* like free-lance punditry. To be sure, this is typical CSL, and *The Abolition of Man* is the result when he brings to his rhetorical project his B-game. (Do remember that the Bambino's B-game remains better than anyone else's A-game.)

And then there is Our Own Fault, our narrow boundaries and proximate horizons. In short, there is our Stubbornness, for we *will* have our Apologist and our Apostle, his Christian World, his Baptized Imagination – above all. Anyway, *I* will. But *exclusively*?

But it isn't: the Conversation on the subject of *The Abolition of Man* has virtually no CSL.

I consider the Bad Guys first, and nearly first among them must be the behaviorist B. F. Skinner, whose *Beyond Freedom and Dignity* (1971) takes Lewis on directly; his title is an explicit reference to *The Abolition of Man* and his book does not so much refute as embrace Lewis' admonition. Skinner is a self-proclaimed Conditioner, proud of it, and he would have the rest of us submit. His candor is bracing. It pales, however, in comparison to Peter Singer's. Singer is the ethicist at Princeton University. In his *Practical Ethics* (1993) he doesn't bother with Lewis or with anyone else. He merely proclaims, " . . . characteristics like rationality, autonomy, and self-consciousness make the difference. Infants lack these . . . killing them, therefore, cannot be equated with killing normal human beings, or any other self-conscious beings . . . . Their species is not relevant to their moral status."

Third is a group led by Richard Rorty, he of the Liberal Project. In his landmark *Philosophy and Social Hope* (paper, 2000) we read the relatively benign (but axiomatically approved by the culture at large), "[that it should] seem bad taste to bring religion into discussions of public policy." The European Union would seem to agree. Its recent Draft Conference on a Constitution for the European Union acknowledges the Enlightenment, along with many other elements of "common European heritage," without any similar reference to Christianity. A gaseous general nod to the "spiritual patrimony" of Europe is "absolutely insufficient," according to Jean-Louis Tauran, a Vatican foreign-policy official. Why insufficient? Because people like Stephen S. Hall, in his *Merchants of Immortality* (2003), write stuff like "constricting our biomedical opportunities in the face of speculative and often ideologically inspired fears is timid, reactive, and bad public policy." He means cloning, abortion, genetic engineering and the like, and he means Christianity.

Remember, of this very recent, prolific, learned and effective group, only the oldest (and now dated) Skinner bothers even to mention C. S. Lewis. But surely the Good Guys – and there are some – are different?

In his *Our Posthuman Future: Consequences of the Biotechnology Revolution* (2002), Francis Fukuyama invokes Lewis prominently, making *AoM* the basis of an entire chapter; and last year, when his book came out, he said in an interview, "when science can offer a father or a mother a prenatal examination of the genetic patrimony of their child and the possibility of modifying it, human nature itself and, what is more, the very dignity of our species, will be at stake." Clearly he has read the right books. And yet his only company in that respect is the adversary B. F. Skinner – from nearly forty years ago!

Two other prominent Good Guys seem not to know CSL. Here is Bill McKibben in his well- and amply-reviewed *Enough: Staying Human in an Engineered Age* (2003): " . . . and now we seem bent on making our own children into devices." Why (McKibben asks) "engineer minds in the first place?" He refutes Rodney Brooks, who professes: "It will allow us a deeper understanding of what we really are"; and Gregory Stock, who is worse: "It will pierce the veneer of inside things, we may reach the naked soul of man"; and J. Hughes, who easily could be a stand-in for Weston: engineering minds (i.e. conditioning Man unto abolition) will "permit us to think more profound and intense thoughts." Where's the Unman when you need him? But no CSL.

And none of him in Steven Pinker, *The Blank Slate: The Modern Denial of Human Nature* (2002), who could easily have had the Appendix to *The Abolition of Man* open at his elbow when he declares, with all the evasive language at his disposal, that we share Cognitive Development, Language Capacity, and an *Emotional Calculus* (i.e. what the properly trained Chest tells us all, my emphasis). This last has four dimensions:

1/ other-condemning (contempt, anger, disgust),
2/ other-praising (elevation, awe),
3/ other-suffering (sympathy, compassion, empathy), and
4/ self-conscious emotions (guilt, shame, embarrassment).

These, you see, all cut across lines of autonomy, community, and divinity. He then refers the reader to Donald E. Brown's *Human Universals* (! [1991]), to which Pinker devotes his own Appendix. Of course, no Lewis, no *Tao*, in either Pinker or Brown.

Antidote? Recover CSL the Philosopher

Lewis' central conceptions – of *Abolition of Man* and well beyond – are supremely valuable and ought to be recovered as such. I mean not only Innovator and Conditioner and the others from *The Abolition of Man*, but Egoistic Castle-Building, Drab Age, the Dangerous Sense (remember that one?), Need Love, the Few and the Many, At/Along, and many, many others. Lewis, after all, is a Big Picture philosopher *tout compris*: in *Miracles*, in the early parts of *Problem of Pain*, in *God in the Dock* (especially Part III), in most of *Christian Reflections* and *Present Concerns*, in much of *Literary Essays* (see "Bluspels and Flanansferes"!) and everywhere in the sermons (for example "Transpositions"!). In short, *before* his theology, there are his ontology, metaphysics, anthropology, sociology (including his political theory), a complex psychology, and underlying all a very sophisticated epistemology.

So we need a CSL Philosophy Project!

I mean we must de-ghettoize CSL, perhaps by consolidating the work of William Luther White, Gilbert Meilander, Lionel Adey, Paul Holmer, and Michael Aeschliman from some twenty and thirty years ago, and that of Don King, Bruce L. Edwards (especially in Thomas L. Martin's *Reading the Classics with C. S. Lewis*), and Doris Myers more recently. And then – most importantly – we must enlarge the Conversation, seeing CSL in fresh light and novel contexts. James Patrick has done this, and Armand Nicholi, and most recently Louis Markos. And we should be bold. How bold? I hold *Till We Have Faces* to be among the greatest modern novels in English; in fact, as a first-person narrator Orual has one, and only one, competitor, and he is Humbert Humbert, anti-hero of *Lolita*. But I say no more about that . . . for now. Instead, I suggest particular and immediate attention be paid to the philosophy that inform CSL's Prophetic Realism, particularly his philosophy of:

1 Being: *What* exists
2 Knowledge, Consciousness and Logic: *How* we know it
3 Personhood: Who is knowing it

Notice the omission of what it *Means* ultimately (theology) and what we *Do* about it (religion and ethics). And here is a hint: In my judgment, and from the perspective I am suggesting, the vast wealth of the sermons and essays has been sorely neglected. Since my original article ("Broadening the Lewisian Context") on this theme in *CSL* more than twenty years ago, I have argued the point hither and yon, urging that Lewis be viewed in larger and more varied contexts than is ordinarily the case. Let us be catholic, *sophisticated* – if you will – in our approaches, contexts, and connections, applying our own version of the Law of Inattention: The more the Philosopher, the richer the Apologist. Neglect of CSL the Philosopher is too high a price to pay for what is, after all, an emphasis on his comforting but *unnecessarily* narrow supremacy! He is no less the Philosopher (in particular the social, epistemological, and metaphysical Prophetic Realist) than any of the thinkers in that Conversation that I have so briefly summarized above. Those writers should know it, and so should everyone else.

We all recall (we all *should* recall!) that the Bambino was the Sultan of Swat. But does the non-fan – or even the average fan – know he was the greatest left-handed *pitcher* of his day? Or that the combination is unique in the annals of the sport? Harry Frazee, who sold the Babe, forgot, putting something ahead of the Big Picture. Well, if you will permit me, CSL is the Babe of intellectual scope, as well as of apologetic depth and achievement. And we are forgetting. *We* are the Few of *An Experiment in Criticism.* It is for us to be as sophisticated as CSL. Linda Bridges began this Weekend with a fitting discussion of *De Descriptione Temporum* and its lessons. Perhaps by next year, the 35th anniversary of our society and the 50th of that great inaugural lecture, we will apprehend and advertise our earthly master more fully than we do now?

Culture and Public Philosophy: Another C. S. Lewis
(Being Finally an Exhortation)

I must not begin without first expressing my deep personal gratitude to Professor Travers for having invited me to "connect and re-connect" and for the richness of hospitality afforded each one of us. Dr. Johnson tells us that "men must be reminded more often than instructed," and here, under the aegis of Professor Travers and his colleagues and associates, we are reminded that we are all members of the Body of our Lord.

Did you know that President Akin's education in medieval philosophy was conducted by a Cistercian monk from a monastery nearby his college? Well then, in *that* light please consider with me some *other* achievements of the medieval monastery. From Thomas E. Woods, Jr., in *How the Catholic Church Built Western Civilization* (Regnery, 2005, *passim*), we learn that Henry Goodell, president of the Massachusetts Agricultural College, held that, " . . . the work of these grand monks during a period of fifteen hundred years . . . saved agriculture when no one else could save it. . . . They labored with their own hands, drained morasses, and cleared away forests. By them [the land] was rendered a fruitful country." Gregoire, Moulin, and Oursel, authors of *The Monastic Realm* (Rizzoli, 1985), go further: "[The monks] were the skillful and unpaid technical advisors of the third world of their times. . . . There is no activity . . . in which the monks did not display . . . a fertile spirit of research." The regnant view was expressed best nearly one hundred years ago (1909) by Flick, in *The Rise of the Medieval Church*, explaining that the monasteries ". . . converted the wilderness into cultivated country. . . . " That is (from *cultus*) they beheld a field, "a sodded place fit for tilling and providing for growth" – thus making a *culture*.

I posit these assessments for a personal and, I admit, quirky reason: whenever meeting in conference on the subject of C. S. Lewis I delight in imagining my fellow conferees as medieval monks and nuns and our venue as a monastery. Of course, here at Southeastern Baptist Theological Seminary the irony of this *amuse-esprit* is not lost on me. But consider: Are we not surrounded by a world largely bereft of manners and morality? Do we not seek to till that landscape so as to replenish it and thus grow the old faith anew? Do we not seek links to other such enclaves? Moreover, is not Lewis rather like our Father Abbot Jack who, providing purpose and direction, above all cultivates that indispensable fruit which is Hope, thereby motivating us to even greater cultivation? That Lewis we know best – the enduring apostle of Hope; the lay theologian, fantasist, and Narnian; the Christian *Romantic* (in Lewis' own lexicon) and apologist; and, of course, the literary steward, to whom a dwindled few pay any attention these days – *that* Lewis is the father abbot whom we commonly spirit from monastery to monastery, now and again dispatching him into the larger world (the West End, Broadway, PBS, Hollywood) for what good he may do.

But there is another Lewis, an un-romantic chap who, unlike the monks within the monasteries, has directly engaged his massively ruined and ruinous landscape. This Lewis is the Public Philosopher who acknowledges few temporal demarcations and submits to no school; who strikes opportunistically, even improbably, especially journalistically; and whose voice – here, as always, direct and proximate – differs from the familiar and inviting Narnian's. By no means is this other persona unrecognizable: as is the case with most deft and supple writers, Lewis' voices interpenetrate each other. Like the Renaissance ("so-called," I hasten to add, in deference to the master) with its chronological neighbors, there is no bold line of demarcation separating one persona from another. Rather, my argument is, first, that the tone of this public philosopher's voice *concentrates* certain features which in the popular Lewis' voice are more temperate and diffuse than in the former and are thus less noticeable – in fact, more tolerable – than in the philosopher's. (I will designate those features presently.) Second, this concentration of tonal features in the public philosopher accompanies *a)* distinctive subjects, *b)* disparate (and often surprising) views on those subjects, and *c)* is tuned to readers more closely fitted to those subjects than are conventional Lewis readers. Third, this *concentration* of features, subjects, views and audience gives rise to a literary persona somewhat less . . . *comforting* . . . than that of the much better-known – we might say, the iconic – Lewis.

But the plot thickens. As a public philosopher Lewis presents two broad aspects, that of a Prophetic Public Philosopher and that of a Social one. I will deal with both, for both evince that concentration of tonal features I've alluded to. These features are rhetorical and logical severity, a daunting perspective and cultural capaciousness (unbound by time, space or school), a lack of sentimentality that can be downright chilling, and an unrelenting intellectual seriousness undistracted by the trendy or the iron-clad "ism."

However, just as Lewis' Christianity and his popular defense of it cost him both the support and the serious attention of the intellectual elite of his day (e.g. Empson, Cooke, Orwell, Russell – their name is legion), I suggest – this being the final prong of my four-prong argument – that owing to that discomfiting quality I've alluded to this other Lewis persona has dampened, not only popular attention (preponderantly) to the public philosopher but our own scholarly attention as well. Certainly scholars among us have labored mightily towards an understanding of the prophetic species of the public philosopher – David Mills, Victor Reppert, Michael D. Aeschliman, Gilbert Meilander, William Luther White, and James Patrick (*The Magdalen Metaphysicals* being my personal favorite) – and they have succeeded, to an extent. But they are few, and the public philosopher – especially the Social Public Philosopher – remains ignored by mainstream public intellectuals (see the third preface to *C. S. Lewis at the 'Breakfast Table,'* now titled *Remembering C. S. Lewis*) and by the reading public, *including Lewis' own*. Might, then, part of the blame be ours?

In short, as Lewis has enacted *his* Great Knock (the legendary, relentlessly logical and beloved pre-Oxford tutor W. T. Kirkpatrick), we have largely neglected an aspect of our own Knock – oh, not the apologist and transcendent religious thinker, nor the seminal scholar, and certainly not the Christian romantic and fantasist who, frankly, takes up far too much of the available popular oxygen, but the public philosopher, especially he of the social variety.

Now, unlike us, in our neo-monastery, public philosophers (or "public intellectuals") are free to walk about the culture, to pick their spots; properly speaking, they are more *preaching friars* than monks. That is, our neo-friar is within the culture, not removed from it. Public philosophers come from the university, the law, journalism or the think tank, though on occasion they freelance the intellect. Often they seek to modify a cultural agenda or radically to change it: they often speak adversarially. In doing so they are confident that ideas – ideas are the raw material of this figure – are the seeds of cultural change. Who are they? A varied group, to be sure. From the eighteenth-century (when journalism, not coincidentally, came into its own) to now they have been people such as Addison and Steele, Swift, Dryden, Pope, and Dr. Johnson; the Adamses, Paine, the *Federalist* writers Madison, Hamilton and Jay; Tocqueville; William F. Buckley, Norman Podhoretz, Richard Rorty, Peter Singer, the Kristols, Stanley Fish, Thomas Sowell, the

Himmelfarbs, and Jean Kirkpatrick. Many of Lewis' own period are in this well-worn tradition as well: Cooke, Orwell, Belloc, Chesterton, Mencken, Dewey, Russell, Wells, Muggeridge, Shaw, Hook, and the prototype himself, Walter Lippmann, who first publicly philosophized on the nature and importance of public opinion and the role of the public intellectual in its formation (*Public Opinion*, 1922).

What *was* the cultural milieu like during Lewis' time, roughly the middle third of the twentieth century? Nearly his entire life was lived during one of the worst declines in human history. Did I say *one* of the worst? Let me not be cautious for caution's sake: the twentieth century offers mostly ruins and constitutes a net moral and cultural loss. So I ask: could that – that cauldron of infernal depredation – be to some small measure the result of cultural idolatry? After all, which of our modern, twentieth-century cultures was most elevated if not the German? Hitler could quote Schopenhauer from memory. In *The Fall of Berlin, 1945* Antony Beevor tells us that on the night of April 12, 1945, as the Red Army began its final assault on Berlin, the philharmonic was performing Beethoven's Violin Concerto, Gruckner's Eighth Symphony, and the finale of Wagner's Gotterdammerung. "After the performance," he goes on, "the Nazi Party had organized Hitler Youth members to stand in uniform with baskets of cyanide capsules." Wolf Lepenies's *The Seduction of Culture in German History* describes an intellectual attitude that can be observed throughout German history: the overrating of culture. Surely Lewis' wonderful application of the phrase "enemy-occupied territory" to Western culture must come to mind.

To be sure we have witnessed cultural idolatry before. But it seems the differences of degree that marked the twentieth century have added up to a difference in kind. Now when freedom is equated with license *the equation is celebrated*. For example, just how do we "ism"? Let me count the ways: relativism, subjectivism, nihilism; narcissism, scientism, solipsism (*Self* magazine!); Madonna praised, not as singer or dancer, but as self-inventor (every man his own creator!); emotivism and sentimentalism; and the belief that technologism + scientism = "progress." These may be no more than twitches, instances of a sort of cultural Tourets; but they take their massive toll, and we pass them on. After all, that is what "education" does; it transmits. In short, John Dewey (such a good man, too) has won. The function of education, he argued, is to *challenge* the received notions of Western civilization, such as Judeo-Christian religious belief, since religion is socially dangerous, seeking (as it does) to mold conduct in light of norms beyond temporal society. For Dewey, reports Jude B. Dougherty in *John*

Dewey and the Decline of American Education, "The function of education is to challenge, not perpetuate, the inherited."

Has Lewis' Great Divorce *ever* been greater? How has man *not* been *abolished*? Baby Boomers are still babies, and they are booming. Certainly our catalogue of depravities is prodigious, and they do predate the twentieth-century. No, our problem is not novelty but *proliferation*: mass adolescence + mass technology = a massively misshapened landscape. But I hear myself – I am in the middle of a Jeremiad! So I ask: is there nothing to redeem the century? So I look, and I find . . . the advent of movies, the maturation of baseball, and the ready availability of ibuprofen, for those of us delusional enough to think we can still play the second instead of merely watching the first.

But they are the depredations of the century, not its saving graces, that bring us to Lewis – and Lewis to us, for he is a Providential man if ever there was one.

Owing to the enduring vitality of two staggeringly visionary works, the prophetic Lewis is, as I've avowed, much better known than his social counterpart. He looks ahead (though the prophetic philosopher is not to be confounded with a prophet). And what Lewis saw he said unsparingly in *The Abolition of Man* and in *That Hideous Strength*. Putting aside *Miracles* (as is our wont, alas), in which Lewis writes more or less classically as a philosopher in response to David Hume's philosophical rejection of miracles, the prophetic philosopher is the Lewis most people usually know if they know Lewis as a philosopher in the first place.

In that light, and for our shared recollection, I review this Lewis' features: an aspect of Chesterton may come to mind. In addition to that unalloyed seriousness I've mentioned, the prophetic philosopher is 1/ broadly moral, 2/ keenly, even intuitively, attentive to culturally subterranean assumptions, 3/ intellectually fresh, penetrating, and analytical, 4/ anticipatory, and 5/ typically admonitory. He offers dispositive statements on natural law and human nature, and on the working of these in the realm of practical events (ethics) and on aspects of the broader culture (education). He anticipates (though not in detail, of course; prophetic philosophers leave matter, method and dates to the pure prophet): cloning, legalized and epidemic abortion, legalized euthanasia, genetic engineering, and the rampant redefinition of fundamental, axiomatic premises (e.g. 'family'). He reminds us that values are premises not conclusions; introduces new, telling concepts, such as the Innovator and the Conditioner; and instructs us respecting what, exactly, is at stake in the debate – freedom and dignity – and the consequence of their disappearance not so far into the future, the abolition of man.

That is the Prophetic Philosopher, well-(if-not-widely-)known, thanks to the scholars I've mentioned earlier. In contrast is the Social Philosopher, who is neither. I turn to him now, but with an apology both to him and to you for the brevity of my treatment – a Cook's Tour, but not therefore unrepresentative of the whole landscape. Perhaps there is here a prospective dissertation- or book-writer looking for an apt subject?

Rather than looking ahead, the *social* public philosopher is a diagnostician, looking around and, in Lewis' case, often by first looking back. Alas, our attention to this Lewis does not match his to the culture. Too infrequently, for example, do we read or cite, let alone examine carefully, such essays and sermons as "Modern Man and His Categories of Thought," "Is History Bunk?", "On the Reading of Old Books," "On Living in an Atomic Age" and "Is English Doomed?" (all conveniently collected in Lesley Walmsley [ed.], C.S. Lewis *Essay Collection: Volumes I and II*, HarperCollins, 2000).

This neglect includes *The Pilgrim's Regress* and is thus particularly anomalous, even unpardonable. In this, the first book Lewis wrote as a Christian, we have nearly all of Lewis and his hard features at once: the romantic examines *Sehnsucht*, the apologist defends the claim of its Christian etiology, the parabolist allegorizes its application, and the philosopher (under both species) lays waste to its opponents both direct and oblique, temporal and spiritual, physical, psychological and intellectual. Lewis would come to describe it as being of "an uncharitable temper"; I describe it as severe, unsentimental, serious, realistic, capacious . . . I describe it as The Lewis Template. Here is how Jane Spence Southron described it in the *New York Times Book Review* (December 8, 1935):

> A modern man's intricate journey . . . and the highly complex mental processes that distinguish him from creatures of a different order are resolved, here, into the utmost simplicity. . . . He is . . . an intellectual of our own day, who is not content to take anything in life at its face value and who makes use of the stored-up knowledge of the past and the possibilities of practical adventures in living to help him in his explorations. . . . The language, throughout, is plain, straightforward and leanly significant.

With the exception of some of the Augustans – particularly Dr. Johnson and Swift – no public philosopher comes close to achieving the perspective – the cultural scope and intellectual reach – that Lewis achieves in this one book.

As for the essays and relevant sermons, take, for example, "Learning in War-Time," preached at the Church of St. Mary the Virgin on December 22, 1939:

> The war creates no absolutely new situation: it simply aggravates the permanent human situation so that we can no longer ignore it. Human life has always been lived on the edge of a precipice. Human culture has always had to exist under the shadow of something infinitely more important than itself. . . . Life has never been normal. . . . I reject at once an idea . . . that cultural activities are in their own right spiritual and meritorious.

This insistence on a *long* perspective – an insistence which subverts unspoken, and often unexamined, assumptions respecting our exceptionalism – is typical of Lewis, of course, and it is severe: it practices no attenuation of thought, offers no rhetorical mitigation.

And he just does not let up. Five years after that dismissal of Matthew Arnold's cultural idolatry would come a classic double jab, the first at Deweyism (though Lewis may not have known of John Dewey) and the second at F. R. Leavis. In "The Parthenon and the Optative" (Notes on the Way, *Time and Tide*, XXV, March 11, 1944) we read:

> The one [the 'optative', standing for the tough study of a difficult language] begins with hard, dry things like grammar, and dates, and prosody . . . the other [the Parthenon is a discussion of the Greek temple], begins in 'Appreciation' and ends in gush. . . . [It] fails most disastrously when it most succeeds. It teaches a man to feel vaguely cultured while he remains in fact a dunce. It makes him think he is enjoying poems he can't construe. It qualifies him to review books he does not understand, and to be intellectual without intellect. It plays havoc with the very distinction between truth and error. . . . Mr. A [just down from reading English with Dr Leavis at Cambridge] pours out his personality – in pure non-factual Appreciation to his form.

Most pieces in "Notes on the Way" are brief, journalistic, and semi-occasional; thoughtful, usually non-religious and written quite accessibly. Lewis is cognizant of venue and audience. I suppose these pieces did not have a wide "adversary" circulation. Neither do they seem to have circulated widely among us.

More typical of Lewis-as-public-philosopher are "The Necessity of Chivalry," "Bulverism," "Democratic Education," and "Priestesses in the Church" (I omit "Delinquents in the Snow" as the work of an aggrieved, and soon to be grieving, man): all unsparingly diagnostic – and all, by the way, substantially unrefuted (as opposed to sneered at). One of my personal favorites, though, is "Sex in Literature" (*Sunday Telegraph*, 87, September 30, 1962). I recall my surprise followed by delight when first I read it. If you do not know it, I wonder if you will share either the delight or the surprise:

> It is a bad thing that the results of trials should depend on the personal moral philosophy of a particular jury rather than on what has been proved in court. . . . When the prevalent morality of a nation comes to differ unduly from that presupposed in its laws, the laws must sooner or later change and conform to it. This is the case with "obscene" literature: masturbation, perversion, fornication and adultery were great evils; now the intelligentsia are not sure, but even if the acts are evils, they do not think the law should be meddling. My own view . . . is that they are evils, but that the law should be concerned with none of them except adultery . . . because it offends the Hobbesian principle 'that men perform their covenants.' . . . The lesser of the evils now before us is to abandon all moral censorship. We have either sunk beneath or risen above it. If we do, there will be reams of filth. But we need not read it. Nor, probably, will the fashion last forever.

That happens to be a rare instance of Lewis causing me to believe that he is sometimes naïve and that, in fact, I know better. But instead of ourselves as typical readers of this essay, we should think of other public philosophers. What can they make of this, coming, as it does, from the dogmatic, theology-soaked, popularizing fantasist? Why, they say nothing. And scarcely do we.

Two essays that appeared in remote, if not quite esoteric, venues *have* gotten our attention. In "Vivisection," a pamphlet first published by the New England Anti-vivisection Society in 1947, then by the National Anti-vivisection Society in 1948, Lewis tells us, " . . . the victory of vivisection marks a great advance in the triumph of ruthless, nonmoral utilitarianism over the old world of ethical law. . . ." He did not use the locution "Old Western," as he does so prominently elsewhere, but he might just as well have; having looked around, he concludes by looking back, invoking the concept of a natural moral order. In "The Humanitarian Theory of Punishment," published in Australia (*20th Century: An Australian Quarterly Review*, 1949) because he could not publish it elsewhere, we note Lewis' characteristic subversion of contemporary unexamined assumptions (about the nature of justice and human accountability), cultivating instead Old Western assumptions respecting both human nature and the role of the state:

> The Humanitarian theory removes from Punishment the concept of Desert. But the concept of Desert is the only connecting link between punishment and justice. It is only as deserved or undeserved that a sentence can be just or unjust. . . . Thus when we cease to consider what the criminal deserves and consider only what will cure him or deter others, we have tacitly removed him from the sphere of justice altogether; instead of a person, a subject of rights, we now have a mere object, a patient, a 'case'.

Those are two pieces which, though not entirely obscure to us, were certainly so at the time of their publication and have remained so to the world-at-large. No matter their standing, they are classic Lewis in their severity and especially in their unsentimentality.

Going where the argument leads when given certain premises, as well as stating them, are the tasks of philosophers, public or otherwise, and constitute a pronounced Lewis strength. The question is whether or not anyone beyond the monastery pays attention. For his part Lewis does not always make it easy; in addition to the usual tasks, he brings not only his signature severity (characteristics of effective abbots and preaching friars, by the way) but some confoundedness too. He can be full of surprises. Five essays epitomize this Lewis, and all appeared prominently. Noteworthy is this refreshing, and perhaps unsettling, fact: Lewis rarely has a "side," as we now conceive sides. The "Old Western Man" of his famous inaugural lecture at Cambridge does not necessarily equal Conservative.

Does Lewis have a *moral* objection to obscenity? Not if we read him in "Prudery and Philology" (*Spectator*, January 21, 1955):

> It is the words, not the things, that are obscene. That is, they are words long consecrated (or desecrated) to insult, derision, and buffoonery. You cannot use them without bringing in the whole atmosphere of the slum, the barrack-room and the public school. . . . When authors rail too much . . . against public taste, do they perhaps betray some insufficiency?

Well then, because of his class and upbringing, is he a bigoted elitist, a man fearful of "the revolt of the masses"? Not if we read him in "Private Bates" (*Spectator*, December 29, 1944):

> We must get rid of our arrogant assumption that it is the masses who can be led by the nose. As far as I can make out, the shoe is on the other foot. The only people who are really the dupes of their favourite newspapers are the intelligentsia. It is they who read leading articles: the poor read the sporting news, which is mostly true.

So then, having deposited this body of faith in "the common man," Lewis might, we would expect, defend democracy on their behalf. But he does not – not on their behalf. And his reasoning is quite simple: he regards a zeal for equality as nothing more than a superstition. He tells us as much in "Equality" (*Spectator*, August 27, 1943):

> I am a democrat because I believe in the Fall of Man. . . . I don't deserve a share in governing a hen-roost, much less a nation. Nor do most people. . . . This introduces a view of equality rather different from that in which we have been trained. I do not think that equality is one of those things (like wisdom or happiness) which are good simply in themselves and for their own sakes. I think it is in the same class as medicine, which is good because we are ill. . . . When equality is treated not as a medicine or a safety-gadget but as an ideal we begin to breed that stunted and envious sort of mind which hates all superiority.

Of course, we've always known how seriously Lewis take the Fall of Man. His political application of the belief, however, is unforgiving (so to speak), another example of his logical severity. In "Willing Slaves of the Welfare State" (*The Observer*, July 20, 1958, No. 2 in the series "Is Progress Possible? [a reply to C.P. Snow's "Man in Society."]) he makes clear the basis of his objection to all collectivist paradigms:

> Now I care far more how humanity lives than how long. Progress, for me, means increasing goodness and happiness of individual lives. For the species, as for each man, mere longevity seems to me a contemptible idea. . . . It seems childish not to recognise that actual government is and always must be oligarchical. Our effective masters must be more than one and fewer than all. But the oligarchs begin to regard us in a new way. . . . Let us not be deceived by phrases about 'Man taking charge of his own destiny'. All that can really happen is that some men will take charge of the destiny of the others. They will be simply men; none perfect; some greedy, cruel and dishonest. The more completely we are planned the more powerful they will be. Have we discovered some new reason why, this time, powers should not corrupt as it has done before?

Whether in the thirties (Auden's "low, dishonest decade"), forties, or fifties, such unrelenting, rhetorically unadorned, and inexorably counter-dominant public thinking would have made Lewis unpalatable to the regnant verbal class – but far too cogent to permit of refutation.

One aspect of Lewis' career is not merely largely, but near-universally, ignored (though Walter Hooper is about to remedy that – and soon, we hope). For all of his professional life Lewis was, if not exactly a prolific, then certainly a trenchant and durable book reviewer. And in his reviews we see the same severity of thinking, along with his untempered willingness to lay it out. The difference, perhaps, between his book reviews and the essays noted above is their greater economy-of-expression. "Hardly possible," one might say; yet true. Here is a sampling, and though I've taken some elliptical liberties, there are none that accelerate Lewis' style or deceptively abbreviate his thinking. Do note that these four range over four decades.

On December 6, 1928, he reviewed W. P. Ker's *Form and Style in Poetry* for *Book News and Reviews*: "There is . . . a cooling [sic] card here and there for those who believe too intemperately in the Renaissance." Well, we certainly will hear more of that in years to come! Six years later, in the midst of the decade made low and dishonest by its ruling left-wing intelligentsia, he reviewed T. R. Hen's *Longinus and English Criticism* for the *Oxford Magazine* (December 6, 1934): "It is rather an attempt to relate his [i.e. Longinus's] teaching to the 'advanced' criticism of the Cambridge Left Wing – the diagrammatic, psychological and 'practical' school." The next review is of a book which he thought variously flawed but could not help liking, indeed, virtually adopting. In June of 1940 he reviewed de Rougement's *Passion and Society* for *Theology*. His last sentence is actually a quotation from Rougement, though it is unquoted, and, I believe, Lewis would lift it wholesale and insert it into *The Screwtape Letters* (I do recall his citing it with admiration in a letter): "M. de Rougement . . . maintains with eloquence the incompatibility between the Christian conception of marriage and the modern notion according to which every marriage must have 'falling in love' as its efficient, and worldly 'happiness' as its final, cause. . . . but all of us need to learn, almost daily, that Eros ceases to be a demon only when he ceases to be a god (p. 321)."

Not long before his death he was no less penetrating than he had been forty years earlier. Note his impatience with prudery, his anger over avoidable ignorance, his analytical acuity, and his impatience with certain modern methodologies in this review of David Loth's *The Erotic in Literature* for *The Observer Weekend Review* of March 4, 1962.

> He gives a pretty full and very damaging history of the law's confused and largely futile attempts to control, or even to define, pornography. He also casts serious doubts on common assumptions as to what will or will not corrupt the young reader. . . . They [who answer

questionnaires] betray their abnormality by the very act of answering.
. . . Anything which mentions copulation – for whatever purpose, in
whatever tone – is for him 'pornography' – a hymn from a Sumerian
fertility rite, the story of Judah and Tamar, Sophocles's "Electra." It
ought to be made impossible for the repressive party to include the
scatological under the pornographic or to call a book immoral because
it offends their taste. It should be equally impossible for the other party
to make a remark that 'sex is innocent'. If *sex* means the biological
fact, it is no more innocent or guilty than a turnip. If it is meant that
human sexual behavior is all, and all equally, innocent, we want to be
told why. No one claims a similar liberty for all economic or political
behavior. . . . when the morality embodied in the law departs too
widely, either for better or worse, from that really current in a society,
the law must sooner or later either sink or rise into conformity. Till it
does, confusion and inconsistency are inevitable. . . . The author treats
erotica as a singular and *orgiastic* as the adjective of orgasm.

The last line here is the last line of Lewis' review: except during actual combat, it seems Lewis did not take prisoners.

And so we have Lewis the Social Public Philosopher, he who laid waste to chronocentrism and its snobbery, not merely seeing through trends and movements but restoring some perspective for those of us who know so much less cultural history than he; the man who could write, "I believe I just proved that the Renaissance never happened and that, if it did, it didn't matter!" In short, our favorite fantasist was fundamentally that serious realist, both philosophically and rhetorically, and realism can hurt. Indeed, when expressed severely and unsentimentally it surely does become God's megaphone to a fallen world. In eschewing "isms," and by seeing instead the quiddity of things and apprehending their currency, Lewis became a providential time traveler, seeing the ruins, certainly, but seeing beyond them as well. Skeptical of received opinion and trendy abstraction, he is not merely unsentimental but anti-sentimental. This is a father abbot to be reckoned with, a friar to be heeded.

So I will attempt to reckon. The public philosopher – especially he of the social aspect – seems somehow . . . different. Capacious in his perspective, severe in his thinking, unrelenting in his combativeness, and rhetorically uninsulated, this unflinching realist is, as I've suggested earlier, not entirely unfamiliar to us. He is the "ruthless dialectician who insists that reason not stop short of its goal: truth," as Richard Cunningham so cogently puts it (and much else) in his ground-breaking *C. S. Lewis: Defender of the Faith*. He knocks as greatly as ever did his master. But we are unaccustomed to such concentrated doses of these qualities, to the subjects they vivify and the views they convey, and even to the audiences they address: somehow not us. What sort of persona, then, gives rise to such a voice? It is not the voice of that familiar, benevolent persona who has comforted us, often as though shoulder-to-shoulder, even cozily, and so abidingly. Not exactly. This persona is *sophisticated*. And he is . . . off-putting.

One of the tricky meanings of that tricky word is *mixed* – not necessarily with impurity or inauthenticity, but mixed by experience (the OED tells me), in fact worldly-wise, "subtle, discriminating, refined, *cultured*." Certainly Lewis' humors were mixed, but so was that magnificent and magnificently furnished, nuanced, supple, and dextrously militant intellect. This Lewis may no longer be *of* that culture, but he certainly was, once; and the public philosopher is certainly *in* it. Not a snob, though he was once, and priggishly so; and not condescending, though he once was a master of condescension, this Lewis is nevertheless not the romantic Narnian, and there is certainly nothing *mere* about him. We recall that near the end of his life this Lewis taught us how to read and judge literature. That lesson from *An Experiment in Criticism* is simple: read in "the same spirit as the author writ." Are we up to the challenge when reading the public philosopher? After all, much is at stake: Lewis also insists that the proper way to judge a book is by what good readers say about it. I am suggesting not only that we read this Other Lewis but that we read him "in the same spirit as the author writ."

Why so, and urgently? Because in the twenty-first century *insula such as ours – such as this very seminary, and this very conference – are, in fact, counter-dominant neo-monasteries*. Remember? " . . . [T]he work of these grand monks . . . saved agriculture when no one else could save it. . . . They labored [and] drained morasses. . . . By them [the land] was rendered a fruitful country." "[The monks] were the skillful and unpaid technical advisors of . . . of their times. . . . There is no activity . . .. in which the monks did not display . . . a fertile spirit of research." The monasteries ". . . converted the wilderness into cultivated country. . . ." That is, they beheld a waste and made a *culture*. And why not? Our own severity, long perspective, and seriousness – our own conveyance, not only of Lewis as our father abbot-romantic apologist but as our preaching friar-public philosopher, indeed *our very own sophistication*

– will engage a waste that needs him . . . and us, and this very Center, as Prof. Little's review last evening of its mission made pellucidly clear. Lewis will always remain our apostle of Hope, the much-studied and popular Lewis. But he must again be *our public philosopher who "happens to be a Christian"*: an *emissary* to the wider culture and as sophisticated, speaking its unsentimental language. *That* Lewis simply must have his oxygen, which is for us to deliver.

And the culture may be waiting. In 2002 Jurgen Habermas, he of Cultural Criticism and De-constructionism and as Leftist an atheist as we've ever had, seems dis-positively to have refuted the facile Dewey, suggesting (*Religion and Rationality: Essays on Reason, God, and Modernity*, ed. Eduardo Mendieta, MIT) that the culture in fact should "perpetuate the inherited":

> [F]or the normative self-understanding of modernity, Christianity has functioned as more than just a precursor or a catalyst. . . . the ideals of freedom and a collective life in solidarity, the autonomous conduct of life and emancipation, the individual morality of conscience, human rights, and democracy, is the direct legacy of the Judaic ethic of justice and the Christian ethic of love. . . . The search for reasons that aspire to general acceptance need not lead to an unfair exclusion of religion from public life, and secular society, for its part, need not cut itself off from the important resources of spiritual explanations. . . .

Lewis agrees, of course, and typically has provided a context for the insight – his signature long perspective. It is from *Punch* (July 9, 1958). In it we witness Lewis' reach, disinterested devotion to truth, and his penetrating diagnostic power. The essay is "Revival or Decay?":

> Is there a homogeneous 'West'? I doubt it. Everything that can go on is going on all round us. Religions buzz about us like bees. A serious sex – quite different from the cheery lechery endemic in our species – is one of them. Traces of embryonic religions occur in science fiction. Meanwhile, as always, the Christian way too is followed. But nowadays, when it is not followed, it need not be feigned. That fact covers a good deal of what is called the decay of religion. Apart from that, is the present so very different from other ages or 'the West' from anywhere else?

The doctor, as they say, is in, and I remind myself that, as with "learning in Wartime," Lewis did *not* write that in the twenty-first century; that he did not write that *yesterday*.

Our avatar of the abbot, friar, emissary, and apostle of hope remained true to his "rule," selecting and occupying a "tillable *cultus* suitable for growth," notwithstanding opposition, ridicule and neglect. Intellectually and spiritually, and publicly so, he was a brave man – he certainly is a hero of mine – who fought the good fight, ran the race, and kept the faith, and did so "to the ruddy end." But this we already knew.

And we – we have swamps to drain.

Disobedience and Self-discovery
Reflections on Meaning in *Till We Have Faces*

We must be grateful to C. S. Lewis that Orual, the first-person narrator of *Till We Have Faces*, finally died when she did, even in mid-sentence; for had she not, then surely she would be prattling on to this very day, troubling us and all around her and delaying her own resurrection to boot. I believed that more than thirty years ago when I first read the book and I still believe it; but unlike Orual, for better or worse, I persist. Thus have a handful of Grand Explanations come and gone, so that now my only certainty about this very great work is this: you can never say it all, so do not even try.

Of course, this novel is – as the author himself believed – Lewis' supreme literary achievement, at once utterly typical of his thought (in fact, a compendium of it) *and* so thoroughly uncharacteristic of the working of his imagination. The former is so because Lewis' thought is everywhere whole and here that integrity is proven; the latter, because this work is not only a novel but a distinctly *modern* novel: Lewis' only one, as opposed to romance, allegory, parable, satire, or fairy tale. In fact it stands with the very best of its category. It is in that spirit that I have reduced my central thesis about this book to a single premise that gives rise to a single proposition (though I give thanks for corollaries).

But for now the premise: *Since meaning is connectedness, and Ultimate Meaning is connectedness to the Ultimate, then the meaning of all human existence is the utter connectedness of a self to God.* Now, for one who believes in our providential and loving Creator, the God of Abraham, this is nothing new. But why, with respect to human existence, a *self*? Just this: a self is our irreducible, concrete minimal axiom; the most satisfying, treacherous, and promising of ambivalent challenges; the most elusive of the many elusive ambiguities in all His creation. It is at once God's image of Himself in us and His instrument for turning His creatures into His children. That is the premise. The proposition is this: *Nothing less than this high Turning – its ingredients, recipe, and flavors; its tortuous subversions; its charity, sacrifice, and promise of glory* – nothing less than all of these constitute the central theme of *Till We Have Faces*. And such is Lewis' artistic audacity *and* spiritual acuity that he allows his protagonist almost to *talk herself out of it*.

1. Mimesis

First, wherefore uncharacteristic of his imagination? In its modernity, Lewis' use of the first-person narrator is the equal of any of Henry James' (James being the godfather of such use and of its theories); his psychological reach is as penetrating, and possessed of as much *gravitas*, as that of Flannery O'Connor or Walker Percy; Part II certainly echoes Borges and directly foreshadows the Magic Realism of, say, Garcia Marquez and rivals that of his progenitor Faulkner. Moreover, Lewis' suggestion of historical actuality strongly suggests comparison to the greatest twentieth-century religio-historical fiction, Sigrid Undset's *Kristin Lavransdatter*. But Lewis has established an atemporal order that conditions our own; amidst a trial that issues in grace, that order warrants our eventual transcendence of time. We see how we might get out of time and *over there*. And whereas Lewis' usual technique is to mythologize (or to re-mythologize), in *Till We Have Faces* he is *de-*mythologizing, painting an intimate portrait of a brilliant, willful and resentful mind who is angry with the gods for not existing (to paraphrase Lewis about himself). Glome is *not* another world and does not exist in another dimension; we do not discover – as we do in *Perelandra* or in the short story "Forms of Things Unknown" – that the myth is historically accurate. We remain on Earth (in Thrace, perhaps, or near the Caucasus), as we and Orual are shown that *the received myth is factually false*. Lewis' great fifth chapter on myth in *An Experiment in Criticism* simply does not apply here.

But the difference of narrative perspective, which is unlike any we are accustomed to in Lewis, is the most important of all differences. Doubtless we have seen the first person elsewhere (*Perelandra, The Great Divorce*), but that is always "Lewis"; here, the first person is a stranger, and a woman, and a not-very-likable woman: self-serving, belligerent, and filled with militantly anti-divine delusions. She is not only uncharacteristically ugly (or putatively so) but ambivalent, too.

Thus the exclusion of traditional elements and the inclusion of a strikingly new one should serve to forewarn us. Orual, or the self she is projecting like the Tragedian on the fringe of Heaven in *The Great Divorce*, is not quite whom she seems to be, least of all to herself. In the end it is she who – *on her way to eternity* – will be found out.

On the other hand, thematically *Till We Have Faces* is Lewis from beginning to end. The god and his castle, for example, are concrete, though intangible and invisible to Orual; in fact more real than Orual, who comes to realize that she was but a shadow compared to them. Can the peroration of *Miracles* not be called to mind? Or the denouement of *The Last Battle*? Or the premise of *The Great Divorce*, wherein the heavenly rain is so real it drills through the ectoplasmic bodies of the visiting Shades? We have been prepared for Orual's possessiveness by *The Four Loves* and *The Great Divorce*, where we are shown a woman like Orual and are told that Hell should not be allowed to blackmail Heaven. And Psyche, who always longed to live on the mountain, as though it were her *real* home: is she not like John the Pilgrim regressing? Is she not also surprised by Joy? Many other distinctly Lewisian themes abound, such as the nature of "divine semantics" and of the divine personality, of love and atonement, and the validity of reason *complementing* the reliability of imagination. But three ideas, which are evident in much of Lewis' thought, I believe to be at the center of the web of connectedness in *Till We Have Faces*: 1/ grace, the unmerited gift that transcends argument, accounts for the "improbability" of the change in Orual in Book II; 2/ membership, the purposeful functioning of a part within the Mysterious Body, allows for the interchange of labors; and 3/ the Law of Inattention (which Orual violates wholesale), that antidote to excessive attentiveness to one's own emotional state.

A furter, and pivotal, difference between this book and others is its structural intricacy. One might regard Part I simply as a question, with Part II the answer. But ought not answers be at least as clear as their questions? Or we might divide the narrative into the stages of its teller's life. Then we would have five parts: 1 /Orual from childhood to queen; 2/ Orual as Queen to the writing of her book (several decades that seem narratively slighted, to say the least); 3/ the writing of the book (which brings about such wholesale change – exactly one paragraph!); 4/ the first three tasks (Bk. II, ch. 1-3); and 5/the final task and the denouement (Bk. II, ch. 4, the last chapter). This division helps us immediately to note the *dis*proportion between the length of treatment of a section and its apparent importance in terms of temporal duration – a noteworthy disporportion, as it happens nowhere else in Lewis.

In his seminal *The Rhetoric of Fiction*, Wayne Booth identifies three narrative features that compel us to a conclusion: *intellectual* engagement, a sort of cognitive recreation marked by curiosity; *qualitative* allure, the desire for a completion of a pattern; and *practical* concern, our need to witness success or failure with respect to a difficulty of serious moment encountered by the protagonist. In *Till We Have Faces* the cognitive element is high indeed, owing not least to Orual's commanding intelligence and overbearing personality; she is out, first to make a case, then to solve a problem – and she will not relent. The telling of the story is as lean as the structure is ostensibly simple, making for an inviting forensic (for Orual has undertaken that very branch of classical rhetoric, that of the law court) pattern. Lewis' achievement in these respects is noteworthy, for the more we accept the invitation, the more we realize how much richer, and therefore challenging, the patterns are.

I invite the reader to consider merely the double helix of transmuted meaning formed by the inter-animation of, for example, the words 'fear' and 'holy', or 'marry' and 'eat'; or the surpassing audacity of chapter ten, in which Orual, having finally found Psyche on the mountain, has the tables turned upon her when Psyche *a/* wins the debate, *b/* uncharacteristically commands herself rather than allowing herself to be commanded, and *c/* comforts the confused and vulnerable Orual! These complications of character and of plot, both of which heighten suspense and considerably exacerbate Orual's practical problem, make the reader uncertain with respect to Orual's ultimate success or failure. Indeed, they call into doubt what constitutes either since, audaciously, Lewis makes our view of his protagonist more and more ambivalent as the story progresses. Such are the perils of any protagonist taking the stand on her own behalf.

And here, precisely in applying Booth's categories, do we discern the three cornerstones of Lewis' great edifice: 1/ foreshadowing, 2 /the distortion of time, and 3/ irony – the great device, mimetically perfect in mirroring the dark glass that is Orual's soul and the distortions that result from trying to see through it. Even more to the point, these three elements are intertwined; indeed, barely separable. Remember Trom's killing of the boy servant at Psyche's birth? It foreshadows Orual's brutal ordering of the death of the insufferable Batta. Or recall Trom's lament (which Orual regards as deeply cynical, yet admirable in its tactical aptness) that Psyche has been torn from him: rather like Orual complaining that she has lost her sister "three times over." But note further that the foreshadowing implants the great irony: that Orual is an image of her hateful father. (Much later she will literally see herself as Trom.) Trom, too, complains about the gods as first driving you to an act then punishing you for the same act. Very early on Trom cries out "faces, faces, faces," echoing Orual near her end, when she sees numberless rows of them. Then, not long after the removal of Psyche, Orual sets out veiled for the first time, though not yet permanently. And note, too, that these foreshadowings form nothing less than a commentary on signs, the presence in this world of God's evidence, both of Himself and of His will.

But in case we, like Orual, *miss* the signs, we are given the story no fewer than four times, each in a different modality of time. The first is Orual's ordinary telling; the second, the telling by the priest whom she meets in the forest; the third, the time of the visions, the spiritual enactment (if you will) of what this world has been palely imitating; and, finally, the time – or timelessness – of Orual's reading and re-reading of her complaint, the interval that mattered most for Orual's destiny. In short, the further away we get from time as we know it (that "gaping wound," as Lewis has called it) and the closer to eternity, the truer and less ironic our seeing. Of course, in eternity there is no foreshadowing, since there are no shadows and, by definition, there can be no "fore."

But instances of irony not only abound but persist (as they must) until the very end. Redival, for example, of all people, is the first to discern Psyche's burgeoning status. Trom turns out not to be such a bad fellow after all, when he is around other fellows. "I could not rule myself," says Orual at early on, "a sort of pride." Then there is the widow Ansit, seeing that Orual also loved Bardia. And Psyche, the "accursed," is the "perfect victim." The list could go on and on. Instead, I'll cite the most telling, which occurs as Orual is making her climb to the Holy Tree where, she believes, the remains of Psyche are located. She is high above Glome, and the vista is breath-taking:

> And my struggle was this. . . . I came on a sad errand. Now, flung at me like frolic or insolence, there came as if it were a voice – *no* words – but if you made it into words it would be, "Why should your heart not dance?" . . . The sight of the huge world put mad ideas into me, as if I could wander away . . . see strange and beautiful things, one after another to the world's end. The freshness and wetness all about me . . . made me feel I had misjudged the world; it seemed kind, and laughing, as if its heart also danced. Even my ugliness I could not quite believe in.

Of course, the irony is all Orual's own: clarity taken as confusion. She will not believe her own eyes. But *could* she? She never questions the reliability of the feeling, only its propriety and *usefulness*, for were she not to struggle against it, "how should [she] ever again believe that [she] had loved" Psyche? She can never be friends with "this god-haunted, plague-breeding, decaying, tyrannous world. I had seen," she continues, "I was not a fool." And so, because "Reason called for it" – meaning not Reason of course but dry logic based on false premises – "I ruled myself."

Here – *right here* – is Orual's first great act of disobedience, ironically an act of disobeying what is reasonable – her participation in the Logos – in the name of Reason: a blaspheming act of willfulness, and one that foreshadows the greater disobedience, the one in the valley in the presence of the very "gold and amber" palace, that follows presently.

2. To the Brink

The most thorough study of the book is Peter Schakel's *Reason and Imagination: A Study of 'Till We Have Faces'*. Even when you think Schakel wrong, his argument is rich and greatly advances our understanding. Chad Walsh's chapter in his *The Literary Legacy of C. S. Lewis* is indispensable, really, for its appreciation of the contingent unpredictability of the novel; and Walsh knows it *is* a novel, *not* a myth. The most trenchant commentary on *Till We Have Faces*, however, comes – I am delighted to say in his presence – from Tom Howard, who grasps the aspect of what can only be called the novel's "thickness" of meaning and design as no other critic. (I lament that his reading is limited to a single chapter of his superb *C. S. Lewis: Man of Letters: A Reading of His Fiction*.) I cite Tom's penetrating incision into the pulsating tissue of meaning with respect to my *proposition*, that turning of the self:

> The thing which has thickened and hardened in Lewis' version of the Cupid and Psyche story is an idea, or rather a set of ideas, about freedom. It might go something like this: the thing that stands between the human soul and final freedom is not the malice of the gods, nor bad luck, nor handicaps, nor anything else like this. It is quite simply that soul's grim insistence on having freedom on its own terms. Independence. Autonomy. Self-determination.
>
> Give it a hundred names, but it comes to the same thing. The irony is that what that soul supposes is the enemy, or at least the set of obstructions between self and freedom, is the love of the gods. But, alas, the only way of discovering that is to stop fighting and surrender. The one condition of joy is obedience.

We know that Psyche commits one, terrible, act of disobedience, when she illuminates her husband. But what of Orual? I have called her denial of ordinate feeling disobedient: what else would you call going the wrong way on a clearly marked one-way street? She not only deceives herself but the Fox and Bardia as well, for of course she *does* see the palace – and within the next thought is rationalizing away what she has seen. Yet this denial (in the psychoanalytical sense) is not the worst of her disobedience. That begins (or rather is foreshadowed) when, before starting out for the valley, she indulges the fantasy that Psyche is her greatest enemy. At least she is still calling it a fantasy, and it does occur in a feverish vision (yet more foreshadowing). But upon recovering, Orual admits that the visions "left behind them only a settled sense of some great injury that Psyche had done me." What more excuse does she need, then, to motivate her reprehensible act of emotional blackmail, the threat to kill herself if Psyche does not disobey her husband?

In his first letter to the Corinthians, immediately following his soaring encomium to love, St. Paul tells us, "for now we see through a glass, darkly; but then face to face: now I know in part; but then I shall know even as also I am known." Time, then, is not a window, originally meaning a glassless "eye to the wind" or to a moving breath, a spirit. No. We are murky even, especially, to our own selves. Perhaps Lewis would have preferred Keats's metaphor: "A man's life of any worth is a continual allegory," he wrote, "and very few eyes can see the mystery of his life – a life like the Scriptures, figurative – which . . . people can no more make out than they can the Hebrew Bible." Well, I believe Lewis himself was wrong in saying that the story is about a woman corrupted by the dark seeing of possessive love. He gave this sort of corruption very great emphasis in several places, pre-eminently in *The Four Loves*: "It is the reaction to a desertion, even to robbery," he writes of, say, a sibling's response to the other's conversion. He continues, "someone or something has stolen 'our' boy (or girl). He who was one of Us has become one of Them. What right had anyone to do it? He was *ours*."

Such a depiction may be all he intended, but he produced very much more. Near the beginning of his wonderful autobiography, *The Golden String*, Dom Bede Griffiths (first Lewis' pupil, then friend, and finally co-convert to Christianity), writes that people "will not be converted by words or arguments, for God . . . is the very ground of existence. We have to encounter him as a fact of our existence before we can really be persuaded to believe in him. To discover God," he continues, "is not to discover an idea but to discover oneself. It is to awake to that part of one's existence which has been hidden from sight and which one has refused to recognize." Then he concludes, "the discovery may be very painful; it is like going through a kind of death. But it is the one thing that makes life worth living." *That is what this book is about, and there is nothing false in this tale.* If read correctly it can enlarge any reader – especially a post-modern one. It requires no Christian belief and addresses a question which nearly monopolizes the contemporary mind: What is Personhood and what does it *mean*?

The book gives an answer, as does much of Lewis' work. It is so basic that it underlies the rest of the entire grammar of Lewis' thought. It is, to paraphrase him, what the story is about, his version of a person in despair, not knowing it, but on the brink and finally being brought over, "kicking and screaming." She has projected an Open self, nurtured a Hidden self (she spends virtually all of her adulthood behind a veil), avoided her Blind self, and denied her Unknown self, her version of a Deeper World. It is Orual's own *Surprised by Joy*, with both books ending in exactly the same place – their narrators making a leap of Faith. Lewis vindicates Dom Bede's insight by confessing to these very difficulties. His poem "Legion" addresses them:

> Lord, hear my voice, my present voice, I mean,
> Not that which may be speaking an hour hence
> (For I am Legion) in an opposite sense,
> And not by show of hands decide between
> The multiple factions which my state has seen
> Or will see. Condescend to the pretense
> That what speaks now is I; in its defence
> Dissolve my parliament and intervene.
> Thou wilt not, though we asked it, quite recall
> Free will once given. Yet to this moment's choice
> Give unfair weight. Hold me to this. Oh strain
> A point – use legal fictions; for if all
> My quarrelling selves must bear an equal voice
> Farewell, thou hast created me in vain.

The problem arises when we pay improper attention to the lens, or window, forgetting that the best one is the plainest, the "poorest" in adornment and complication, and thus the clearest. When we are not only known by God but *assent* to being known, "then," Lewis writes in *Letters to Malcolm*, "we treat ourselves, in relation to God, not as things but as persons. We have *unveiled* [emphasis added]." George MacDonald, Lewis' master, sums up beautifully. This is from his book of devotional poetry, *Diary of an Old Soul*, for November 7:

> Wilt thou not one day, Lord? In all my wrong,
> self-love and weakness, laziness and fear,
> This one thing I can say: *I am content*
> *To be and have what in thy heart I am meant*
> *To be and have.* In my best times I long
> After thy will, and think it glorious-dear;
> Even in my worst, perforce my will to thine is bent.

Orual systematically disobeys her reason, her imagination, the pull (at one point) of her own will, family affection, the law of charity, the bond of friendship, and memory itself, all in the service of *her* imperial self. All the *foreshadowings*, all the *distortions of time*, all the *ironies* – even the very greatest – are not enough to rouse her from the most dangerous formula of all: Intelligence + strong willpower + an enlarged self of nearly-insatiable appetite = *vigorous self-delusion*.

That is, these three cornerstones of Lewis' great edifice are insufficient *per se*. But before examining how Orual is finally overcome, we must look at a last, most prominent, aspect of Lewis' fabric and of Orual's intelligence, the one she disastrously might yield to, even at the very end, but for the intervention of death itself.

3. Silence?

According to John Donne there is a twofold clothing, putting on Christ as a garment and putting on His person. "That is, we shall so appear before the Father, as that he shall take us for his owne Christ; we shall beare his name and person. . . . in all our mindes, his *Agonies*; in all our hearts, and actions his *Obedience*." Earlier he had preached, "The organ that God hath given the naturall man, is the *eye*; he sees God in the creature. . . . The habituall, and manifold sinner, sees nothing aright; Hee sees a *judgement*, and cals[sic] it an *accident*. . . . And as under water, everything seems distorted and crooked, to man, so does man himself to God, who sees not his own Image in that man, in that form as he made it."

Donne's antidote is an appreciation for the proper design of language in preparation for one's full participation in God's design: *"Breath is speech*, but *Breath is life too."* Our speech is the manifestation of God's spirit at work in us Thus, language "apparells" God, and the very material of language is sacred. "That therefore you may the better know him, when you come *to see him face to face, then,* by having *seen him in a glass now* . . . we thus proceed in the handling of . . . words. . . . But in heaven our sight is *face to face*, And our knowledge is *to know, as we are knowne.*" Would that we had the time to discuss fully the concept and reality of Donne's essential subject, nothing less than *Logos*; instead I must simply posit it as the *instrument* of all meaning: thought, word, image, and intuition, and the conjunction of the these: *the ground of all connectedness.* And it is that which Orual most deeply and momentously disobeys, for at the heart of *Till We Have Faces* is obsessive volubility, an unrelenting rhetoric that conceals when it does not distort.

Consider just two names, the Fox's real name and Orual's nickname, respectively Lysias and Maya. Lysias was one of the great sophistic rhetoricians of ancient Greece, an opponent of the Thirty Tyrants, contemporary of Pericles, and well-known logographer (really a ghost-writer); in a calm and idiomatic style he wrote more than 200 forensic (or courtroom) speeches. That is, the man after whom Orual's dear Greek tutor is named was a specialist in precisely the sort of Book Orual is writing, as she proclaims at its very beginning. She will accuse, so that the wise Greek (us?) may judge. In short, she is writing a classic Complaint, an indictment in this case, a quintessential forensic statement. From the first paragraph we are plunged into Rhetoric, that art of discourse that the Fox would teach. And what sort is it? Well, it is the sort that holds, as the Fox does, that "everything is as good or bad as our opinion makes it"; or that allows him to take both sides when giving advice to Trom; or that would allow Orual to say of her teacher that Greeks love words (and that men especially love their own). It is the sort that will justify the Fox's final admission that all his sayings were "a prattle of maxims."

Now, we know Lewis loved words, that he lent his life to their study and deployment. They are, after all, the Talking Beasts who are most valuable in Narnia; and it is Nonsense – Logos debased – that brings down the N.I.C.E. of *That Hideous Strength*; Screwtape dedicates himself to distortions of language; and Ransom is a philologist, who therefore can learn Old Solar and thus communicate with the creatures of Malacandra and come to know their dearness and nobility. But for us (on the Silent Planet) there is a great impediment, a sort of internal disobedience that intrudes between us and meaning, or the Logos. Owen Barfield (Lewis' great friend and solicitor and a formidable philosopher in his own right) believes that "we have *ceased to identify ourselves with our thoughts* – at any rate, with such thoughts as can be expressed in words. . . . We distinguish between thinking and believing." This has resulted, of course, from an evolution of consciousness, the Ego developing into the "Consciousness Soul," the epitome of self-consciousness, "the point at which the individual feels himself to be cut off from the surrounding cosmos. . . . complete self-consciousness – at the cost of practically everything else." The result is the painful experience that words and thought must be transferred: objects, meaning and experience are his – cut off from any outward, objective meaning. (Perhaps this is why Lewis also aborts language at crucial moments in so many of his narratives). If words cut you off from objective meaning, then be quiet and act. Is not this, finally, what Orual understands at the very end of her tale when she laments, "words, words, led out to do battle against other words"? Verbal distortion demands silence. But who – what sort of person – can fall silent?

We are left with Orual's nickname, Maya. The classical Maya was the daughter of Atlas, the mother(!) of Hermes, and the protector of Dionysus(!) – oh, Irony, thy name is surely Orual! But in Sanskrit 'maya' means *nescience*, lack of knowledge, particularly of one's self; in short, *no one*. Lewis' old, ambivalent view of rhetoric thus intimately mirrors his equally ambivalent view of one's self and the Christian demand that it be transcended, or excavated, or perhaps *transfigured*. What he finds discomforting – even alarming – is its hold upon him, and that this hold symptomizes an inability to let go of an old, needful theatrical ego. In his chapter on Pride in *Mere Christianity*, "The Great Sin," he tells us that God is trying to make us humble for own sakes, "trying to take off a lot of silly, ugly, fancy-dress" of self-conceit that we are wearing. And then he confesses, "I wish I had got a bit further with humility myself: if I had, I could probably tell you more about the relief, the comfort, of taking the fancy-dress off – getting rid of the false self, with all its 'Look at me . . . '." Not "no one" but Legion.

An alternative to Lewis, Maya, and Barfield comes from Viktor Frankl: in effect, "tension is not something to avoid unconditionally, and peace of mind, or peace of soul is not anything to avow unconditionally." Such tension is aroused by some meaning wanting fulfillment, a tension created by direction. "One must recognize that being human profoundly means being engaged and entangled in a situation, and confronted with a world whose objectivity and reality is in no way detracted from by the subjectivity of that 'being' who is [as the existentialists say] 'in the world'." "*The possibility of error* does not dispense man from *the necessity of trial*." "The supra-meaning is no longer a matter of thinking but rather a matter of believing. We do not catch hold of it on intellectual grounds but on existential grounds, out of our whole being, i.e., through faith." What we need is unconditional faith in unconditional meaning, such as Habakkuk's. His granaries empty, he could chant this hymn of triumph: "Although the fig tree shall not blossom, neither shall fruit be in the vines; the labor of the olive shall fail, and the fields yield no meat; the flock shall be cut off from the fold, and there shall be no herd in the stalls: Yet I will rejoice in the Lord, I will joy in the God of my salvation." Dom Bede would have understood.

Yet another alternative comes from Philo. The great historian of religious ideas, Harry Wolfson, tells us that for Philo the Jew the Logos is conceived as identical to the intelligible world and hence with ideas which constitute that world. Their existence as real beings is a fundamental teaching of Moses – a foreshadowing of the beginning of John's fourth Gospel, wherein The Trinity harmonizes the Logos by Unification, so that thinking and ideas are one and Incarnate. Those who deny the reality of ideas are, according to Philo, condemned in Scripture as "impious" and "unholy;"

For Lewis, let alone for Orual, Frankl's tension was a very great challenge, the improbability of achieving Philo's unification a source of despair. In another poem not published during his lifetime, "The Apologist's Evening Prayer," the dilemma of self-denial v. self-exploitation brought him to the brink of despair:

> From all my lame defeats and oh! much more
> From all the victories that I seemed to score;
> From cleverness shot forth on Thy behalf
> At which, while angels weep, the audience laugh;
> From all my proofs of Thy divinity,
> Thou, who wouldst give no sign, deliver me.
> Thoughts are but coins. Let me not trust, instead
> Of Thee, their thin-worn image of Thy head.
> From all my thoughts, even from my thoughts of Thee,
> O thou fair Silence, fall, and set me free.
> Lord of the narrow gate and needle's eye,
> Take from me all my trumpery lest I die.

The spiritual dilemma, for Orual, Lewis, and all of us "wise Greeks," is clear. When rhetoric and the possibility of redemption meet in the self, one or the other must give way, since the former requires a voluble ego, the latter its death – an antecedent act of obedience that Orual very nearly misses.

4. *The Eighth Day*

As she approaches the brink, Orual is at her most disobedient. She realizes, early in her talk with Psyche, that "if this is all true, I've been wrong all my life"; and so she chooses, finally exhausted at "fluttering to and from between two opinions." Now, since an opinion is a mere rhetorical touchstone, as Fox-Lysias would have it, then a choice respecting the objective validity of one over the other is utterly baseless: Orual instantaneously makes the self-serving choice. In this light, her denial of a true vision of the palace can be no surprise, but note her thought process. She first ponders the possibility of the vision having been "a sign" then dismisses that very possibility with, "I'll not grant them that. What is the use of a sign which is itself only another riddle?" Her rejection of faith, reason, and eyesight – this disobedience – is dispositive when, in spite of admitting that "it might have been a true seeing," she resolves never to mention it; since it is "a seeming that can't be tested" she will see to it that it is not. Finally, Bardia, who has heard the whole tale *except* for the sighting, allows the he does not "well know what's *really*, when it comes to houses of gods."

This, the climax of the book, continues some forty pages later when Orual sees the god of the mountain; or, rather, is seen by him. Here there can be no denial, for Orual is judged, judged by one with the ability and authority to do so with utter justice and certainty, and she knows it. She "also shall be Psyche," wandering in exile, and when again she hears weeping she unerringly know it is she who is to blame for it. Upon returning she does not merely withhold the truth from the Fox but lies to him, wishing at once that she still wore her traveling veil. The Fox, intuiting the lie, does not blame, let alone badger; instead he says, "friends must be free." It is Orual's shame, then, which prompts the next act: to go about veiled in perpetuity. To be sure, shame is about the self; in Orual's case it is the start of obedience. Redemption begins here, with a specific act, in our actual time, at a decisive moment.

As it must, for the narrativity and concreteness of the novel form are unique: something is happening in time. After all, continues Walker Percy, the central fact of our civilization is that something big *has* happened in time. The novel communicates that "deeper truth about the way things are, the way people are; in a word, a truth about the human condition." He continues:

> Judeo-Christianity is about pilgrims who have something wrong with them and are embarked on a search to find a way out. This is also what novels are about. It is no accident that the novel has never flourished in the Eastern tradition. If Buddhism and Hinduism believe that the self is illusory, that ordinary life is misery, that ordinary things have no sacramental value, and that reality itself is concealed by the veil

of *maya*, how can any importance be attached to or any pleasure be taken in novels about selves and happenings and things in an ordinary world? Show me a young California novelist raised in Taoism who spends his life meditating on the Way and I'll show you a bad novelist. Show me a lapsed Catholic who writes a good novel about being a young Communist at Columbia and I'll show you a novelist who owes more to Sister Gertrude at Sacred Heart in Brooklyn, who slapped him clean out of his seat for disrespect to the Eucharist, than he owes to all of Marxist dialectic.

In other words, we can – as Percy says elsewhere – *possess /a clear /problem* or we can *participate/* in a *rich/ mystery*. "Holy places are dark places," Orual tells us, and so "nothing that can be said clearly can be said truly."

Orual's mystery is enriched by her tasks, undertaken in some other mode of time than the one in which she begins to be obedient. By way of them she becomes Psyche, and by way of that emergent identity irony begins to wane. These tasks seem to me to represent love, contrition, and grace, with the last (the fourth, undertaken by Psyche) symbolizing redemption: Orual, who was Trom and Ungit – *as are all of us who, far from being the wise Greek judge, are on the brink with Orual* – has her beauty (withal, her face, her personhood) restored. How? "The idea that the whole human race is, in a sense, one thing," Lewis wrote in *Mere Christianity*, makes us like separate organs working in the same body, all sharing in the common health. But "things which are parts of a single organism may be very different from one another."

The earlier judgment that sent Orual into exile is shown to have been a mere . . . foreshadowing; now her case will be heard, she will be brought to the judge, she will be uncovered, and she will read her complaint. Finally, all the disobedience will pour forth. About loved ones, Orual says to the judge (no longer the "wise Greek"!), "We'd rather you'd drank their blood than stole their hearts. . . . But to steal her heart from me, to make her see things I couldn't see. . . ." This rant builds, of course, until we arrive at the heart of the truth: "The girl was mine. . . . We want to be our own. I was my own and Psyche was mine and no one else had any right to her. . . . She was mine. *Mine*. Do you know what that word means? Mine!" Within moments, Orual understands herself to have been repeating the complaint over and again, and when she is stopped she apprehends that "there was given to me a certainty that this, at last, was my true voice," from amidst the legion.

"I was a gap," an empty, isolated self, Orual had said before her reading, and thereafter, "I was no one." At last, she admits "the Divine Nature can change the past. Nothing is yet in its true form." She had described herself as being "with book," but now would be the end of all "narrativity," for that requires a flow of time: There are no novels in Eternity. Nor, since there is no "mine," is there possession: "Never again will I call you mine," Orual tells Psyche. In his chapter entitled "The New Men," in *Mere Christianity*, Lewis writes, "the principles runs through all life from top to bottom. Give up your self, and you will find your real self; lose your life and you will save it. . . . Keep back nothing." He concludes his book with, "look for yourself, and you will find in the long run only hatred, loneliness, despair, rage, ruin, and decay." After a tortuous and torturous journey, like Orual's, we are brought to the brink of Eternity. No less than a restoration of meaning – a renewed confidence in an inter-connected wholeness and thus in the ability of a transfigured self obediently to apprehend the Ultimate, in Eternity – is Lewis' achievement in *Till We Have Faces*.

Works Cited

Augustine, St. *The City of God.* Trans. Gerald G. Walsh, *et al.* New York: Doubleday, 1958.

Barfield, Owen. *Romanticism Comes of Age.* London: Anthroposophical Publishing Company, 1944.

Booth, Wayne C. *The Rhetoric of Fiction.* 2nd Ed. Chicago: The University of Chicago, 1983.

Frankl, Victor E. *The Will to Meaning: Foundations and Applications of Logotherapy.* New York: Meridian, 1988.

Griffiths, Dom Bede. *The Golden String.* Springfield, Illinois: Templegate, 1980.

Howard, Thomas. *C. S. Lewis: Man of Letters.* San Francisco: Ignatius Press, 1987.

Lewis, C. S. *The Four Loves.* New York: Harcourt, Brace and Company, 1960.

___. *Mere Christianity.* New York: Macmillan Publishing Company, 1952.

___. *Poems.* Ed. Walter Hooper. New York: Harcourt, Brace & World, 1964.

___. *Till We Have Faces.* Grand Rapids: Wm. B. Eerdmans, 1956.

___., ed. *George MacDonald: An Anthology.* New York: Macmillan, 1947.

Percy, Walker. *The Message in the Bottle.* New York: Farrar, Straus and Giroux, 1975

___. *Signposts in a Strange Land.* New York: Farrar, Straus, Giroux, 1991.

Schakel, Peter J. *Reason and Imagination in C. S. Lewis: A Study of Till We Have Faces.* Grand Rapids: Wm B. Eerdmans, 1984.

Stanwood, P.G. and Heather Ross Asals, edd. *John Donne and the Theology of Language.* Columbia, University of Missouri, 1986.

Walsh, Chad. *The Literary Legacy of C. S. Lewis.* New York: Harcourt, Brace, Jovanovich, 1979.

Wolfson, Harry Austryn. *Philo: Foundations of Religious Philosophy in Judaism, Christianity and Islam.* Cambridge: Harvard University, 1962.

___. *Religious Philosophy: A Group of Essays.* Cambridge: Harvard

16

The Screwtape Letters
of Evil, and Its Antagonists

How brief and penetrating; how witty; how easy, familiar and true. How horrible. Lewis believed in this Horror because he knew the Devil believes in us, because he had met the Devil in himself, had seen him paying so very much attention to how he and the rest of us are put together. So Lewis decided to pay some attention of his own and asked, Just what does this malignity see? The result is a report: a small, ostensibly simple, whistle-blowing amusement, that both entices and engages. We are enticed by the appeal of eavesdropping; these are *intercepted* letters after all. And we are engaged by the clever device of a reversed point-of-view. In short, we have secret information, it is about us, and we can figure it out.

How admirable that literary conceit; how clever the ruse. But notwithstanding the conceit, it is no ruse; and the Devil is *not* amused. His cover blown, his *soi-disant* majesty mocked, and his tactics neutered – *he* knows better. An agent of the Enemy is behind the lines (a favorite Lewis image), he has stolen the secrets of the kingdom, and he has spilled the beans! The diabolical paroxysms of anger must have been towering, the vows of retribution terrible. It is no wonder that Lewis never wrote another letter of the sort in this book. Having produced one of the great satires in the language – at once a psychological thriller, a theological taxonomy, and a satire mocking the great Adversary himself – he knew to get out while the getting was good.

What sort of stand-up genius pulls this off and incites such fury? How did he do it? And what Evil is this, to know us so well, to recognize a ruseless ruse when it sees one, and to take such umbrage at being mocked? Much goes into the making of a masterpiece.

Elsewhere (*Branches to Heaven: The Geniuses of C. S. Lewis*) I've argued that Lewis' presiding genius – the chairman of his board of geniuses, so to speak – was *rhetoric*. Whether by argument, description, exposition or imaginative enticement, Lewis was ever persuasive, and persuasion, as Aristotle has taught us, is the heart of rhetoric. Always Lewis marshaled language in adaptation to his subject, venue, and type of communication: sermon, review, lay theology; the public address, the BBC, a book; fiction, letter, short commentary, extended non-fiction. But especially he adapted his language to his particular audience, so that, for example, the voice of Lewis-the-academic-reviewer differs pronouncedly from that of the Narnian. In short his was a militant intellect, and he a warrior in words who knew to scout his terrain and adjust accordingly. That is the sort of genius he was.

In the instance of *The Screwtape Letters* we behold Lewis deploying a collection of characteristic devices. I offer an abbreviated sampling with a brief comment on each. *1/ Reversal.* The cleverness of the device, which invites our own cleverness – which is itself so satisfying – has a deeper purpose than mere engagement. In *Out of the Silent Planet*, for example, we look back on Earth from Mars, and from Martian eyes; in *Screwtape* God Almighty is the Enemy, Satan Our Father Below. This intellectual smack is refreshing; seeing things from the outside unsettles our unexamined assumptions. *2/ Obliqueness.* Related to reversal but common enough in Lewis to be named separately: Lewis never directly argues for the veracity of any given doctrine (as opposed to its plausibility) and often connects theology to psychology, ideas to us, by way of some contrivance, often involving a surrogate or surrogates. This connecting he does best in his parabolic works, those using literary genres that are visionary or allegorical (e.g. *The Great Divorce* and *Pilgrim's Regress*) or others that turn out to be at some variance from claimed actuality (i.e. *Letters to Malcolm*, which turn out not to be actual letters, and *A Grief Observed*, which though emotionally true shows many signs of rhetorical contrivance). *3/ Humor.* Of course nephew Wormwood is a knucklehead, Hell is a bureaucracy (and therefore *bound* for inefficacy), and Uncle Screwtape, an academic and a bureaucrat, is thoroughly vexed – a lovely turning of the tables, that, given how often *we* are commonly vexed by bureaucrats.

So we have intellectual engagement, the self-satisfaction of rising to that challenge, the unsettling thrill of self-recognition, laughs, surprise, the delights of glimpsed intimacy, and grave insight respecting that thorn that matters most, temptation: a rhetorical mixture all stirred by a knowing master. And have we noted the concision and brevity of this brew? All in all, a very, very difficult concoction to resist. But here a caveat. The wonderful Sugar Ray Robinson, the greatest boxer who ever lived, was once asked how he felt about being so good at something he loved so much. His answer:

"What would make you think I love boxing?" Lewis' sort of genius was rhetorical, a genius that largely defined his public life. So how did he feel about being so good at something he loved so dearly? Well, he didn't. Love it dearly, that is.

Certainly he *knew* rhetoric inside out: its works and workings, from ground level to a view from thirty thousand feet. His professional discussions of it in, for example, *Preface to Paradise Lost*, *The Discarded Image* and elsewhere, are penetrating; I've found them more useful in my teaching of the subject than many a primary source. Consider from the *Preface* this one summary description of the art: "The *differentia* of Rhetoric is that it wishes to produce some practical resolve . . . and it does this by calling passion to the aid of reason . . . because the end of Rhetoric is in the world of action . . . in Rhetoric imagination is present for he sake of passion." There in a nutshell are fifteen hundred years worth of rhetorical theory! Yet he admits to finding the art uncongenial, and he often uses the word pejoratively in unpublished work – as when remarking upon a revision of his own narrative poem *Queen of Drum* as "rhetorical."

And we know that rhetoric – its power *and his facility with that power –* troubled him. Upon hearing a speech by Hitler picked up and simultaneously translated by the BBC Lewis wrote (July 20, 1940), "I don't know if I'm weaker than other people, but it is a positive revelation to me how while the speech lasts it is impossible not to waver just a little." He concludes, "statements which I know to be untrue all but convince me . . . if only the man says them unflinchingly." A philosopher may be reminded of Plato's *Gorgias*, in which the eponymous character brags to Socrates over his ability to gets his physician brother's patients to take their medicine, even though he, Gorgias, is utterly ignorant of medicine. In a poem unpublished during his lifetime Lewis gave a less bemused, far more grave, and much more personal expression to his misgivings than he did in the letter of 1940. "The Apologist's Evening Prayer" is less a complaint than it is a *cri de coeur*. "While angels weep, the audience laughs," laments Lewis, referring to his many triumphs. Finally, scanning the whole body of his apologetic work, he begs, "Lord of the narrow gate and needle's eye, / Take from all my trumpery lest I die." No wonder, then, that when his characters are faced with overwhelming rhetorical force, Lewis often – and abruptly, sometimes in mid-discourse – resorts to *silence*, either violently (as when Ransom strikes the Unman in *Perelandra*), self-sacrificially (as when Puddleglum badly burns his foot to silence the witch-queen of Underland in *The Silver Chair*), or fatally (as when Orual dies mid-word at the end of *Till We Have Faces*). Now, and not exactly by-the-way: Do *you* recall the end of *Screwtape*?

More on the ending anon. Meanwhile, I note the beginning of *Screwtape*, on the very day after Lewis heard Hitler's speech. July 21, 1940 was a Sunday, and Lewis was attending the Communion service at Holy Trinity Church in Headington Quarry. Sometime during that service he was struck by the idea for a book he tentatively called *As One Devil to Another*, in which "the idea would be to give all the psychology of temptation from the *other* point of view." (My bet for that moment: the Consecration of the Eucharist; at least, that is when I'm most under assault.) In describing in a letter his example, which deals with someone at prayer, Lewis becomes the consummate debater: he shows how *any* occurrence following human prayer can be used as an argument against its efficacy or – in deceiving the praying person into believing something he did brought about the occurrence – how answered prayer can become a source of something more potent than disbelief, namely, Pride. The epistolary performance, virtually *ex tempore*, is staggering. That must have been some Communion service. (Lewis was a devoted believer in the Real Presence.) Lewis would deliver all thirty-one letters by Christmas to the *Guardian*, a religious weekly that published them serially from May through November of 1941.

Uncle Screwtape was an immediate hit. Bles published the book in Britain in 1942, Macmillan here in 1943. In *The Saturday Review of Literature* Leonard Bacon spoke for most reviewers on both sides of the Atlantic when he called *Screwtape* (April 17, 1943) "remarkably original" and declared, "there is a spectacular and satisfactory nova in the bleak sky of satire." By 1947 Lewis was on the cover of *Time* magazine, the image of a small devil on his shoulder. *That* is how easily rhetoric came to Lewis; how thoroughly it worked *for* him. And that is why it would trouble him so.

As it happens the manuscript of *Screwtape* is relatively nearby, in the Berg Collection of the New York Public Library on Forty-second Street, and decades ago I had a close look at it.[1] I will not impose upon you the burdensome details, but some of the *unburdensome* ones merit our attention. The paper, Lewis' manner of filling the surface and of numbering the letters (same distance from the left of the page and from the top), the length of each letter, even his method of marking his own left margin – all are impressively uniform. Sometimes Lewis actually catches himself in the middle of a word and switches to another. (None of that these days with word processing!) He did read through the text at least once, for through to the end he must change "Slimtrumpet" to "Scabtree" or to a different character, "Slumtrimpet"; he

---

1   A thorough description is in *CSL: The Bulletin of the New York C. S. Lewis Society*, vol. 11, no. 12 (October 1980), pp. 2-7.

The Screwtape Letters: of Evil and Its Antagonists — 121

had not made that change along the way. Including these changes, there are one hundred and eighty-seven emendations, which sound like a lot – until you realize that the preponderance are minor and that all are made on the original manuscript; there is no whole revision. Lewis' composition, like the working of his mind generally, is unrelenting.

I remember my amusement at finding tea stains over some text and seeing that the tea had so obscured one word that Lewis used the stain as the obliteration allowing for change: he did not need to bother rubbing out the original word. The most amusing single change, though, occurs in the first letter. At one point Lewis uses the word "fix," which had always struck me as the perfect stylistic choice: short, punchy, immediately unmistakable. But he had at first written "revit." That's "r-e-v-i-t." Now, we know he knew that is wrong, because he tried to spell "rivet" correctly twice more – in fact, he even got it *right* on the second try but didn't know it! So he struck out his last effort and in bold hand wrote 'FIX' followed by an exclamation point. So much for stylistic genius. A much more important, and telling, change occurs in Letter XX. There Lewis alters "celestial" to "terrestrial.," "You will find," Screwtape writes (and we read post-alteration), "if you look carefully into any human's heart, that he is haunted by at least two imaginary women – a *terrestrial* and an infernal Venus." We cannot know for sure why Lewis made the change, but I have my guess: he simply would not permit, let alone invite, any confusion with The Blessed Mother, who is as "celestial" as any woman could ever be and utterly unsuited to the brief point concerning lust that follows. By the way, not being a man particularly troubled by the use of the male pronoun generically, I do see a solecism in Lewis' emended sentence. For surely he means "if you look into any *man's* [rather than "any *human's*"] heart," especially as a reference for the "he" that follows and the passions he describes? Withal, perhaps Lewis has some slack coming his way. Remember: he was tutoring, lecturing, writing other books and articles, keeping up a growing correspondence (though not yet Gargantuan), and contending with both evacuees and the increasingly difficult Mrs. Moore – all as he was polishing off *Screwtape*. He would finally secure a copy of the manuscript with his friend Sister Penelope, to protect it from a blitzing.

In short, there was a whirlwind around Lewis who, in the midst of his driving composition, with its penetrating insight, remembered to include a . . . *plot* . . . which *we* often forget. A young man – the "patient," not quite callow but certainly not Christian – is in a big city during wartime. Unbeknownst to him, he is under spiritual attack by an apprentice tempter, one Wormwood, who is both invisible and inaudible to the young man.

Wormwood can influence the man's intellect and imagination but cannot work directly on his will; that is, the man is always a free agent. As it happens, Wormwood is something of a bumbler, which bumbling becomes all the clearer as his mentor, Uncle Screwtape, becomes increasingly undone. That – I believe these days it's called *de-compensation*? – becomes more and more laughable, since Screwtape's self-important and increasingly predatory voice is the only voice we hear. In fact the one exception must be regarded as the result of a full-blown psychotic break, occurring when a letter must be resumed by Toadpipe, the secretary, upon Screwtape's rage transforming him into a centipede.

And the bumbles are, after all, catastrophic, at least for Wormwood. Very early on the patient becomes a Christian, falls in with the wrong crowd, begins to have fun, and then falls in love – with a Christian woman no less, and from a Christian family, she being a "simpering" type, a "virginal, bread-and-butter miss," according to Slumtrimpet, the woman's tempter. Then, though the patient fears war, he nevertheless does his duty bravely, and finally, *while there is still time to snatch him as food for Our Father Below*, he – did you remember the ending when I asked earlier? – he . . . *dies*! No more temptation, no more talk. The patient is done with rhetoric, especially his own. That, right then, is very Bad for Wormwood. But there is Worse: at the moment of death the patient *sees* Wormwood, as well as his own guardian angel, and understands the battle that has been going on around him – all is clarity as he and we see what and whom Screwtape has been up against, what forces all along have been marshalled on behalf of the "patient." And then the Worst: the patient sees what no tempter, no matter his ranking in the Lowerarchy, can see: he sees not only the angels but the Enemy Himself, for the patient has been saved. A Catholic ending, I think, the patient not finally saved at baptism but remaining subject to temptation unto to the moment of death – a susceptibility requiring some scrubbing (Letter XXXI is quite clear on this) but not one that cost him his place in the Communion of Saints.

Yet the story is not done, for all along there has been a subplot, a second helical strand spiraling downwards around the patient's strand winding upwards. Owing to Wormwood, Screwtape has lost a great and expected asset, a meal for the boss. The result? As it happens, Hell is a zero-sum operation: there's a meal to be had, and someone must be eaten . . .

Since the debut of Uncle Screwtape there have been many imitators. Among the best is a short series by the late Wayne C. Booth, a pivotal rhetorical critic and a dean at the University of Chicago in, of all decades, the Sixties. His eight short letters are addressed to Harley P. Sellout, Vice-President,

Surrogate University. It seems that some administrators are actually in the service of the our father below, who has his own ideas about a new church of the university! Here are a very few of this Screwtape's many points. I wonder what you think? First this generally: "Now that with your appointment the university has eight vice-presidents and fourteen deans," Screwtape exults, "your opportunities to create confusion are practically unlimited." And then this, a principle: "Every faculty member and every student should be forced to see that everything is done" – and why? – "for the sake of something else and nothing for its own sake." In fact, "you might give an award," Screwtape continues, "to any student . . . or faculty member . . . who could show that he never *wasted* any reading – always [looked to] some . . . exam." And my favorite: ". . . many a student and faculty member has been effectively saved from an afternoon of reading or thought or love making or listening to music or genuine conversation" – how? – "by a well-organized, brainless faculty tea" or (I add) "leadership" meeting!

From time-to-time The New York C. S. Lewis Society has conducted its own Screwtape competitions, for which one winner took a highly novel approach. In her perfectly pitched letter, Jennifer Swift (and what a satirically worthy surname is that!) has *Wormwood* write to his uncle describing his own . . . escape! And with whose help? Why, with the help of Wormwood's escaped patient, who appears as a witness on behalf of his former tempter. After an artful debate with an Inspector, and in response to Wormwood's inquiry, the saved soul explains, "you made yourself unfit for Hell the moment you cried out for the mercy of Heaven." I cannot help thinking that Lewis would have approved. That letter, though, remains my second favorite "sort-of" Screwtape letter. Here is my first:

My Dear Wormwood,

You are mistaken to think that causing the boy to slap his sister is "terribly good." That accomplishes little, though you are on the right track.

The slap is good. That, however, takes the patient no further from the Enemy – which is always the whole and only point! – than to have him argue honestly with his mother. When he merely slaps the girl he is not committing a serious sin. But if you make him enjoy the act, cause him to look for opportunities to perform it – if you compel him to do it more and more – then it is even better than "good."

The little things his sister does which annoy the boy should be kept in mind, in *his* mind. Keep repeating those venial habits which so irritate him, remind him of all her irksome mannerisms and idiosyncrasies. Do not let him forget these things. Let *these* stay in his head, and like festering wounds they will drive the patient to violence in the form of striking his sibling.

That way you will find you can control him easily; exacting a smack will not be a matter of tempting him – it will only be a matter of *reminding* him. Thus will he be safely on his way to our Father's house.

Your affectionate uncle,

Screwtape

Chilling, that, don't you agree – especially you parents of differently-sexed siblings? Well, I remain as chilled today as I was twenty-four years ago – when my twelve-year-old son wrote it.

Chilling because insidious; that is, subtle and stealthy, marked by a persuasiveness that hides persuasion. (Remember Screwtape's outrage at the dying patient *seeing* Wormwood and thereby apprehending what all along had been at work.) In that light, have you noticed that Lewis never depicts Satan himself? Always there is an agent at work, but never the Prince of Darkness *per se*. The witches of *The Chronicles of Narnia* are certainly avatars of evil but not Evil itself; and they all work through deception. The obscene horrors of *That Hideous Strength* are wrought by Powers and Principalities, but not directly by the Prince of Liars. Even the single most repulsive, concrete, and direct depiction of evil agency in Lewis, the Unman of *Perelandra*, is just that, an agent. And he is, for me, the most interesting. How, after all, does he seek to tempt the Green Lady into disobedience? By debate, of course: open, honest debate! And how does our hero Ransom stop him? It's certainly not by winning the debate but rather by the antithesis of debate: he throws the most satisfying straight right hand since Joe Louis clocked Max Schmelling. In other words, *the time for rhetoric had expired*. Earlier, though, that Unman had confronted Ransom. Perhaps because merely an agent, he could not do so with fire, brimstone, or a terrifying display of overwhelming power; so instead he used . . . delicacy. Do you remember his device? Droolingly, he offers Ransom – who has come upon the creature by following a trail of eviscerated, but still living, frogs – a frog-victim of his own to rip to pieces. Ransom realizes then that though revolting against the very throne of heaven this agent and this act, representing the core of evil, is made ecstatic by the satisfaction it receives from the infliction of banal, even if hideous, physical torture. Ransom concludes that Evil is inside out; the closer you get to its center, the more hollow it is.

Lewis' use of surrogacy in his depictions of evil can be explained, I think, by two factors. The first I'll call proximate recognition. How often are *we* tempted by Satan visible? On the other hand, how often are we tempted by surrogates, and in those stealthy, subtle ways depicted in the *Letters*? The temptations and tempters in Lewis – even the Unman – are nearby and recognizable, unlike my second factor. We kneel to Our Lord, who is the only Person we know (I discount Luther) to have been tempted by Satan himself. We don't merit such direct agency, and, I believe, Lewis would do nothing to let us think otherwise. For Lewis, though not picky about hooves, horns, and the pointed tail, believed pronouncedly in the Devil. He is neither to be ignored nor obsessed over.

We too have our very own surrogate, the unnamed Patient, who would be hardly more than a foil except for one thing: free will. You will have noticed my avoidance, more or less, of particular letters, each of which holds a lesson worthy at least of a sermon, maybe (in some cases) of a book, even of an entire dissertation. Instead, I note what I make out to be a few paramount lessons. Take Letter VIII. "I know we have won many a soul through pleasure. All the same, it is His invention, not ours: all our research so far has not enabled us to produce one." The devil, in other words, is a parasite: he creates nothing. Thus he must have us avoid real pleasure (in Letter XXII we will learn that the God is "a hedonist at heart"), and avoid pain too, because they smack of reality, which always brings us closer to God. And this, again from Letter VIII: "Do not let him suspect the law of undulation. Let him assume that the first ardours of his conversion might have been expected to last, and ought to have lasted, forever, and that his present dryness is an equally permanent condition."

And what makes for the perfect object of attention? Why, feelings of course. For example, we might ask, Are they the *right* ones? You see, truth matters less than feeling good about ourselves, and that matters less than the state of our Inner Life – as opposed, say, to doing our duty. We might continue to believe that "being in love" requires a tumult of emotion. We might encounter not Jesus himself but rather the *Historical* Jesus. And if we are Christians our creed must be diluted, so that we come to believe in Christianity *and* . . . whatever. Finally we learn that the devil does not understand love: "if only we could find out what he is really up to," complains Screwtape respecting this inscrutable act (and *act* it is) of selfless, unconditioned giving. We must not know that we are made for God and may rest only in Him. In his *Pensees* (nos. 136 and 139) Pascal notes the disease: "The only [pleasurable] thing for men therefore is to be diverted from thinking of *what* they are, either by some occupation which takes their mind off it, or by some novel and agreeable passion . . ." where we remain trapped. That is evil in Lewisian, and in most Christian, literature: a Self trapped in its own babble.

Letter after letter not only advances the plot and contrapuntally unwinds the subplot, but mocks the devil by allowing him to take himself with the utmost seriousness – as Wormwood subverts the bureaucracy with comedy-skit incompetence. (In two headnotes, Lewis cites both Luther and St. Thomas More to the point that the devil "cannot endure to be mocked.") But most important is that, along the way, and as though incidentally, Lewis pins *us* and our abuse of will to the card. Here we arrive at the heart of a masterpiece: a work of art, ostensibly simple, that again and again gives us more bang for the buck than we had reckoned with and finally delivers that straight right hand to *our* chin. How does Lewis know us so? How does he know *me* so? Lewis had taken that look into himself and for our sake had filled his mouth with ashes. I recommend the *Letters* as Lenten reading, when we are especially required to pay some price, for when you find yourself in them then your mouth, too, will fill with ashes.

Just beneath the literary conceit lies that Horror I mentioned at the start. Lewis used a sort of joke but, at the end of the day, is deadly serious. This depiction of evil in Christian literature may be a mere device, but as I avowed earlier it is no ruse. Again, Screwtape's greatest defeat is that the patient sees what all along has been going on; our surrogate finally realizes that a real war is being waged around us. As bumbling as *your* Wormwood may be, his Uncle Screwtape is in deadly, omnivorous earnest, right here, right now; and like the Unman on Perelandra *he does not sleep*. But Screwtape and his master usually fail to reckon with the Church Triumphant and all its angels and saints: neither do they sleep.

Myth and Belief in Perelandra

Perelandra was first published in 1943 and, ten years later, re-issued (by Pan Books) as *A Voyage to Venus*. The most recent (1968) cloth edition is claimed by Macmillan to be its first hardcover *Perelandra*, yet I have seen a Macmillan hardcover dating back at least twenty-five years. With regard to the composition of *Perelandra*, we know very little, though what we do know is interesting: the book was not planned as part of a trilogy (since a trilogy had not been planned); it was originally conceived, and begun, as a space- *and* time-travel story but later abandoned; and we know, finally, that it all started (like *The Lion, the Witch, and the Wardrobe*) with an image, in this case, the image of floating islands.

The book may be organized into five parts: narrative framework (Chs.1 and 2), Perelandran Eden (3-6), Temptation (7-11), Descent (12-14), and Ascent (15-17); these five divisions correspond, in general, to the conventional literary divisions of exposition, development, climax, counterstroke, and eucatastrophe (from John D. Haigh, *The Fiction of C.S. Lewis*, Ph. D. Dissertation, University of Leeds, 1962, pp. 188-89). Though the style of *Perelandra* is typically Lewisian (more strikingly descriptive, perhaps, than any other of his works), its structure is not. In this book Lewis chose to use the *epical* form of address, that form whereby *presumably true events* are *directly* related by a *participant* in those events. In *Perelandra* "Lewis" talks to us directly.

Any number of questions could be asked about *Perelandra*. About the type of book it is – allegory, myth, or science fiction? Or about its themes – exactly what (value, type) does Ransom represent to us? What relationship really obtains between Satan and man, or between angels and man? What is the doctrine, in detail, of not repeating pleasures, or running life backwards, like a film? Is Lewis suggesting (as one Society member asks) a sort of Christian evolutionism, any number of Incarnations which, perhaps, would detract from the absoluteness of what happened on Earth? Or, finally, we could ask questions about specific items within the story: what, for example, is the purpose, or meaning, of the cave-monster?

Well, I propose to answer none of these questions; instead, I would like to indulge an idiosyncracy and ask: What is it about *Perelandra* that is so convincing, which so irresistibly seems to compel belief, either literary belief, or that sort of profound acquiescence to fundamental truths, or – more frequent than we might suppose – *literal* belief? My hypothesis, from among many possible hypotheses, is that the power of Myth accounts for belief. We must first ask, Belief in what? Then we must ask whether or not the author intended such an effect. And finally – the last preliminary: is belief (of one sort or another) indeed an effect of reading *Perelandra*?

There can be no doubt concerning the sense of *Perelandra*. The novel is *not* an allegory; things are exactly what they seem to be, and the only correspondences are symbolical. The subject of *Perelandra* is revealed as Ransom ponders the task before him:

> But when you come to think of it, is it odder than what all of us have to do every day? When the Bible used that very expression about fighting with principalities and powers and depraved hypersomatic begins at great heights. . . . it meant that quite ordinary people were to do the fighting . . . Your idea that ordinary people will never meet the Dark Eldila in any form except a psychological or moral form – as temptations or the like – is simply an idea that held good for a certain phase of the cosmic war. . . .in the next phase it may be anyone's job to meet them . . .in some quite different mode. (p. 24)

Ransom's battle – and the cosmic significance of it – is the subject of *Perelandra*.

So if we are to be taught anything by *Perelandra*, it is that every Christian should make Ransom's battle his own and that every one should be Christian, for the battle is *at least* as real as any stone, or building, or exploding hydrogen bomb.

Lewis liked battle; Barfield told us so. In *Surprised by Joy*, Lewis describes enthusiastically the Great Knock's instruction. The strength of Lewis' mind is immediately attractive; following a Lewis argument, stated a writer in the *Manchester Guardian*, is "like watching a master chess-player who makes a trivial and seemingly unimportant move which ten minutes later turns out to be a stroke of genius."[1] And "Lewis was an argumentative man, in the best sense, and as likely to argue with himself as with anyone."[2] Which is why, most likely, he has his greatest influence upon the "backslidden and the agnostic.[3]

Behind Lewis' choice of genre is a very interesting psychological theory. He believed that a fictive work might be a more successful didactic tool than the Bible because a reader, when attending to fiction, is caught unawares. Though the Bible may be approached correctly, some "unhappy psychological law" causes the original attitude to thwart itself. Such a law may be the reason for not being merry at Christmas, or for not being in love on the wedding day.[4] The dutiful effort prevents spontaneous feeling . . . Make it a fairy-tale and the reader is taken off his guard.[5]

Lewis has explicitly denied ever having explicitly written a story impelled by a moral intention – in spite of the fact that many people believe the Space Trilogy and the *Narnian Chronicles* to be little more than pure Lesson.[6] Ostensibly opposite to this statement are a number of Lewis' letters. He once wrote that the Imaginative Man in him first compelled him toward poetry, then toward criticism, and – finally – toward the embodiment of religious belief in symbolic or mythopoeic form.[7] Relatively early in his career (before the publication of *Perelandra* but *after* the publication of *Out of the Silent Planet*), Lewis wrote that "any amount of theology can now be smuggled into people's minds under cover of romance without them knowing it."[8] Later, while referring to his expository apologetics, he confided that he no longer would write "*directly theological* pieces," that he could now only catch the reader unawares through fiction and symbol.[9] For Lewis, the reconciliation between his public disavowal of didacticism and his private embrace of it could be found in what *he* was; indeed, for Lewis reconciliation was unnecessary – the question was simply not an issue:

> But it is better not to ask the question at all. Let the pictures tell you their own moral. For the moral in them will rise from whatever spiritual roots you have succeeded in striking during the course of your life. . . . *The only moral that is of any value is that which rises inevitably from the whole cast of the author's mind.*[10]

The success of *Perelandra* in eliciting belief is easily documented. Roger Lancelyn Green wrote:

> The imagination, the conception, the description of the Perelandrian Paradise . . . is astonishing and awe-inspiring: Lewis has depicted Venus once and for all, and *it is impossible not to believe his picture* – or to get it out of our minds and visual memories once it has been imprinted there.[11]

Although disagreeing with Lewis' most fundamental beliefs, Leonard Bacon, reviewing the book in *The Saturday Review of Literature*, stated:

> He has a powerful, discriminating and, in the proper sense of the word, poetic mind, great learning, startling wit, an overwhelming imagination . . . and the capacity to express himself best described by saying: 'he can write' . . . One's own fancy, one's own thought, leap after the writer's. Agreement, dissent, analogy wake in the lethargic mind. . . . Mr. Lewis' romance, or better myth, for Mr. Lewis' imagination (as has been said of a very great poet) is equal to the manufacture of myth, is . . . *provocative of the suspension of disbelief* . . . He knows how to make the fantastic explicit.[12]

Moreover, many readers found *Perelandra* so convincing that they wrote Lewis asking him for the philologist's address; it seems they wanted to compliment him on his heroism. Other – perhaps more sophisticated – readers complimented Lewis for his "realism of presentation" adding that he certainly gave the Devil a "'good run for his money.'"[13]

Thus we can see that Perelandra is a) primarily about the Christian myth; b) intended, at least in part to teach; and c) successful. The question, again, is Wherefore successful? The answer lies with two notions of myth, Lewis' own and another, very tentative, hypothesis.

The most difficult kind of world to impose upon a reader is a mythic one, for such a world has its own rules, its own history, and its own ambience; its life is utterly foreign to the life we know on earth. It is most truly another world, which is why Lewis chose a literal *other world* (Venus) to embody the Christian Myth, and which is why he wrote:

> No merely physical strangeness or merely spacial distance will realize that idea of otherness which is what we are always trying to grasp in a story about voyaging through Space: you must go into another dimension. To construct plausible and moving "other worlds" we must draw on the only real "other world" we know, that of the spirit.[14]

The reader quickly discovers Perelandra is a Paradise; it is that *kind* of a world. And he discovers many times over what are the *qualities* peculiar to a Paradise – the Illusion is intensified to an irresistible degree. When Ransom looks at the Un-man, he returns the look, and the reader is thrilled and terrified by what he sees in that face.

> It looked at Ransom in silence and at last began to smile. We have all spoken – Ransom himself had often spoken – of a devilish smile.

Now he realized that he had never taken the words seriously. The smile was not bitter, nor raging, nor, in any ordinary sense, sinister; it was not even mocking. It seemed to summon Ransom, with horrible naivete of welcome, into the world of its own pleasures, as if all men were at one in those pleasures, as if they were the most natural thing in the world and no dispute could ever have occurred about them. It was not furtive, nor ashamed, it has nothing of the conspirator in it. It did not defy goodness, it ignored it to the point of annihilation. (p. 110)

Of course, the reader struggles right along with Ransom as he attempts to rationalize the situation, as he is beset with doubts, and as finally he comes to realize that he knew all along what is right and what needs to be done. The most exciting episode in the book, however, is the Debate. The battle is real, the stakes enormous. Ransom is frightened, the enemy is only too real – and the subject is orthodox Christian doctrine doctrine. The Un-man says,

"He has not told you that it was the breaking of the commandment which brought Maledil to our world and because of which he was made man. He dare not deny it."

"Do you say this, Piebald? asked the Lady.

Ransom was sitting with his fingers locked so tightly that his knuckles were white. The unfairness of it all was wounding him like barbed wire. Unfair . . . unfair. . . .

"Do you say this, Piebald?" the Lady asked a second time.

The spell was broken.

"I will tell you what I say...Of course good came of it. Is Maledil a beast that we can stop his path, or a leaf that we can twist his shape . . ." He turned to the body of Weston . . . "Tell her *your* joys."[15] (p. 120-121)

C.S. Lewis has stated (quite parenthetically) that a myth is "a not unlikely tale" "an account of what *may have been* historical fact", not "a symbolic representation of non-historical truth."[16]

The manner in which Belief may be a function of Myth has been described by two men whose collective influence has run high indeed, Sir James George Frazer and C.G. Jung, with the latter attempting, as well, to account for that function.

Frazer's *The Golden Bough*[17] is an attempt to demonstrate the commonality of religious practice and belief among cultures varying widely in time and place. The similarities between much of that data and many events occurring (or accepted) in *Perelandra* are striking. The idea of an incarnate God – Maledil himself when he came to Earth – was common to the Washington Islands, Egypt, India, Polynesia, and Greece.[18] Tree worship – the earthly parallel of the Green Lady's understanding concerning the Fixed Land – was an ancient and wide-spread practice.[19] That a well-endowed woman could provoke vegetation (and the *sacred nuptials* could lend even more bounty to whatever land) was a belief widely held (though most predominant in Central America).[20] The tastes and smells of Perelandra are sufficient testimony to that world's fertility; and the wedding of the Green Lady to the King will permit those two to "'be fruitful and multiply'" – a command not entirely fulfilled by their Thulcandran counterparts – in magnificent and (to fallen creatures) nearly incomprehensible ways:

> "We will fill this world with our children. We will know this world to the centre. We will make the nobler of the beasts so wise that they will become *hnau* and speak . . . When the time is ripe for it…we will tear the sky curtain and Deep Heaven shall become familiar to the eyes of our sons. . . . I set forth even now on ten thousand years of preparation – I, the first of my race, my race the first of races, to begin. I tell you that when the last of my children has ripened and ripeness has spread from them to all the Low Worlds, it will be whispered that the morning is at hand." (p. 211-13)

A number of items less important than these basic instances are also worthy of note. A major conceit of *Perelandra* is the occupation of Weston's body by the Devil, an occurrence terrifying because of its importance and imminence. Frazer tells us that an old and widespread belief holds that a body may be victimized by an alien spirit after its own soul has departed.[21] During Ransom's journey upward through the mountain, Weston's body is finally destroyed when it is thrown into a raging blaze (fire imagery is important throughout this scene), and only *after* this ascent through darkness and fire is Ransom prepared for the glory which follows. Frazier tells us that Fire Festivals were common in Europe, their purpose being either destruction of evil spirits or purification.[22]

The significance of these parallels is difficult to ascertain. The historical practices are perhaps *too* scattered to hold much meaning. But we must remember that we are *not* dealing with literary phenomena. The practitioners of the rites described by Frazer are not fictive creations. And the genuinely fundamental beliefs are not literary as they appear in *Perelandra*, for Lewis posits them as *axioms* in the real world (the world of Ransom and of 'Lewis') to be accepted *a priori*. The book *qua* book therefore fails to supply links between ancient practice and rhetorical effectiveness. We turn to Jung.

Since art derives from psychic motives,[23] "we would expect a strangeness of form and content, thoughts that can be apprehended only intuitively, a language pregnant with meanings, and images that are true symbols because they are the best possible expressions for something unknown – bridges thrown out towards an unseen shore."[24] These "expressions" (primarily representations of the psyche) become Myth when taken together. They picture external phenomena which are not mere allegories but rather "inner and unconscious psychic drama that becomes accessible to human consciousness by way of projection."[25] These individual constituents are known as archetypes, primordial images that constantly occur in the course of history and appear wherever *creative fantasy* is freely expressed.[26] They are, from the beginning, surrounded by numinosity.[27] Essentially they are mythological figures; the moment of their appearance is always characterized by a peculiar emotional intensity, "as though chords in us were struck that had never resounded before, or as though forces whose existence we never expected were unloosed."[28] Does it sound like your response to *Perelandra*? At such moments "we are no longer individuals but the race . . . Whoever speaks in primordial images . . . evokes in us all those beneficent forces that ever and anon have enabled humanity to find refuge and to outlive the longest night."[29]

The twentieth century view of the universe should be especially hospitable to archetypes, for although "heaven has become an empty space to us, a fair memory of things that once were," our heart nevertheless "glows, and secret unrest gnaws at the roots of our being."[30] We should (practically and morally) accept archetypal symbols, not as arbitrary or intentional signs standing for known and conceivable facts, but as "an admittedly anthropomorphic – hence limited and only partly valid – expression for something supra-human and only party conceivable."[31] Though few such symbols may appear in a particular work (i.e. *Perelandra*), if they are well-chosen their cumulative effect should be almost irresistible.

One of the cost impelling images is the life of Christ, which describes in symbolic images the events in the conscious (and transcendent) life of a man who has transformed his higher destiny. As the reader shares in this victory, he reacts strongly against the Satanic (fourth) element of the Trinity-archetype.[32] That the drama of Christ is clearly the center of all of us is a *psychological* fact.[33] And immediately below this numinous level lives the King, the carrier of Myth who represents a superior personality, "the statement of the collective unconscious."[34] The King "represents the daylight of the psyche,"[35] – this, I remind you, is Jung, not Lewis – whereas his disappearance represents the rise of the unconscious or the descent of the ego into the unconscious.[36]

Apparently, Man has no choice concerning archetypes. "'Principalities and powers' are always with us; we have no need to create them even if we could. It is merely incumbent on us to *choose* . . . We do not *create* 'God' we *choose* . . .him".[37] Ransom's formulation merits repition:

> "You are feeling the absurdity of it. Dr. Elwin Ransom setting out single-handed to combat powers and principalities . . . But when you come to think of it, is it odder than what all of us have to do every day? When the Bible used that very expression about fighting with principalities and powers . . . at great heights . . . it meant that quite the ordinary people were to do the fighting." (p. 23-24)

Quite explicitly, then, we have no escape, for the "ideas of moral law and of the Godhead are parts of the indestructible constituents of the human soul."[38] Represented syllogistically, the argument would be:

Major Premise

Psycho-racial archetypes, described by Jung as permanent residents of the human spirit, are rhetorically effective when posited in a work.

Minor Premise

The critical symbols of Perelandra closely correspond to psycho-racial archetypes, observed by Frazer to be historical phenomena.

Conclusion

The critical symbols of Perelandra effect a strong and affirmative response, i.e. are rhetorically effective.

So much for my hypothesis; but do note that I am *not* claiming literary influence.

But what of Lewis' own notion of myth? A myth is that "particular kind of story which has a value in itself – a value independent of its embodiment in any literary work"[39] and (I might add) is independent of any particular doctrine. Lewis has listed six characteristics common to all myths, and *Perelandra* (as I hope to demonstrate) possesses each one of them. Yet, "the same story may be a myth to one man and not to another,"[40] for most of Lewis' criteria describe a reaction. I would submit that my reactions, though only my own, are not atypical. Above all, a myth is extra-literary; its simple narrative may be got at through any number of authors. Of course, no one but C.S. Lewis has told the story of Perelandra, but I will present a brief synopsis of that story, containing no literary merit whatever – certainly none of Lewis' particular kind of merit – and see if it can "make a powerful impression on any person of sensibility."[41]

> On the planet Perelandra – a beautiful Paradise of water, floating islands, and Fixed Land – there dwelt a Green Lady and her King. Maledil, Maker of All Things, gave them all they could want, but He forbade them ever to remain on the Fixed Land during the night. The Green Lady and the King returned Maledil's love and obeyed Him. Then it happened that the Lady and the King became separated. At that time the Dark Power of Earth, enemy of Maleldil and all of His creatures, came to the Lady. He tried to persuade her to disobey Maledil, and he might have succeeded had not Ransom, one of Maleldil's loyal servants from Earth, intervened. In spite of the danger to himself and at the cost of great suffering, Ransom fought the Dark Power and drove him into the Deep. And so it came to pass that the Green Lady and the King, because they had not disobeyed Maleldi, were raised to high glory as the Father and Mother of a new Beginning. This was told by the man called Ransom.

Although *Perelandra* does possess the narrative elements described by Lewis, these elements are not responsible for the effects elicited by the story of Perelandra. Whether or not we see through Lewis' strange names to the figures identified or are able to recognize Biblical parallels, most readers of *Perelandra* share a numinous experience. Because Myth and actuality are equally true – with Christianity representing the supreme degree of *both* – literature should be judged according to the criteria or Mythopoeia. Only myth "conveys the meaning embodied in itself."[42] Furthermore, although we do sympathize with Ransom – even, in one sense, identify with him – a projection of ourselves into the character is unnecessary for mythic purposes, for mythic characters "are like shapes moving in another world. We feel indeed that the pattern of their movements has a profound relevance to our own life, but we do not imaginatively transport ourselves into theirs."[43]

Myth always deals with impossibles and preternaturals, as does *Perelandra,* and though the experience it effects may be sad or joyful it is always grave.⁴⁴ And though these are formal qualities they are, in some way, responsible for the final quality of myth:

> The experience is not only grave but awe-inspiring. We feel it to be a numinous. It is as if something of great moment had been communicated to us. The recurrent efforts of the mind to grasp – we mean, chiefly, to conceptualize – this something, are seen in the persistent tendency of humanity to provide myths with allegorical explanations. And after all allegories have been tried, the myth itself continues to feel more important than they.⁴⁵

So it is that *Perelandra* gives the impression of having hit rock bottom, of having exposed some Reality with which there can be no dispute. To be sure, the myth is not itself the Reality, but after experiencing it we are compelled to say, "these images have struck roots far below the surface of my mind"⁴⁶ – they do, indeed, depict something which "*may have been* historical fact."⁴⁷

Perelandra appeals to all of us, for even if we would not care to live there, it yet manages to arouse those "lineaments of ungratified desire." The generosity, charity, and innocence, the commerce with animals and with spirits, and the delicious and willing sensual pleasures – each stimulates in us a vague longing, or desire. Lewis used the German word *Sehnsucht* to describe that feeling of want, a feeling attendant upon a realization that no particular thing, no matter how much we thought we really wanted it, can ever genuinely gratify a desire. It is a longing which brings pleasure, because all longing (no matter what the particular object) is for the same thing: God and heaven. Put another way, *Sehnsucht* is "spilled religion,"⁴⁸ and the drops may be full of blessing to the unconverted man who licks them and begins searching for the cup whence they spilled.

Thus, the power of *Perelandra* to evince belief may derive from the fact that it offers a convincing portrayal of that Truth which, knowingly or not, we have always wanted. This Reality and the longing it arouses exist permanently, independently, and unconditionally. That is why this utterly extra-literary phenomenon (what Lewis call the Dialectic of Desire), if "faithfully followed, would retrieve all mistakes, head you off from fake paths, and force you not to propound, but to live through, a sort of ontological proof." *Perelandra* provokes, provides us with, and is precisely that proof.

Endnotes

1 Clyde S. Kilby, *The Christian World of* C. S. Lewis (Grand Rapids, 1964), p.11.

2 Owen Barfield, "C. S. Lewis," transcript of an address delivered at Wheaton College, October 16, 1964.

3 J. D. Douglas, "The Legacy of C. S. Lewis," *Christianity Today*, December 20, 1963.

4 Letter to Don Holmes, Feb. 17, 1959, in the Archives of Wheaton College.

5 Letter to Allan C. Emery, Jr., August 18, 1959. In the Archives of Wheaton College.

6 ⁶ "Sometimes Fairy Stories May Say Best What's to be Said," in *Of Other Worlds*.

7 Letter to the Milton Society of America; in *Letters*, p. 260.

8 Letter to Sister Penelope, August 19, 1939. In the Archives of Wheaton College.

9 "On Three Ways of Writing for Children," in *Of Other Worlds*. Emphasis mine.

10 Ibid.

11 Roger Lancelyn Green, *C. S. Lewis* (New York, 1963), p. 29. Emphasis mine.

12 Leonard Bacon, "The Imaginative Power of C. S. Lewis," *The Saturday Review of Literature*, April 8, 1944, p. 9. Emphasis mine. A sampling of other reviews: "Since Perelandra is a planet much resembling Paradise, he has accomplished a peculiarly difficult job – that of representing the sights, sounds, smells and all the unfamiliar physical sensations of a state of perfection" (Marjorie Farber, The New York Times); "There . . . is . . . the rare power of inventive imagination, and something of the graphic vigor of language. Mr. Lewis is an idealist." (*Times Literary Supplement*).

13 Walter Hooper, letter to the author, February 7, 1968.

14 "On Stories," *Of Other Worlds*, p. 12.

15 *Perelandra*, pp. 175-84.

16 *The Problem of Pain*, p. 64. Emphasis in original.

17 Originally published in 1890: released in twelve volumes between 1907 and 1915. All of my references are to the one-volume abridgment originally published in 1922 (MacMillan, New York), paperback edition 1963, third printing 1967.

18 *The Golden Bough*, pp. 105-111.

19 Ibid., pp.126-127.

20 Ibid., pp. 157, 164.

21 Ibid., pp. 706, 745, 761.

22 Ibid.

23 C.G. Jung, *The Spirit in Man, Art, and Literature* (New York, 1966), p. 65.

24 Ibid., p. 76.

135 207.

32 Ibid., pp. 157, 191.

33 *Mysterium Coniunctionis*, p. 455. Emphasis in original.

34 p. 258.

35 Ibid., p. 357.

36 Ibid., p. 371.

37 *Psychology and Religion*, p. 87. Incidentally, C. S. Meier in *Jung and Analytic Psychology* (Newton Centre, 1959), p. 65, has stated that Jung, in the second half of his life, never cured a patient unless he had experienced the "religious Function."

38 *Psychological Reflections*, p. 300.

39 *An Experiment in Criticism*, p. 41.

40 Ibid., p. 45.

41 Ibid., p. 65.

42 Ibid., p. 44.

43 Ibid.

44 Ibid.

45 Ibid., p. 49.

46 See note 15, above.

47 *The Pilgrim's Regress*, pp. 7-9.

48 "Christianity and Culture," in *Christian Reflections*, p. 23.

18

C. S. Lewis in Milton Criticism

During the past four decades, the following charges have been brought against *Paradise Lost*: God the Father is a vengeful, jealous tyrant; Satan is a genuine hero, deliberately degraded by a poet who lost artistic control of his creation; a general lack of human interest prevails throughout the poem;[1] Adam and Eve are actually the helpless victims of an inherent weakness in human nature; the Garden of Eden is really nothing more than an absurd greenhouse; the Fall is justifiable, not only because it results in the Incarnation, but because morality is better than innocence; Adam's fall is not sinful but rather a manifestation of perfect human love;[2] Eve is not really condemnable for wanting to be superior to Adam.[3] In short, we have Milton Criticism transformed into that forty-years war known as the Milton Controversy. The question is, What is Lewis' place – its quality, magnitude, and importance – in that controversy?

To answer that question accurately, we must realize that Lewis' *Preface* is not only about Milton's poem; in fact Lewis tells us much about the art of poetry and about poetry in the West. In reviewing the book, Denis Saurat reminded us that

> Milton is one link in a very long chain. Many more points could be discussed; it is a great feat that Mr. Lewis causes them to arise, and often suggests a solution . . . Mr. Lewis' book is also a brilliant link in a long chain which is a credit to English thought.[4]

So the first point to be made when weighing the value of Lewis' *Preface* is that it very well may say more (about poetry in general) in less space than any work since Aristotle's *Poetics*. The second point is the more pertinent to our topic and was articulated by Edward Wagenknecht in his review of the book for The *New York Times*: "But his most valiant service is to protect us against the many students of Milton who have not been able to see the woods for the trees."[5]

Since the publication of the *Preface* in 1942, virtually all students of Milton have had to take account of Lewis, usually (though not invariably) in favorable terms. This phenomenon is sterlingly exemplified by William Empson, who (in *Milton's God*) devotes no fewer than forty-eight pages (of 277) to Lewis' *Preface*, mostly in refutation.[6] On the other hand David Daiches (neither less respected nor less influential than Empson) includes in his book, *Milton*, a number of favorable references to Lewis and frequently relies upon his very judgements Of course, Lewis' most famous adversary – and one of the greatest of all Milton critics – is E. M. W. Tillyard, whose *Milton* prompted the famous controversy set down as *The Personal Heresy*. In *Studies in Milton* Tillyard attacks Lewis' views three times, though he does add "Lewis has written very well on Milton and Hierarchy."[8]

The single most controversial issue of the entire debate probably has been Milton's treatment of Satan, and the single greatest advocate opposing Lewis on this topic has been A.J.A. Waldock, who in *'Paradise Lost' and its Critics*[9] referred to Lewis on forty-four (of 147) pages. In a magnificent chapter entitled "Satan and the Technique of Degradation" Waldock argues that Milton can manage the decline of Satan's image only by a nasty form of narrative intrusion, "information-giving":

> It is a pretended exhibition of changes occurring; actually it is of the nature of an assertion that changes occur. The changes do not generate themselves from within: they are imposed from without. Satan, in short, does not degenerate: *he is degraded.*[10]

It is now generally agreed[11] that Waldock's position is wrong, and Lewis' magnificent description of Satan's decline is worth reading again and again:

> From hero to general, from general to politician, from politician to secret service agent, and thence to a thing that peers in at bedroom or bathroom windows, and thence to a toad, and finally to a snake – such is the progress of Satan.[12]

Perhaps Lewis' greatest accomplishment with regard to Milton criticism was to define the genre of *Paradise Lost* as that of Secondary Epic, wherein the theme is great, unchanging, and remote, and the manner is ceremonial.[13] This placement explains most of the poem and thus puts to rest much difficulty, though a number of troublesome problems do arise. For example, Lewis characterizes the narrator as a Blind Bard (pp. 59-60). Yet this remote and, above all, decorous figure is not above pettiness, as when he criticizes metaphysical debate (II. 555-61), or quarrelsomeness, as when he collects in the Celestial Garbage Bin symbols of Roman Catholicism (III. 489-97). And a second example: Lewis cites many passages from *Paradise Lost* which are singularly mythic (e.g. our impression of Paradise as we approach it with Satan) yet does not account for the singularly *un*mythic questions, such as whether or not angels eat, digest, and evacuate in a manner similar to human beings (V. 407-13).[14]

These criticisms may be as petty as those of the Blind Bard, and no doubt others could be found, but just as we should not forget that Milton's poem is a Secondary Epic, so we must not forget that Lewis' book is a preface; that is, a work which establishes the grounds for, and direction of, criticism. Insofar as the book engages the very most fundamental questions with regard to *Paradise Lost* (and, let us not forget, to poetry in general) it is of considerable scope, and insofar as it engages them superbly (clearly, comprehensively, convincingly) it is of high quality and, thus, of very great importance. Milton criticism inevitably goes on; and as it does, we can be sure that Lewis' work will inspire great allies and great adversaries, perhaps the soundest criterion by which a man's work can be judged.

Endnotes

1 Notwithstanding Helen Gardner's opinion to the contrary in *A Reading of "Paradise Lost"* (Oxford: Clarendon Press, 1965), p. 50.

2 John Peter, *A Critique of "Paradise Lost"* (New York: Columbia University Press, 1960), p. 131.

3 Ibid., p. 128. This list is, of course, not exhaustive. Peter gets much of his ammunition from the great antagonist A.J.A. Waldock, *'Paradise Lost' and its Critics* (Cambridge: The University Press, 1964), who provides what I have omitted.

4 *New Statesman,* 24 (1942), p. 325.

5 May 23, 1943, p. 10.

6 (London: Chatto & Windus, 1961), see index.

7 (London: Hutchinson University Library, 1957), see index.

8 (London: Chatto & Windus, 1964), p. 141.

9 (Cambridge: The University Press, 1961), see index.

10 Ibid., p. 83. See also Anne Davidson Ferry, *Milton's Epic Voice: The Narrator in "Paradise Lost"* (Cambridge: Harvard University Press, 1963), pp. 44-66.

11 This seemed to be Professor Roberts' attitude in his address to the Society; see also Allan H. Gilbert, *On the Composition of "Paradise Lost"* (New York: Octagon Books, 1966), ch. VI.

12 (New York: Oxford University Press, 1961), p. 99. For an outstanding summary of the debate see John M. Steadman, *Milton's Epic Characters* (Chapel Hill: The University of North Carolina Press, 1959), ch. VI.

13 Lewis, pp. 33-52; this question is analyzed and responses to it reviewed in Patrick Murray, "*Paradise Lost*: Milton's Intention and the Reader's Response," *Milton: The Modern Phase* (New York: Barnes & Noble, Inc., 1967), pp. 19-115.

14 Lewis' responses to the mythic elements are convincing, but a more thorough (and surprisingly sympathetic) argument on this matter is Isabel B. MacCaffrey, *"Paradise Lost" as 'Myth'* (Cambridge: Harvard University Press, 1967).

The Book Reviewer
An Enjoyment

Generally book reviews are shortcuts to the shelves of mini-libraries, so I am an inveterate fan. If I were to make the ridiculous calculation comparing how much I've learned from reading books to how much I've learned from reviews of them, I would not be surprised if the split only slightly favored books. That calculation, however, does not apply to Lewis, whose books have taught me more than anyone else's, who has taught me nearly as much by what he has had to say about the books that he read, and who has talked me into reading more books than anyone else. He goes very far beyond the mini-library. We know that C. S. Lewis *had* a very large personal library: thousands of volumes, most of them amply annotated by him. But we can say further that Lewis himself *was* a massive library, his mind furnished with perhaps as many books as he owned. So my claim to having learned from Lewis should seem reasonable to those who have read much of him: the more Lewis wrote and spoke about the books he read, and the more people listened to him and read what he wrote, the smarter those people have become; and the larger too.

Of course Lewis did not always infect us as he is infected. *The Worm Ouroborus* did not, does not, and most likely will never speak to my imagination; Lewis and I are so far distant from each other on this book that I fail to understand how he liked it, though his blurb for *The Mezentian Gate* (*The Worm* being the first book) tells me what he liked: "nowhere else shall we meet this precise blend of hardness and luxury, of lawless speculation and sharply realized detail, of the cynical and the magnanimous. No author can be said to remind us of Eddison," to which I append, that's for sure. So Lewis' own enthusiasm sometimes exceeded the merits of the book that aroused it, at least in the eyes of many a reader who had rushed to the book because of Lewis' enthusiasm. For me, though, notwithstanding *Ouroborous*, that response has been rare. I *have* gotten the preponderance of what Lewis has to teach, and I know I preach to the choir. Or do I? Many who have read a good deal of the master have yet to read the literary historian and critic, and even those who do read that Lewis read very little of him. Those readers are perhaps a *distant* choir. Here in the true church most of us have read every aspect of Lewis and many of us have read all of him. In doing so we have found . . . Lewis: his engagement and enthusiasm, intellectual consistency, and no straitened voice, though it is sometimes restrained; he observes acutely and argues assiduously.

Certainly these features mark *The Allegory of Love* (did you not just want to *run* for your copy of *The Romance of the Rose*?), *Preface to 'Paradise Lost'*, *The Personal Heresy* (how often I would have interrupted had that debate been live and I present). The qualities are present even in his *History of English Literature in the Sixteenth Century*, where he is less making a case than establishing an objective record for a wider range of readers than is normally the scholarly case. None of the literary essays are exceptions. As Walter Jackson Bate said of Dr. Johnson, I would say of Lewis: "what draws us to him is his perennial power to shake the insignificances out of a subject," and as Johnson himself said of good criticism Lewis makes possible the reception of "the stability of truth."

This choir's hymnal, though, is missing more than a few hymns. Through no fault of ours, four decades of Lewis book reviews have been largely inaccessible. Soon they will be accessible. Walter Hooper is now editing them. Lamentably, they will be the last batch of unified, uncollected Lewis we will have between boards. But right now thirty-seven of the forty-two reviews are available only in their original venues – or by way of the Wade Center, my immediate source. (The five exceptions already in books are reviews of *The Hobbit* and *The Lord of the Rings* and two reviews included in *Studies in Medieval and Renaissance Literature*.) The entire boodle turns out to be as interesting as we would expect; in my view, more so. Knowing what Lewis thought of any book is valuable for its own sake; but in this instance there is value added. For the intellectual and academic classes of the middle-third of twentieth-century England, the Lewis known directly and widely was the scholar and critic who was the reviewer. In other words, for this class *our* Lewis *was* the Other Lewis. For us, then, there is a Lewis to be met.

Between 1928, when he reviewed Evelyn Waugh's *Rossetti: His Life and Works* for *The Oxford Magazine*, and 1963, when he wrote "Rhyme and Reason" in review of Dorothy L. Sayers' *The Poetry of Search and the Poetry of Statement* for the *Sunday Telegraph* (that December 1st issue, as it happens, appearing a week after his death), Lewis wrote forty other reviews; he also wrote blurbs for six additional books, including Arthur C. Clarke's *Childhood's End* and Mervyn Peake's *Titus Alone*. In short, he was a persistent reviewer but not a promiscuous one. We must conclude that he picked his spots, of which there were fourteen. His most favored venue was *The Oxford Magazine*, which began publishing in 1883 and is still in business, although it is now a glossy and otherwise slick. His second favorite is a tie between the mid-highbrow *Times Literary Supplement* (still, as *TLS*, the best weekly review in the business – at least in my opinion) and *Medium Aevum*, a foundational scholarly journal. *Time and Tide*, *Theology*, *Sunday Telegraph*, and *The Cambridge Review* have multiple reviews (for the last, only one before he went to Cambridge).

The books he reviews are broadly literary (poets, poetry, periods, genres, criticism), philosophical (Boethius), and cultural (three on some aspect of *eros*). Of the authors he reviewed, the names that most abide are Waugh, Harold Bloom, George Steiner, Douglas Bush, Denis de Rougement, R. S. Loomis, and Robert Fitzgerald, among others: no I. A. Richards, Empson, or Orwell. And we note tellingly eleven reviews of books by friends: four on Tolkien (two on *The Hobbit*), two on Williams (both on different volumes including *Taliessen through Logres*), two on Barfield, two on Sayers and one – unfavorable and close to the longest – on Lord David Cecil.

Rarely is a review longer than two wide columns; sometimes it is only one column or, when in a newspaper, a single three-column page. The exceptions are those in *Medium Aevum*, all of which are really review-essays in which Lewis engages (rather than merely reports upon and assesses) the book under review in one way or another. The roughest of guesses puts the cumulative word-count at fifteen to eighteen thousand (certainly fewer than twenty thousand). His busiest reviewing year is 1962 (five), a datum that invites some speculation. From 1960 to his death in 1963, Lewis published eleven reviews. In all of the Forties he published twelve; in the Fifties, only six. I infer that he was, to say the least, busy in the Forties and that, in the Fifties, he was otherwise occupied, that being the decade of Joy. Finally, the longest spans without any reviews are 1929-1934, the years of his conversion (I note, suggesting without declaring cause-effect), and 1957-1960, the years of Joy's recurrent cancer that culminate in her death in 1960.

What we experience in the reviews are Lewis' exceedingly high levels of objectivity, wit, clarity, and sophistication: Lewis is certainly *in* the world of his class of readers. Moreover, he is severe in his demand that others be as clear as he. This combination of demand and achievement is not unique to Lewis; the reviewing tradition of which he partakes is . . . different . . .

than the one we, for the most part, now know. But Lewis is unrelenting, his thinking especially concentrated, fat-free, and incisive; and he makes it seem so easy. In reading Lewis' reviews I recall one of the great lessons, double-pronged, that he taught me decades ago: not only how to think to "the ruddy end" but, dammit, to do so, always. In short, he is as close to a Great Knock as I've ever had, and never more so than in these reviews, notwithstanding the professional restraints of cordiality and even-handedness that the genre imposes (or should impose) upon its practitioners.

Since one way or another we have become familiar with Lewis' views of his friends' books I will here put those aside. Most of those were his cups of tea and he thought them very good cups indeed. The reader might suspect that Lewis has a stake in welcoming the books; withal, he always defends his judgments, never his personal tastes, let alone his personal loyalties. Still, he can be rough.

Take his review of Lord David Cecil's *The Oxford Book of Christian Verse* (*The Review of English Studies*, January 1941). Perhaps Lewis was first annoyed by the same passage from Lord David's preface that annoys me: "hymns are usually a second-rate type of poetry. [Hymns are usually second-rate poems? Or hymns are generally second-rate? Might they not still be first-class hymns?] Composed as they are for the practical purpose of congregational singing, they do not provide a free vehicle for the expression of the poet's imagination, his intimate soul," which "free vehicle" therefore assures first-rate poetry? (xxiii).

In the event, Lewis early suggests what he would have included, hurries to say "I think it better to leave all detailed criticism unwritten," and completes his first paragraph with a promise to "discuss instead certain questions arising out of [the editor's] preface." About Lord David's claim that good Christian poetry is rare and that the rarity is owing to the poet's feeling "it profane to show himself in all his earthly imperfections," Lewis says, "this seems to me precisely the reverse of the truth"; and by the end of the second paragraph we agree with him that "it is the sacred poetry which gives us life in the raw. For whatever else the religious life may be, it is apparently the fountain of self-knowledge and disillusion, the safest form of psychoanalysis." He notes the "incivility with which the sacred poets sometimes treat the Almighty" and how they are eager to celebrate the "paradox of their faith." The penultimate paragraph tells us, "the 'devout persons' of Lord David's preface who are stifled by the difficulties he mentioned, are stifled not because they are devout but because they are not poets." We await a study of Lewis' concluding sentences, even those of internal paragraphs; as intellectual punctuations they are virtually epigrammatic, and they can be merciless.

About some books, however, Lewis does seem to have reined himself in, his professional courtesy showing. His review of Pearsall Smith's *Milton and His Modern Critics* (*The Cambridge Review*, February 21, 1941), for example, is not dismissive. Rather, he shows that F. R. Leavis – one of Lewis' most pronounced critical adversaries, whom Pearsall Smith attacks – is closer to Milton than is Smith, who is *defending* Milton for the "charm" and "enchantment" of his words only. Lewis ends the review with, "I do not mean to be insolent but a great matter is at stake." Well, Lewis in fact has not been insolent – in the review. But in a letter to Brother Every (January 28, 1941) he writes, "I've just written a review of Pearsall Smiths [sic] *Milton & His Modern Critics* for the *Cambridge Review*. What a perfectly ghastly book! I hope you understand tht [sic] if I thought Smith's case for Milton the real and best one, I shd. join Leavis [!] at once. Against all that bilge Leavis, Milton and I almost stand together: and Milton wd. resent *this* defence more than the attack." Now, that's the sort of expression one *does* see, *these days*, in the daily or weekly press.

What Harold Bloom thought when he read Lewis' review of *The Visionary Company, a Reading of English Romantic Poetry* (*Encounter*, June 1963) is anybody's guess. I enjoy and have profited from Bloom's criticism; he's nuts, true, but he's also unfathomably cultured and very smart; so smart, in fact, that I used to think my inability to get my brain around a passage such as the following was my fault. Bloom (p. 417 of 1971 edition, not the one reviewed by Lewis) is referring to Keats's "Ode on a Grecian Urn": "They [foliage, song, singer, lover, beloved] can scorn the complexities of blood and mire, the common bird and the human singer, and the lover who moves in flesh. The art of Keats triumphs in the line 'All breathing human passion far above,' for to Keats nothing more is to be desired than 'breathing human passion,' the sexual experience, which heightens nature to its own limits."

Lewis does not cite that passage, but surely he had it in mind when he began his review with, "this is one of the most difficult books I have ever read; harder than Romans and ten times harder than Aristotle. . . . Perhaps the best I can do is to cite a few of the expressions which puzzled me and leave the reader to judge." He goes on to say the likes of, "I can make no sense at all," "I can hammer out a meaning, but I don't know for sure if it is Mr. Bloom's," "I can find no evidence for this in the text" (that the Ancient Mariner "is a haunter of wedding feasts"), and the subtle, "he finds in Blake many ironies which have not, I think, been seen before." Bloom is smart – but now I know that he is also a bad writer.

David Loth's *The Erotic in Literature: A historical survey of pornography as delightful as it is indiscreet* comes in for harsh treatment (*Eros on the Loose*, The *Observer*, March 4, 1962); Lewis seems provoked (perhaps by the absurd sub-title). I think it a slightly better book than does Lewis, who allows that Loth is a thorough researcher who has turned up interesting historical facts. Here, for example, is a rare instance (not cited by Lewis) of someone directly attributing his perversion to corruptions produced by reading: ". . . Gilles de Rais embarked upon an unsurpassed career of sex and other crimes, including murder of children under horrible circumstances. When he finally met his end, he declared that he got some of his ferocious ideas about mutilating small boys and girls from reading Suetonius . . . who was not considered specially obscene although he did write about the crimes of his contemporaries" (p. 213).

Yet Lewis is unpersuaded, and finally the reader is broadly persuaded by a scalpel-wielding Lewis. "The ghost story and the erotic book," Lewis points out, "merely provide a channel for what would have made its own channel without them" – a typical display of Lewis-the-anthropologian's penetrating insight. When disputing Loth's reliance on polls, Lewis is brutal: "[Respondents] betray their abnormality by the very act of answering." In response to Loth's insistence that "sex is innocent" Lewis replies, "it is no more innocent or guilty than a turnip." He continues, "if it is meant that human sexual behavior is all, and all equally, innocent, we want to be told why," which is reasonable enough but not, for Lewis, the point, which he makes: "no one claims a similar liberty for all economic or political behavior." How trenchant and obvious – once Lewis has said it. Now, just in case his reader still does not know that Lewis dislikes this book, he deliver that final sentence, and with an absolutely straight face: "The author treats *erotica* as a singular and *orgiastic* as the adjective of orgasm." Ba-rum-bum.

Most of the books Lewis reviewed, though, brought him some pleasure. He delights in praising a work, exercising less restraint (it seems) than when damning. An example is his review of Douglas Bush's *'Paradise Lost' in Our Time: some Comments* (*The Oxford Magazine*, February 13, 1947). By the time of the review he had already written three letters to Bush, the last being in 1943. (Bush has completed his OHEL volume, *English Literature in the Earlier Seventeenth Century 1600-1660*, and Lewis is at work on his own OHEL.) His first letter had saluted Bush as "Professor," the second as "Mr.," the last as "Bush (if we may now drop the honorifics)." They evidence much mutual respect and kindredness of critical spirit. In the second letter, March 28, 1941, for example, Lewis writes a long, detailed and exceedingly cordial commentary on Bush's *The Renaissance and English Humanism*. He concludes, "once again, thanks & congratulations. If we both live and civilisation remains" – surely a reference to their shared OHEL-writing Purgatory as well as to ordinary mortality or to the War – "we may blow a lot of nonsense out of the way."

The review begins, "it is packed with good meat, and its zest and wit . . . are a pleasing proof that the author's spirit has not been broken by his late gigantic labours for the *Oxford History of English Literature*." He professes early that, as he is on Bush's side, he "cannot be a neutral judge," but I note he avoids here the word *objective*. He quotes a sentence by Bush that he might have written himself: "there are always critics who, seeing the surface of the ocean smooth, take it for a pond." And he agrees with Bush's major distinction between Rationalists and Dynamists (Reason v. Will). Given the following (not quoted by Lewis), how could he not? Bush favorably quotes Benjamin Whichcote, a Cambridge Platonist: "To go against Reason, is to go against God; it is the self same thing, to do that which the Reason of the Case doth require; and that which God Himself doth appoint: Reason is the Divine Governor of Man's Life; it is the very Voice of God." Is that not Lewis beginning to end? Lewis notes a sentence (saying that for certain seventeenth-century thinkers "God and nature are one") as "simply false," but concludes, "my own gratitude takes the form of a wish that [Bush] may hereafter deal more fully with some of the points touched. . . ."

So much for straightforward blame or praise. But what of the mixed review? A book that brought from him considerable approval is one he found half bad; it is also the most important book Lewis ever reviewed, in *Theology* (June 1940). It is Denis de Rougement's *Passion and Society* (1940), which would become *Love in the Western World* (1956). In a letter to his brother (March 29, 1940) he writes, "the other thing I've been busy on this week is a book called *L'amoure et l'Occident* by one Denis de Rougement, apparently a French Protestant [in fact a Swiss Catholic and Nazi Resistor], wh. I have to review. It contains a thoroughly bad historical thesis about medieval love, and an absolutely first class moral thesis about the utter incompatibility of *l'amour passion* with Christian marriage, happiness, or even enjoyable physical sexuality. He's a corker of a man, tho' with some bogus elements in him: I've written to him today. [This letter has not turned up.] If, as I suspect, he is now a [a soldier], my letter may give a moments [sic] happiness." Lewis tells us that the historical thesis is that Courtly Love was not an expression of sexual passion but a "wish for death and pain arising from Eros-mysticism . . . through the Catharist heresy."

As it happens, Lewis has read *both* the French and English versions of the book and notes that the former contains a statement of Rougement's basic assumption missing from the latter: since the Cathari were repressed "documents are naturally lacking." Lewis makes short work of this nothing-proving-something but seems otherwise annoyed. The cause may be the sort of assertion (which Lewis does not cite) from Chapter IV, "Petrarch, the Converted Rhetor": "[The poet's description of his memorable passion for Laura was quickened by] an entirely pagan breath! Pagan, and not in the least heretical! Petrarch stands at the antipodes not only of Dante, but also of the rhetors whom Dante attacked . . . . The language of love had at length become the rhetoric of the heart" (176). Pronouncedly *not* Lewis' cup of tea, and not least owing to Rougement's use of *rhetoric* as a term of praise.

Here I must declare my own interest. I've elsewhere described what I regard as Lewis' telling impatience with, and distrust of, rhetoric. Pre-dating those descriptions is my own abiding affection for J.W.H. Atkins' *English Literary Criticism: the Medieval Phase* – precisely because Atkins makes clear that the history of criticism is the history of rhetoric; that is, rhetoric gets its due, especially in light of its dispositive influence (traced by Atkins) on Chaucer. But what does Lewis say (*The Oxford Review*, February 10, 1944) of the Atkins? Why, he says that Atkins "makes it abundantly plain that the history of criticism is at first place *merely* [my italics] the history of rhetoric." Tricky word, *merely*, don't you think? Lewis goes on to say the unsurprising, "I do not always agree with Atkins' interpretation of Chaucer" but ends with the gracious, "perhaps after a few years I should not agree with my own." Alas, he never did.

So much for the historical thesis – and for my rant. It is the "first class moral thesis" that compels Lewis to write of the Rougement, "nevertheless this book is indispensable." Why so? I wonder if you will recognize the key line from the following section (not cited in full by Lewis): "Yet Eros could lead [the natural man] but to death. But a man who believes the revelation of Agape suddenly beholds the circle broken: faith delivers him from natural religion. Now he may *hope* for something else. . . . And thereupon Eros in turn has been relieved of its fatal office and delivered from his fate. *In ceasing to be a god, he ceases to be a demon* [emph. orig.]. And he finds his proper place in the provisional economy of Creation and of what is human" (321). Certainly Lewis' meat. In a letter dated April 16, 1940, he writes to Dom Bede, "[sensual love] ceases to be a devil when it ceases to be a god" and adds "isn't that well put?" But the quoting did not stop there. We read the sentence again in "Christianity and Culture," in one other letter, and several times in *The Four Loves*. In short, it has become a touchstone for Lewis (and, I'd wager, for very many others).

Having noted one Lewisian touchstone, a second might be welcome. In *The Times Literary Supplement* of May 29, 1937, Lewis reviews Dorothy M. Hoare's, *The Works of Morris and of Yeats in Relation to Early Saga Literature*. Apparently Ms. Hoare gets one of Lewis' favorites (Morris, not Yeats) wrong. I have never found the master convincing on Morris, but even I bristle at her glib condescension, here dismissing Morris's *The Life and Death of Jason*: "None of the strangeness of the unknown creeps into the narrative, though it deals with matters strange enough. There comes . . . no new experience, no sudden fresh angle of vision, no feeling of the pity of things; the world is not enlarged. . . . Morris' nature avoids tragedy. He turns instinctively to the soft, the pretty, the pathetic – 'piercing sweet pathos' is his own phrase" (37, 41). After not quite dismissing the book (when Hoare admits to a need to "hesitate" Lewis writes, "it is on a certain hesitation that much of the value of her book depends"), Lewis not-so-faintly damns with even fainter praise. Hoare has admitted that, despite the *Jason* flaws, one "somehow" keeps reading, only discovering its defects when she is done, "in other words," Lewis writes, "when she passes from imaginative experience to literary theories." (How typical of Lewis to choose the concrete over the abstract: we are reminded that even in *An Experiment in Criticism* Lewis did not write, let alone abide by, "literary theory.") Then comes that fainter praise, a characteristic concluding sentence. Referring to Hoare's admissions of hesitation and of "somehow" managing to finish a bad book, Lewis allows, "it is a great thing to remain true to the facts under severe strain."

Finally Lewis offers his defense of Morris, providing that second touchstone: "the endless dithering and thithering of natural desire, the irrepressible thirst for immortality, and its inevitable recoil to the familiar – the sweet familiar whose very sweetness must once more reawake the rebel passion." Do we see where Lewis is heading? "It is this *dialectic of desire* [my emphasis], presented with no solution, no lies, no panacea, which gives him his peculiar bittersweet quality, and also his solidity." And then the characteristic intellectual punctuation: "there are greater writers than Morris. You can go on from him to all manner of subtleties and sublimities which he does not offer: but you cannot go behind him." Rougement's may be the most important book to Lewis that Lewis ever reviewed, but for readers of Lewis, this may be the most important review, for here has given us . . . Joy.

Smaller joys than this abound everywhere in these reviews: surprises, distinctions, wit, refutation, congeniality, cold courtesy, and – *errors*? George

Steiner has long been a commanding literary critic and theorist, not least on tragedy, beginning with his *The Death of Tragedy* (1961). There he writes ". . . that representation of personal suffering and heroism which we call tragic drama is distinctive of the western tradition. . . . we forget what a strange and complex idea it is to re-enact private anguish on a public stage. This idea and the vision of man which it implies are Greek. . . . The fall of Jericho is . . . merely just [because "it has defied God"], whereas the fall of Troy is the first great metaphor of tragedy . . . brought about by the fierce sport of human hatreds and the wanton, mysterious choice of destiny" (3-5).

Forty years ago this seemed to me, and still does, epiphanous. But not to Lewis, who in "Tragic Ends" (*Encounter*, February 1962), amidst high praise and some very gracious and wise dissent, writes "the moral I would draw is that *tragedy*, taken as a common essence of which all 'tragedies' are instances, is a phantom concept." *A phantom concept*! Tragedy! Lewis continues, "they share a common name for historical reasons; as the Postlethwaits are all so called not because they all exhibit a common character of Postlethwaiticity, but in virtue of their genetic connections." And then that intellectual punctuation: "An Athenian knew whether the play he had seen was or was not a 'tragedy' by far coarser and more objective criteria than ours; more as a modern man knows whether he has been watching rugger or soccer." Now, surely Lewis is wrong simply to dismiss a major category of Western artistic philosophy and criticism?

But he does not stop with tragedy; he goes on to Aristotle. On John Jones's *On Aristotle and Greek Tragedy*, in "Ajax and Others" for *The Sunday Telegraph* (December 16, 1962), we read this characteristically peremptory dismissal: "I also wonder whether [Jones] would, as I would, go a step further and say that Aristotle, that very great man, was never less great than in the 'Poetics.' It is difficult to think well of a book which, however diversely interpreted, has always had a bad influence on criticism and dramaturgy." But ought we to be surprised? After all, we know what he thought of the Renaissance (here I resist the temptation to write "so-called"). Did we know how early on he thought it? Reviewing W.P. Ker's *Form and Style in Poetry* (*The Oxford Magazine*) with enormous respect, he writes "there is of course far more . . . a cooling card here and there for those who believe too intemperately in the Renaissance." That is from February 6, 1928, nearly thirty years prior *De Descriptione Temporum*, the statement most closely associated with his denial of the Renaissance.

In his review (*Medium Aevum*, 1957) of W. Schwarz's, *Principles and Problems of Biblical Translation; Some Reformation controversies and their background* (1955) there is a different sort of denial – more neglect, perhaps. He engages the book heartily, as though with a colleague in robust conversation, always a sign that he likes a book a good deal. Of course his professional favor does not compromise his professional duty, as he notes "the most obvious defect of the book . . . the imperfections of its English." He then ends the review by citing, and immediately minimizing, other "trifles," concluding "the book is welcome." Now, none of this qualifies as neglect, and perhaps the following does not either. Perhaps its omission from Lewis' review is merely discretion; but given the year of the review I cannot but believe that it caught Lewis' eye. Schwarz writes, "in 1489, when about 11 years old, Conrad Pellican heard that in a disputation a certain doctor of theology had been confuted by the answers of a Jew and even of a Jewess. The fact that a Jew got the better of the argument in a religious disputation (a fact hardly ever recorded) made a deep impression on the boy. . . . All these experiences aroused his wish to learn Hebrew" (69). We do not know that Lewis set himself to learn Hebrew systematically. He probably did not. But we do know he loved a Hebrew-speaking Jewess – and not least for her disputatiousness – and a Jewess who, more than once, must have "got the better of the argument"!

There are so very many gems of Lewisian insight and expression in this neglected cache that we must delight in the prospect that soon we will be able to have at it for ourselves. Then I look forward to Lewis readers comparing analyses and judgments – and favorite passages. You have seen mine, except for these assorted few self-indulgences which I offer for the sheer pleasure they afford.

On Hugh Kingsmill's *Matthew Arnold*, in *The Oxford Magazine* (November 15, 1928), a final sentence to relish: "If after two hundred odd pages of this sort of stuff the reader is tempted to ask why Mr. Kingsmill, hating Arnold, hating the Nineteenth Century, and hating poetry, has found it necessary to write the life of Arnold, he will find his answer in [a jejune] cautionary tale on page 54. . . .The blurb on the inside of the jacket justly remarks that Mr. Kingsmill writes 'with unusual courage.'" On *Ronald Arbuthnot Knox: A Selection from the Occasional Sermons*, for *TLS* (May 20, 1949), again Lewis' ready generosity of spirit to a writer he admires: "If it is complained that Monsignor Knox lacks the colour and melody of the Authorized Version, he can reply, '*Salva reverentia*, so did St. Paul.'" On *The Odyssey Translated by Robert Fitzgerald*, in "Odysseus Sails Again" for *The Sunday Telegraph*, September 9, 1962, some disparaging, but gentle, wit, with an especially witty last word: "The prevailing taste [to achieve a contemporary music] is like a stencil: it lets through some Homeric qualities and excludes others. . . . [So] I have a special reason to be cautious. I know some Greek, but I know very little American. . . . But then I am a confessed square."

I must not close, however, without indulging twice more, both passages by Lewis applying equally to Lewis himself as to his authors. This first, for its delicious irony. Do you recall the early mention of Lewis' sometimes unwarranted enthusiasm? Here is Lewis reviewing *The Mirror of Love: a reinterpretation of 'The Romance of the Rose'* by Alan M. F. Gunn ((*Medium Aevum*, 1953):

> We are now at the heart of the book and Professor Gunn writes with a fervour and exaltation which will arouse suspicion in some but which I myself have found curiously impressive. In these glowing pages, seeing the *Roman* through Professor Gunn's eyes, I certainly feel the presence of an 'esemplastic' imagination imposing unity on a great wealth of attractive material. [All following emphasis mine!] *What is hard to decide is whose imagination it is*. Are we being shown at last the poetic whole which Jean de Meun made out of chaotic experience, *or are we being shown the poetic whole which Professor Gunn has made out of the chaotic Roman*? Either way it is excellent reading: but as scholars we should like the question to be settled. *At the same time it is not easy to see how the methods of scholarship can settle it.*

Well well: so Jack knew what it felt like! Good for Gunn, better for Lewis, best of all for us.

And finally this, on another critic's excellence. As I have suggested, Lewis' audience for these reviews was not the apologist's or the avuncular fantasist's. Please do not misunderstand: this Lewis is recognizably ours. But our Lewis was not, and is not, recognizably theirs – the intellectual and academic elite for whom Lewis wrote these reviews. Perhaps, unlike us, they are the provincials? Not Lewis. Writing on W. P. Ker in review in *Form and Style in Poetry* for *The Oxford Magazine* (December 6, 1928), Lewis tell us: "no scrap of Ker's writing does not embody the quality of his mind as a whole, and no scrap therefore is negligible. . . . No writer in modern times approached so nearly to that critical ideal of being 'like God – easy to please and hard to satisfy.'" Surely *there* is C. S. Lewis the book reviewer.

The Critical Principles of C. S. Lewis
(Pronouncedly Pre-Post-modern)

I would like to begin with a question. How many of you first loved in Lewis, or especially love in him now, certain intangible qualities, characteristics of style or voice, if you will, which seem as much a part of the *man* as any doctrine he ever expounded? On the Society questionnaire and at Society meetings, each of us has responded to a like query with such words as *brilliance, clarity, veracity, Britishness, nobility, humility,* and *joy.* One of our members has praised Lewis as a "lovable, warm person, not a phony"; another, as a man of great patience; and yet a third as a "sophisticate." And apparently each of us is correct, for those who met Lewis personally and have addressed the Society have all remarked upon these very same qualities. As Thomas Howard put it, he was "down to the last molecule the man I would have expected."[1]

As for me: my experience was at once similar and very, very different. I was struck by these qualities and came to love both the writings and their author because of them. But I had read neither his apologetics nor his fiction. I was originally introduced, and drawn, to CSL – in fact, I might almost say, without exaggeration, reconfirmed in my faith – by his literary criticism. This body of work seemed to me to synthesize form and content, manner and matter, to such a startling degree that it became, as Alexander Pope has written in his An *Essay on Criticism* (II.299-300), "Something, whose truth convinc'd at sight we find,/ That gives us back the image of our mind."

I therefore contend that, in a very genuine and essential sense, all of you really do know the criticism, even if you have not read it. My purpose this evening is not to offer an exhaustive study but to introduce you to the major *topoi* which CSL addressed in his criticism. A secondary purpose is to get you to read that criticism, or even to re-re-read it. Two days ago an ex-dean of mine – a learned, humane man, and a devoted admirer of Lewis – stopped me to ask whether or not I had seen the Narnia review printed in the *New York Times* of 21 February. (By the way, I had urged this man to join the Society and, in response to his protest, insisted that few of us were what he called "joiners"; but he would have nothing of it.) Well, I had seen the review, so for a while we discussed it excitedly. I then took the opportunity to describe our next topic and to invite him to this very meeting, whereupon he answered that he had read nothing of Lewis-the-literary-critic. I was amazed and asked why he had not. "Because," he responded, "there is so much in his other writings, why press on to the criticism?" This paper is my attempt at an answer.

I propose to discuss two general areas: the nature of literary criticism, classical and modern; and the principles and practice of C. S. Lewis the literary critic. As I progress, I would like you to keep in mind, and to help me to struggle with, this question: Do Lewis' own creative writings (the Ransom trilogy, Narnia, *Till We Have Faces*) conform to his own set of literary principles?

In 1924 Lewis received a temporary appointment at Oxford as a lecturer in Philosophy; thirty years later he was elected Professor of Medieval and Renaissance English Literature at Cambridge. The Chair had been created especially for him. His first major critical work, *The Allegory of Love: A Study in Medieval Tradition*, won for him the Gollancz Memorial Prize; and students regularly stood in auditoriums filled to capacity (a rarity at Cambridge or Oxford) in order to hear his lectures. Nevill Coghill, CSL's friend, colleague, and successor, has lamented the

> loss of his living force in the kind of study in which [he was] engaged, the study of English, of which he was easily the greatest teacher of our time in his chosen fields.[2]

And Jeffrey Hart at once summarized Lewis' influence and justified it ten he wrote:

> To most university students and their professors, C. S. Lewis is well known as a scholar and a literary critic. His two books on medieval literature, his books on Milton and on sixteenth-century literature, and his widely ranging essays, have firmly established his authority in the Academy.[3]

Moreover, these singular achievements become all the more striking as we review the number and variety of his critical works, for in this school-ridden age of ours, CSL eschewed all schools – and was praised nevertheless.

The Allegory of Love, for example, was described by William Empson (a great critic in his own right) as "learned, witty, and sensible . . . , in the first flush of renewed admiration for the *Romance of the Rose* I tried to read the Chaucerian version. . . . Far better to read Mr. Lewis";[4] and a critic for the *London Times* wrote that *The Allegory of Love* was a "scholarly, fascinating and original book. . . . Mr. Lewis is both interested and skilled in the history of human psychology. He is obviously qualified to write literary history of the best kind; for his book is an example of it."[5] What CSL did in *The Allegory of Love*, an example of what has been called socio-cultural criticism, was to trace the rise of a literary genre, the medieval love allegory, to cultural circumstances.

Lewis himself was fond of what he called the "all hail!" (or "oh, Hell!") volume, his contribution to the Oxford History of English Literature entitled *English Literature in the Sixteenth Century. Excluding Drama*. With this volume Lewis satisfied both the literary historians and critics. A reviewer for the *London Times* wrote:

> Learned, vivacious, individual, this handbook is a notable performance. Few critics of recent years have so wide a knowledge both of the classical literatures and of French and Italian literature. . . . And Mr. Lewis, be it said, knows how to make his learning felt – you feel, reading him, that he has read what he is talking about. Even so, what is best in his book . . . is the lively, individual quality of it.[6]

And just so, during the course of three decades, diverse works met with consistent praise: *The Discarded Image* (1964), an intellectual history of the middle ages told from the point of view of a native; *Studies in Words* (1960), a semantic and etymological investigation of such words as 'nature', 'sad', 'wit', 'free', and 'sense'; and *Rehabilitations and Other Essays* (1939), too various and profound a collection to classify. But even so, we have not yet looked upon his greatest theoretical achievement, his momentous controversy with the great E. M. W. Tillyard, *The Personal Heresy* (1939). A reviewer recorded that

> Dr. Tillyard's three studies appear slight when they are confronted with what he rightly calls "the formidable battery of Mr. Lewis' dialectic," and his general position seems scarcely tenable. . . . Driven from position to position, Dr. Tillyard returns, wildly, to his original view; but it is a view that has been . . . thoroughly discredited.[7]

Many essays followed this book; but more than twenty years had to elapse before CSL's theoretical achievement could, in 1961, reach its highest point with the publication of *An Experiment in Criticism*, so unassuming that it has never been taken seriously by professional, let alone academic, critics.

But what of literary criticism in general? Somehow, the words 'literary theory' do not belong with the words 'socio-cultural,' 'etymological,' 'historical,' 'semantic,' or, as some critics have added, the grotesque 'psycho-biographical.' For theory implies the application of values, whereas all those other words imply merely their description. Clearly, modern *differentia* are useless; they carry little substantive meaning, and Lewis violates them wholesale. "So," you might ask, "what of our great thinkers? Surely *they* can provide some guidance!" In this instance, unfortunately, I think not. Dryden, for example, wrote in *The Conquest of Granada* that "They who write ill, and they who ne'er durst write,/ Turn critics out of mere revenge and spite."[12] Or perhaps criticism is what George Jean Nathan (*The House of Satan*) has called "the art wherewith a critic tries to guess himself into a share of the artist's fame"?[8] And certainly an abundance of evidence supports Harold Macmillan's observation that "criticism is never inhibited by ignorance ." Very unaccommodating, except, perhaps, for Lewis, to whom it is best we return.

In his inaugural lecture at Cambridge CSL dismissed all the "great divides" of Western Civilization, those, for example, between the ancient world and the Dark Ages, the Middle Ages and the Renaissance and the Enlightenment. These are minor when compared to the real Great Divine, "that which divides the present from, say, the age of Jane Austen and Scott." Our age of machines, political 'leaders' (instead of 'rulers'), religious skepticism and atheism, Dadaists, Surrealists, and Picasso is more foreign to Old Western culture than any period of that culture is to any other period within it. Yet this great change, Lewis went on to say, is not even now complete, and "those who are native to different sides of it can still meet." "I myself," he continued, "belong far more to that Old Western order than to [this one]." And, as usual, he recognized the limits of his affinities, for, he said, "you don't want to be lectured on Neanderthal Man by a Neanderthaler, still less on dinosaurs by a dinosaur." Then, in a peroration which since has become famous, Lewis told why those affinities eminently qualified him for Ms new position:

> And yet, is that the whole story? If a live dinosaur dragged its slow length into the laboratory would we not all look back as we fled? What a chance to know at last how it really moved and looked and smelled

and what noises it made! . . . One thing I know: I would give a great deal to hear any ancient Athenian, even a stupid one, talking about Greek tragedy. He would know in his bones so much that we seek in vain. Ladies and gentlemen, I stand before you somewhat as that Athenian might stand. I read as a native texts which you must read as foreigners. . . . And because this is the judgement of a native, I claim that, even if the defence of my conviction is weak, the fact of my conviction is a historical datum. That way, where I fail as critic, I may yet be useful as a specimen. . . . Speaking not only for myself but for all other Old Western men whom you may meet, I would say, use your specimens while you can. There are not going to be many more dinosaurs.[9]

Clearly, according to Lewis, the appropriate *differentia* is a chronological one; and if it is accurately placed, literary critical theory should divide in two right around the beginning of the nineteenth century. In fact, roughly between 1798 and 1815, that period known as Classical, with its roots as far back as Aristotle, effectively ended, to be succeeded by the post-Classical, or Modern, period. And though Lewis was *of* the first period, he was nevertheless in the second, and not so reluctantly as we might at first suspect. But what were, and are, the values and considerations inherent within each of these periods?

The classical era is more or less consistent and complete. Our authorities for it are, among others, the Greeks Plato, Aristotle, and Longinus, the Roman Horace, and the Englishmen Sidney (an Elizabethan), Dryden, Pope, and Johnson (from the late seventeenth to the mid-eighteenth centuries). If we study them, we discover five elements formulated with near-unanimity. First, a view of reality; second, a view of the fundamental nature of man; third, agreement with regard to the nature of poetry; fourth, opinions regarding the nature of a single poem; and fifth, a view of the function of poetry. Reality, man, the nature of poetry, the nature of a poem, and the function of poetry. As I review them, consider whether or not you conform to the classical view. I suspect there are some dinosaurs among us.

Reality is simply the concrete realm of forms and processes, as opposed to the world of shadows which we inhabit. It is objective, ordered, and harmonious; if the soul of man is itself ordered and harmonious, he may catch a glimpse of it. But, on a more mundane level, man is characterized by three attributes: he takes a natural and lively pleasure in learning; he possesses a natural instinct for rhythm; and, most important of all, he possesses a natural instinct for imitation. Learning, rhythm, and imitation – we seem to sound suspiciously like a bunch of monkeys.

The nature of poetry is not such a simple matter. Think back to those real forms and processes. Well, poetry is supposed to imitate them by shaping something relatively concrete – imaginative events, or characters, or sensations, or feelings – into something that imitates those realities, something which fulfills them, which shows us what they would be like if they were down here instead of up there and inaccessible.

Now a single poem is simply an attempt to carry out this imitation, or fulfillment. An effective poem possesses organic unity, that is, a very purposeful structure based upon probability, harmony, and propriety. But the most important of these is probability, for the poem must show us what its subject (this reality) would *necessarily* look like if it were down here instead of up there. From this idea of what a poem is supposed to do, we derive criteria for judging particular poems: decorum, balance, symmetry and proportion, the harmonious integration of parts, and (if you are Horatian) urbanity, grace and effortlessness. Also moderation, for (as Horace said) mountains should not labor to bring forth mice.

As for the function of poetry, that is simple: it is to communicate, but in a very special way. First, poetry must please. Second, it must bring about a catharsis; that is, some participation on the part of the audience, which arouses certain emotions and then soothes them. Examples are fear of the Unman, love for Aslan, pity for Puzzle the donkey. Third, poetry must provide an awareness of the world, what the Greeks called *psychagogia*, an awakening to moral purpose in actions and desires, though not necessarily an exhortation to pursue that purpose. So the classical view is ultimately reader-oriented, striving to achieve pleasure, catharsis and *psychogogia*.

Lewis accepted all of these principles, but emphasized some more than he did others. An objective and ultimate reality; natural instincts to learn and to imitate; imitation or fulfillment within a structure based on probability and propriety; pleasure; catharsis; *psychagogia*: all of these together form the foundation of CSL's literary criticism.

These are all classical concepts. What of the modern period? It is to the everlasting misfortune of the modern period that it is on the wrong side of every single issue raised in the previous period. The result is a fragmentation so severe that contemporary critics can barely agree upon a common vocabulary with which to argue their disagreements. But this is not to say that they do not raise new issues. Wordsworth, Coleridge, Maritian, and Lewis have told us much about the imagination; I. A. Richards, Philip Wheelwright, Ernst Cassier, and Lewis have provided great insights into the nature and function of language; and Susanne Langer, C. G. Jung, Northrop Frye, Cassirer, and Lewis have delved into the mysteries of allegory, symbolism, and myth.

We can go no further, however, without a survey of that criticism which, in my view, is so great as to accommodate two views that are nearly, but not quite, mutually exclusive. I hope I may illustrate a number of the points raised in my description of the two periods.

CSL's views both of reality and of the nature of poetry are expressed most effectively not in a work of criticism, but in *The Great Divorce*, during that conversation between an artist and an angel:

> . . . all *this*. It's . . . It's . . . I should like to paint this.' 'I shouldn't bother about that just at present if I were you.' 'Look here; isn't one going to be allowed to go on painting?' 'That sort of thing's no good here.' . . . do you mean?' ~ you painted on earth. . . . it was because you caught a glimpse of heaven in the earthly landscape. The success of your painting was that it enabled others to see the glimpse too. But here you have the thing itself. It is from here that the messages.[10]

Drippings, if you will, from the world of reality up there to the world of shadows down here. Now what can we make of this, besides the fact that Lewis is classical in his outlook? Well, recall, for a moment, his concept of *Sehnsucht*, which he describes, in "Christianity and Culture," as "spilled religion."[11] I contend that this concept is as good a theory of poetic inspiration – what Coleridge would call imagination – as any we have ever had, for these drippings, or *Sehnsucht*, convey ultimate meaning, and that is the object of imagination. Listen to this portion of "Bluspels and Flalansferes," Lewis' most provocative essay:

> . . . meaning . . . is the antecedent condition both of truth and false-hood, whose antithesis is not error but nonsense. . . . For me, reason is the natural organ of truth; but imagination is the organ of meaning. Imagination, producing new metaphors or revivifying old, is not the cause of truth, but its condition. It is, I confess, undeniable that such a view indirectly implies a kind of truth or rightness in the imagination itself.[12]

This imaginative experience (shared by many, Lewis believed) is what the artist avails himself of when he makes his poem, and makes it communicable, for "poetry is an exploitation of language to convey the concrete."[13] But rather than myself, let us allow Lewis to demonstrate. Here is that wonderful scene in which is described Ransom's very first awakening in Perelandra. It is lengthy, but this is one group, I am sure, to whom it is not necessary to apologize when quoting C. S. Lewis.

> His first impression was nothing more definite than of something slanted – as though he were looking at a photograph which had been taken when the camera was not held level. And even this lasted only for an instant. The slant was replaced by a different slant; then two slants rushed together and made a peak, and the peak flattened suddenly into a horizontal line, and the horizontal line tilted and made and became the edge of a vast gleaming slope which rushed furiously towards him. At the same moment he felt that he was being lifted. Up and up he soared till it seemed as if he must reach the burning dome of gold that hung above him instead of a sky. Then he was at a summit; but almost before his glance had taken in a huge valley that yawned beneath him – shining green like glass and marbled with streaks of scummy white – he was rushing down into that valley at perhaps thirty miles an hour. And now he realized that there was a delicious coolness over every part of him except his head, that his feet rested on nothing, and that he had for some time been performing unconsciously the actions of a swimmer. . . . As he rushed smoothly up the great convex hillside of the next wave he got a mouthful of water. . . . Though he had not been aware of his thirst till now, his drink gave him quite astonishing pleasure. It was almost like meeting Pleasure itself for the first time. . . . There was a wave ahead of him now so high it was dreadful. . . . It gathered him into itself and hurled him up to that elevation in a matter of seconds. But before he reached the top, he almost cried out in terror.
>
> A horrible crest appeared. . . . Hocks? Foam? Beasts? . . . He turned round. . . . Far down below him in a vast momentary valley he saw the thing that had missed him. It was variegated in colours like a patchwork quilt – flame colour, ultramarine, crimson, orange, gamboge, and violet.[14]

In a letter to a child, Lewis advised never to use abstract nouns when concrete ones would do and that description should always replace "telling" adjectives; responses should be elicited, not pleaded for.[15] And are we not lucky that Lewis followed his own advice? For after reading this passage – with its multi-sensory images so perfectly ordered – who does not feel that he has been there right along with Ransom, whose observations and reactions would surely be our own if . . . if . . . ?

That 'if' is the key word. Reality, poetry, imagination, concreteness: each of these is, ultimately, dependent for its expression, use, or effectiveness on likely and probable 'ifs'. "If you are writing a story," wrote CSL in *Miracles*,

> abnormal events may be bad art, or they may not. If, for example, you are writing an ordinary realistic novel and have got your characters into a hopeless muddle, it would be quite intolerable if you suddenly cut the and knot secured a happy ending by having a fortune left to the hero from an unexpected quarter. On the other hand there is nothing against taking as your subject from the outset adventures of a man who inherits an unexpected fortune. The unusual event is perfectly permissible if it is what you are really writing about.[16]

What is more probable than, for example, Ransom trying to rationalize his presence on Perelandra? What is more likely than that he should find a false security in his casuistic conclusion? And what is more probable than that – at this very moment of triumph – all his reasonings should break to pieces? And *if* any of us ever meets a devil, will he not be exactly as CSL portrays him?

> It looked at Ransom in silence and at last began to smile. We have all spoken – Ransom himself had often spoken – of a devilish smile. Now he realized that he had never taken the words seriously. The smile was not bitter, nor raging, nor, in any ordinary sense, sinister; it was not even mocking. It seemed to summon Ransom, with horrible naiveté of welcome, into the world of its own pleasures, as if all men were at one in those pleasures, as if they were the most natural thing in the world and no dispute could ever have occurred about them. It was not furtive, nor ashamed, it had nothing of the conspirator in it. It did not defy goodness, it ignored it to the point of annihilation.[17]

In a letter to a certain Mrs. Hook, Lewis revealed that *Perelandra* does indeed work out a supposition: What if there were an unspoiled paradise undergoing some temptation? What *if* angels were like unto the Pagan gods? What if? Well, then we would have *Perelandra*.[18]

But we are now moving into a realm of a different order, that of allegory, symbolism, and, very especially, myth. And since it is best not to stay the steed, I will do no more than mention the other topics and their appearances in CSL's criticism. How, in *A Preface to 'Paradise Lost'*, he praises Milton for perfectly imitating, and allowing us to participate in, the great dance of all Christendom, an achievement owing, for the most part, to a decorous and harmonious style. How, in *The Personal Heresy*, he states that the function of poetry is *psychagogia*, though not in the narrower moral sense of didacticism. How he attacks, in *The Personal Heresy* and in such essays as "The Anthropological Approach" and "Psychoanalysis and Literary Criticism," that mode of thought which would violate meaning by taking us out of the structure of the poem and leaving us there, among the ruins of literary excavations, or in the poet's past, or in the garbage heap of the poet's unconscious. Most of these concepts are handled in top-flight fashion in one daring and irresistible essay, "Shelley, Dryden, and Mr. Eliot." Give that one a high priority in your reading plans. But on to allegory, symbol – and myth.

In *The Allegory of Love* Lewis drew a persevering distinction. Allegory results when we invent *visibilia* – characters such as Patience, Wrath, and CSL's own John in *The Pilgrim's Regress* – to represent immaterial facts, such as passions. "But," Lewis continues,

> there is another way of using the equivalence, which is almost the opposite of allegory, and which I would call sacramentalism or symbolism. If our passions, being immaterial, can be copied by material inventions, then it is possible that our material world in its turn is the copy of an invisible world. . . . The allegorist leaves the given – his own passions – to talk of that which is confessedly less real, which is a fiction. The symbolist leaves the given to find that which is more real. To put the difference in another way, for the symbolist it is we who are the allegory.[19]

We should not believe that allegory does not reveal reality, for, in *Reflections on the Psalms*, Lewis tells us precisely the opposite. But it is sacramentalism that carries the real power. Lewis writes:

> It is for most poets and in most poems by far the best method of writing poetry which is religious without being devotional – that is, without being an act of worship to the reader. God . . . appears frequently, but always *incognito*.[20]

The notion of our world as a copy sounds suspiciously like Plato; and the idea of God appearing *incognito* sounds even more suspiciously like Narnia. In fact, put the two together and we have *The Last Battle*. Put the two together, and we have myth, which Lewis hastily defined as "an account of what *may have been* historical fact."[21] It has its roots in metaphor[22] and appeals to the imagination.[23] In *An Experiment in Criticism* he says that because myth can take almost any form and deal with almost any "subject," it must be defined by its effect upon the receiver, which is invariably profound, momentous, everlasting, and, far above all, numinous; though sad or joyful, it is always grave, and, odd though it sounds, human sympathy is at a minimum. It almost always deals with fantastic characters or events and, because it is independent of the usual narrative attractions (suspense, complication, etc.), is exra-literary.[24] In "Shelley, Dryden, and Mr. Eliot," CSL summarizes:

> Myth is thus like manna; it is to each man a different dish and to each the dish he needs. It does not grow old nor stick at frontiers racial, sexual, or philosophic; and even from the same man at the same moment it can elicit different responses at different levels.[25]

And this brings us to the final question, hinted at, perhaps, by the number of references to noncritical, apologetic works, but thus far postponed. We can ask it this way: With regard to myth, whence this power? That is, what ultimate meaning do symbol, metaphor, and myth, as mediated by the imagination, possess?

The simple fact is that critics such as Richards, Frye, and Cassirer are wrong, for something outside of ourselves *does* exist; and not only does it exist, but it sends us messages as well. Authors from the Romantic period to the present have seen it, but only Lewis has insisted upon it with absolute clarity and conviction. Throughout the apologetics, this connection is made clear: There is a Supernature; all mythologies have some truth insofar as they embody elements within the Christian mythology, and this is so because, as Lewis entitled an essay, Myth became Fact – and that Fact was Jesus Christ.[26] In *The Pilgrim's Regress*, John the Pilgrim hears a Voice in the moment of his baptism:

> 'Child, if you will, it is mythology. It is but truth, not fact: an image, not the very real. But then it is My mythology. The words of Wisdom are also myth and metaphor. . . . But this is My inventing, this is the veil under which I have chosen to appear even from the first until now. For this end I made your senses and for this end your imagination, that you might see My Face and live.[27]

And so, in strictly literary terms, Lewis is finally "Platonic." In offering a closed, consistent, sufficient, and detailed system, in transcending petty antagonisms, and in seeing the ultimate source of truth, Lewis achieved a totally unified outlook.

These last few lines may sound like a peroration, but they are not. CSL can offer his own ending, and so I come to two final passages, one from *An Experiment in Criticism*, the other from *The Allegory of Love*.

> My own eyes are not enough for me, I will see through those of others. Reality, even seen through the eyes of many, is not enough. I will see what others have invented. Even the eyes of all humanity are not enough. I regret that the brutes cannot write books. Very gladly would I learn what face things present to a mouse or a bee; more gladly still would I perceive the olfactory world charged with all the information and emotion it carries for a dog.
>
> Literary experience heals the wound, without undermining the privilege, of individuality. There are mass emotions which heal the wound; but they destroy the privilege. In them our separate selves are pooled and we sink back into sub-individuality. But in reading great literature I become a thousand men and yet remain myself. Like the night sky in the Greek poem, I see with a myriad eyes, but it is still I who see. Here, as in worship, in love, in moral action, and in knowing, I transcend myself; and am never more myself than when I do.[28]

All that is valuable in CSL's attitude toward criticism, and all that there is in Lewis to love, is expressed in this passage. And one of the truest things we could ever hope to say about him, he himself said about Edmund Spenser, perhaps his favorite poet. I apply the passage to Lewis:

> His work is one, like a growing thing, a tree . . . with branches reaching to heaven and roots to hell. . . . And between these two extremes comes all the multiplicity of human life. . . .to read him is to grow in mental health.[29]

That, Dean Coogan, is why you should read Lewis' criticism.

Endnotes

1 *CSL*, no. 7 (May 1970).

2 "The Aproach to English," *Light on C. S. Lewis*, ed. Jocelyn Gibb (New York: Harcourt, Brace and World, 1965), p. 65.

3 "The Rebirth of Christ," *National Review*, Dec. 28, 1965, p. 1192.

4 *The Spectator*, CLVII (4 September 1936), p. 950.

5 *The Times of London*, 6 June 1936, p, 474.

6 *The Times of London*, 17 September, 1954, p. 592.

7 J. A. M. Berryman, *Books*, 1 October 1939, p. 18.

8 *Wall Street Journal*, August 13, 1963.

9 "De Descriptione Temporum," *Select Literary Essays*, ed. Walter Hooper (Cambridge: Cambridge University Press), 1969), passim.

10 *The Great Divorce*, (New York: Macmillan, 1946), pp. 77-99.

11 *Christian Reflections*, ed. Walter Hooper (Grand Rapids: Wm B. Eerdmans Publishing Co., 1967), p. 23

12 *Selected Literary Essays*, p. 265.

13 With E. M. W. Tillyard, *The Personal Heresy: A Controversy* (London: Oxford University Press, 1939), p. 114.

14 *Perelandra*, (New York: Macmillan, 1944), pp. 34-37.

15 *Letters*, ed. W. H. Lewis (New York: Harcourt, Brace & World), 26 June 1956.

16 *Miracles* (New York: Macmillan, 1947), p. 118. Emphasis Lewis'.

17 *Perelandra*, p. 110.

18 Letter of 29 December 1958, in the C. S. Lewis Collection, Wheaton College, Wheaton Illinois; by permission of the curator, Prof. Clyde S. Kilby.

19 *The Allegory of Love* (London: Oxford University Press, 1936), p. 45.

20 Ibid., pp. 355-56.

21 *The Problem of Pain* (New York: Macmillan, 1947), p. 64.

22 "Bluspels and Flalansferes," *Selected Literary Essays*, p. 258.

23 *Rehabilitations and Other Essays* (London: Oxford University Press, 1939), p. 29.

24 *An Experiment in Criticism* (Cambridge: Cambridge University Press, 1961), pp. 45-53.

25 *Selected Literary Essays*, p. 205.

26 "Myth Became Fact," *God in the Dock*, ed. Walter Hooper (Grand Rapids: Wm B. Eerdmans Publishing Co., 1970), pp. 63-67.

27 *The Pilgrim's Regress*, 3rd ed. (Grand Rapids: Wm B. Eerdmans Publishing Co., 1958), p. 171.

28 *An Experiment in Criticism*, pp. 140-141.

29 *The Allegory of Love*, p. 359.

Rhetorica Religii

> Rhetoric speaks to man in his whole being and out of his whole past and with reference to values which only a human being can intuit. . . . In the restored man dialectic and rhetoric will go along hand in hand as the regime of the human faculties intended that they should.
> -- Richard Weaver, *"The Cultural Role of Rhetoric"*

1.

Near the beginning of the second book of his *Metaphysics,* Aristotle instructs us that "those who wish to succeed must ask the right preliminary questions." The two never asked of Lewis are, What is he? and, What preponderantly did he practice? The answers would seem obvious, for he is a one-man Argument from Design, so little is there in his life that is not of-a-piece, that does not have about it the feel of inevitability. His rhetorical temper provided a compulsiveness and a posture that could be resolved only in argument. Training, taste and talent equipped him for an academic and apologetic career, to the exclusion of nearly all others. Of course, he could not have remained an atheist, in his case rather an aberration than a settled state; so his conversion added direction to the high apologetic purpose towards which, in the thirties, he had explicitly turned his formidable will. In short, Lewis was the quintessential *Homo rhetoricus,* knew it, acquitted himself superbly at being just that, and yet remained deeply troubled by his own efficacy.

By *rhetoric* I mean that subset of questions and lines of inquiry deriving, first from Aristotle's definition in chapter two of Book One of his treatise, *The faculty of observing in the particular case the available means of persuasion*; and second from the Judeo-Christian tradition of apologetic, characterized (says the *New Catholic Encyclopedia,* closely echoing St. Augustine in Book IV of his *De Doctrina Christiana*) by God's "self-disclosure . . . in the contemporary world," concerning itself with "the relationship between faith and reason." Thus "the apologetic attempt is to persuade, *to translate,* in the literal sense, the Christian demand for faith." [Emphasis added.] The conception that emerged from Aristotle and others is that of a series of systematic adjustments among purpose, circumstances, and strategies. Those circumstances are marked by "exigencies" – some imperfection marked by urgency which demands resolution by persuasion and thus occasions discourse.

There are constraints, of course, inherent to that occasion, the most restrictive being the limitations of what Aristotle called the "judge," any audience empowered to "mediate" the resolution. To these circumstances the communicator brings his resources. Some of these are ready made, such as his pre-existing reputation, whereas others are discovered ("invented") to address the particular question; among these other resources may be some bit of refutation, a definition unique to the subject-matter at hand, but especially proofs – appeals to reason, feeling, or to personal trustworthiness. Together these elements, organized around ideas both general and particular (*topoi*), and embodied in a certain style (for the last century or so our preference has been for *an extension of natural, direct conversation*), make up the tactics and strategy of a given persuasive effort. Finally, of over-riding importance is the nature of rhetoric as an *inherent faculty* of any human being: *an ineluctable feature of everyone's interior landscape.* In short, Aristotle could have begun his seminal *On Rhetoric* with the words, "all people by nature love to, and must, rhetorize."

If Lewis had been around, he would have been Aristotle's (and Augustine's) model. Of the more than forty books he published, all but some poetry and the works of literary scholarship and criticism are either argumentative defenses of the plausibility of Christian doctrine, explanations of it for the purpose of persuading in its favor, or manifestly didactic fictions with Christian intent; six have a veiled intent with the Christian content submerged, but they fulfill precisely the same functions. This assessment applies even to *Till We Have Faces*, though as Lewis' one real novel (as opposed to parable, fairy tale or romance) it differs considerably from its predecessors. The same is largely true of the books published posthumously. In many modes, and at varying levels of intensity and directness, Lewis was relentlessly persuasive. He delivered only a handful of sermons, for example, but they made history. "Transposition" was delivered from the pulpit of Mansfield College, close to the house Lewis stayed in on his very first night in Oxford. "The Weight of Glory" and "Learning in War-Time" were preached to multitudes from the pulpit of The University Church of St. Mary the Virgin: Latimer, Cranmer and Ridley had been tried there, and Wesley, Keble and Newman had preached from the same pulpit. These are impressive venues. But as impressive in their variety and modesty are the venues of some of his greatest essays. Here is a sampling: *St. Jude's Gazette, World Dominion, Electrical and Musical Industries Christian Fellowship, Coventry Evening Telegraph, Bristol Diocesan Gazette, The Month, Breakthrough,* and *St. James's Magazine*; of course there were also *The Saturday Evening Post, The Guardian* (small, but prominent in its day), *Time & Tide, Twentieth Century,* and *Spectator*. No venue was too large for his idiomatic voice, nor audience too small for his concentrated attention.

The subjects he treated were often the most difficult: if Jesus was God, why did he not return, as he seems to have promised, during the lifetime of those who actually heard him? If we are promised that prayers made faithfully will be answered why are they so frequently not? If God is loving why does he permit so much suffering, especially of the innocent – even of the beasts, who were not morally complicit in the Fall? What explanation other than psychosis could explain "speaking in tongues"? In the absence of evidence why should we be "obstinate" in belief? How can we possibly reconcile *dogmatic* belief with the need freely to exercise our reason, presumably God-given? The range of work – in its content, mode, scope, style, and persistence – is unremitting. Surely it came in stages, not unlike Lewis' (or anyone else's) life. In its great array, the whole of the work speaks to a sufficient variety of tastes, intellectual ability, religious doubt, spiritual need, imaginative longing, levels of curiosity, and sheer patience with the written word to satisfy the preponderance of readers, no matter where they break in upon it. In believing that Christ intends for us to be persons (members of His Person), Lewis uses an occasion to offer his audience recognizable facets of personality and to show them what they might become. Having taken seriously the claim that the universe is possessed of meaning, he then provides an image of reality sufficiently coherent and authoritative to make the claim credible.

Lewis' scholarly treatments of rhetoric are both straightforward and a bit unsettled. He discusses the art at length in three places: *English Literature in the Sixteenth Century (Excluding Drama)*, *The Discarded Image: An Introduction to Medieval and Renaissance Literature*, and *A Preface to 'Paradise Lost'*. In the second he provides a dazzling summary of medieval rhetorical theory: thorough, full of telling detail, and replete with apt examples, mostly from Chaucer. Of particular interest here is Lewis' attention to one Geoffrey of Vinsauf, whose *Nove Poetria* of the early thirteenth century achieved commanding influence. It is precisely the sort of rhetoric that would vex Lewis, but the vexation does not show in his description. In his *Preface to 'Paradise Lost'* Lewis exhibits his most impressive grasp of rhetoric, responding to the oldest of all the indictments against it. The passage merits extensive quotation:

> First, as to Manipulation. I do not think (and no great civilization has ever thought) that the art of the rhetorician is necessarily vile. It is in itself noble. . . . Both [rhetoric and poetry] aim at doing something to an audience. And both do it by using language to control what

already exists in our minds. . . . The differentia of Rhetoric is that it wishes to produce some practical resolve. . . and it does this by calling passion to the aid of reason. . . . The proper use is lawful and necessary because, as Aristotle points out, intellect of itself 'moves nothing': the transition from thinking to doing. . . needs to be assisted by appropriate states of feeling. Because the end of rhetoric is in the world of action, the objects it deals with appear foreshortened and much of their reality is omitted. . . . Very roughly, we might almost say that in Rhetoric imagination is present for the sake of passion (and, therefore, in the long run, for the sake of action), while in poetry passion is present for the sake of imagination, and therefore, in the long run, for the sake of wisdom or spiritual health. . . .

Yet, if rhetoric was the prime minister of Lewis' parliament of geniuses (intellectual, imaginative, spiritual, and of the will), he nevertheless found its Classical lineaments and post-Classical emphases entirely uncongenial, even disturbing. His notebooks offer virtually no use of *rhetoric* that is not derogatory; and in his Oxford literary history he writes, "rhetoric is the greatest barrier between us and our ancestors. If the Middle Ages had erred in their devotion to that art, the *renascentia*, far from curing, confirmed the error." He continues with a description of the antiquity and enormous influence of rhetoric, noting its unbroken continuity into the eighteenth century, "not the tyrant, but the darling of humanity, *soavissima*, as Dante says, 'the sweetest of all the other sciences'." Acknowledging that our older poetry was written by people who knew no distinction between poetry and rhetoric, and that they praised "beauties" at best opaque to us, he nevertheless asserts, "this change of taste makes an invisible wall between us and them. Probably all our literary histories, *certainly that on which I am engaged*, are vitiated by our lack of sympathy on this point [emphasis added]." What follows thereupon is a description of a system of education based upon a devoted study of figures of speech and of thought, of the universal enthusiasm for that education, and of its efficacy.

2.

Withal he was as troubled by his own devices as he was impatient with the art behind them. "I don't know if I'm weaker than other people, but it is a positive revelation to me how *while the speech lasts* it is impossible not to waver just a little," he wrote, after hearing a speech by Hitler (the night before he conceived the idea for *The Screwtape Letters*). "I should be useless as a schoolmaster or a policeman. Statements which I *know* to be untrue all but convince me, at any rate for the moment, if only the man says them unflinchingly." But even more telling are the instances when he brings his own fictional rhetoric to a halt. During the debate on Perelandra, the wrong side has the better rhetoric; Ransom "won" only because he acts, non-rhetorically – by punching the Un-man in his mouth. The only passenger on *The Great Divorce* bus to Heaven who stays is the one who stops rhetorizing and exclaims, "Damn and blast you! Go on can't you? Get it over," and presently shuts up. In *The Silver Chair* Puddleglum's affirmation follows his determining *action*: With his naked webbed-foot he stamps on the fire that is complicit in the witch's verbal spell. And at the end of *Till We Have Faces* the queen writes, of what had been her lucid and rather convincing complaint, a rhetorically formal *apologia*, "only words, words; to be led out to battle with other words."

Now, in Christian terms the spiritual dilemma is clear. When rhetoric and redemption meet in the self, one of them must give way, since rhetoric requires a voluble ego and redemption its death, as an antecedent to its rebirth and resurrection. Twenty-five years ago Owen Barfield (Lewis' "second friend," erstwhile mentor, and solicitor) wrote to me that he did not think Lewis' rhetorical persona – his direct, conversational, and confessional familiarity – was deliberately adopted. Rather, "the indifference to self" that came later, wrote Barfield, "may well have been responsible for his *maintaining* the persona throughout the rest of his life, as may also have been the thought of its usefulness for the purpose of argumentative Christian apology." But during his entire life, Lewis used himself as a *datum*, most spectacularly in *A Grief Observed*, but also in *The Magician's Nephew, Till We Have Faces*, and *Letters to Malcolm*, true masterpieces all. Always was he essentially that wary yet energetic, ambivalent yet committed *Homo rhetoricus*. And therein lies the problem. The self upon which Lewis' genius of the will turned its back in his thirties is the very same self so palpably conspiring with his genius of rhetoric, the very same rhetoric that issued forth in response to his *willed commitment to a vocation*. In his chapter on Pride in *Mere Christianity*, "The Great Sin," he tells us that God is trying to make us humble for our own sake, "trying to take off a lot of silly, ugly, fancy-dress" of self-conceit that we are wearing. And then he confesses, "I wish I had got a bit further with humility myself: if I had, I could probably tell you more about the relief, the comfort, of taking the fancy-dress off -- getting rid of the false self, with all its 'Look at me . . . .'"

So the rhetorical genius in Lewis must have presided uneasily, what with all its self-projection. His old, ambivalent view of the art is intimately tied to his equally ambivalent view of one's self and the Christian demand that it be transcended. In the private venue of lyric poetry this alarm surfaces explicitly in "As the Ruin Falls" (unpublished during his lifetime), addressed perhaps to Joy Davidman, perhaps to God:

> All this is flashy rhetoric about loving you.
>
> I never had a selfless thought since I was born.
> I am mercenary and self-seeking through and through:
> I want God, you, all friends, merely to serve my turn.
>
> Peace, re-assurance, pleasure, are the goals I seek
> I cannot crawl one inch outside my proper skin:
> I talk of love – a scholar's parrot may talk Greek –
> But, self-imprisoned, always end where I begin.

And what he finds particularly discomfiting, even alarming, is not only the effect of rhetoric upon his credulity but its hold upon his self, for that hold symptomizes an inability to let go of his old, needful theatrical ego. Listen to this *cri de coeur*, written late and also unpublished in his lifetime:

> From all my lame defeats and oh! much more
>
> From all the victories that I seemed to score;
> From cleverness shot forth on Thy behalf
> At which, while angels weep, the audience laugh;
> From all my proofs of Thy divinity,
> Thou, who wouldst give no sign, deliver me.
> . . . .
> Lord of the narrow gate and the needle's eye,
> Take from me all my trumpery lest I die.

But surely Lewis was too tough on himself. In his *Religio Medici*, Sir Thomas Browne, a physician, sought to "exercise [his] faith in the difficultist point; for to credit ordinary and visible objects is not faith but persuasion" – thereby to reconcile the inquiring skepticism of a scientist with his deep and orthodox religious faith. So is there not for Lewis, along those lines, some *rhetorica religii*? A sort of superordinate *maieusis*, as opposed to imposition? This would not be a new rhetoric, *but it is an existential one*, the sort of thing which St. Augustine, that keen, zealous, and professional rhetorician, approximated as he sought to celebrate "signs of divine presence within the human mind"? I understand that "Existential" might seem odd applied to C. S. Lewis, who had no patience with Existentialism or with such of its embodiments as Kierkegaard, whom he dismissed with exclamatory impatience. But I believe Lewis was wrong and that his rejection may have been preponderantly tonal. In his "Three Kinds of Men" (*Present Concerns*), for example, he describes those who seek pleasure, others who acknowledge a higher claim upon them, and a third for whom, like St. Paul, "to live is Christ"; here the burden of proof is on the Defense to show how this taxonomy is *not* Kierkegaard's aesthetic, ethical, and religious stages, that Lewis was *not* a Knight of Faith incarnate, rejecting the Spirit of the Age to follow God whatever the price, and that Lewis did *not* live a dialectic that found selfhood not given but dependent upon reading the signs and choosing to follow them.

"The Seeing Eye" is the last essay in an early posthumous collection that Walter Hooper edited, *Christian Reflections*, and it is, I think, among Lewis' most useful. In it he ponders the assertion that Russian astronauts have not found God in outer space and goes on to say things which, typically, seem manifestly self-evident, *after* he has said them, of course, but also said them almost peripherally. "If God created the universe, He created space-time" – so far, so obvious. But next comes the *subordinate clause*: "which is to the universe as the metre is to a poem or the key is to music." Well, of course! That *certainly is* space-time. (All along there is a familiar small, soft voice, at least in my head, whispering, "so *that's* space-time.") Thus, Lewis continues, "to look for Him as one item within the framework which He Himself invented is nonsensical." After all, he adds, "a fish is no more, and no less, in the sea" – here he will drive the point home – "after it has swum a thousand miles than it was when it set out. . . . To some, God is discoverable everywhere; to others, nowhere. Those who do not find Him on earth are unlikely to find Him in space. . . ." He concludes, "much depends on the seeing eye," one like Lewis' own.

3.

In "Christianity and Literature," a paper from the thirties also in *Christian Reflections*, Lewis noted that "a cultured person . . . is almost compelled to be aware that reality is very odd and that the ultimate truth, whatever it may be, *must* have the characteristics of strangeness -- *must* be something that would seem remote and fantastic to the uncultured." Or, as Walker Percy has put it, we are shipwrecked and await "the message in the bottle," one that a Seeing Eye discerns and which only the *Homo rhetoricus* can translate for the rest of us who are stranded. In his essay entitled "The Message in the Bottle" Percy (whose summary of Christian existentialism is perfectly applicable to the author of *A Grief Observed*), provides a suggestive image of what a Christian rhetorician does:

> Existentialism has taught us that what man is cannot be grasped by the science of man. The case is rather that man's science is one of the things that man does, a mode of existence. *Another mode is speech* [rhetoric]. Man is not merely a higher organism responding to and controlling his environment. He is . . . that being in the world whose calling it is to find a name for Being, to give testimony to it, and to provide for it a clearing. [Emphasis added.]

Of course the point can be pushed too far. The many dissimilarities between Lewis and avowed, or acknowledged, existentialist writers can be adduced. Over-emphasis on the irrational, for example, or the very fact that he might be grouped with Sartre, bring on a bad case of hives; but there are sub-categories of existentialist writers as there are of any other category. Perhaps that possibility accounts for an exchange I had with Paul Holmer, the author of (I think) the best book on Lewis, a renowned interpreter of Existentialism, and a pioneer in the kindling of interest in Kierkegaard. When I asked him if Lewis was, after all, an existential writer, he answered merely, "if you want him to be."

But this does not require of us a leap of faith, the prototypical existential choice. For example, there exists a related conception, in fact an explanation that can account for just such a choice. It is John Henry Cardinal Newman's idea of the Illative Sense, which has been unaccountably neglected by philosophers and rhetoricians alike. First we doubt, says Newman in his *An Essay in Aid of a Grammar of Assent*, then we infer, and finally we assent, first notionally, then assertively (that is, really) as a "supra-logical judgment" (which closely resembles a claim for our participation in the Divine Logos). This last occurs when finally we recognize *meaning*, whether ratiocinatively or imaginatively, and thus truth: the way things are (e.g. Natural Law). Although it develops as a habit, it originates in our nature, he says, like "good sense," "common sense," or a "sense of beauty." In other words, it conveys us across the gaps that separate evidence from conclusion; it warrants the "therefore" in our reasoning process.

Could there be any more accurate a paradigm for the life and rhetoric of C. S. Lewis? When the Man of Letters speaks with "auctoritee" on myth, metaphor, and meaning in language and in literature; or the Apologist reasons; or the preacher and romancer beckons; or the fellow fugitive reflects, wonders, confesses, and suggests, then he is speaking illatively, his "extension of natural conversation" sufficiently inviting so as to convey us across the gaps. This is no "flashy rhetoric" or "trumpery," but a nuanced, thoughtful, committed religious thinker "speaking well." That is why I have always thought that a couplet from Alexander Pope's *An Essay on Criticism* gets it just right when applied to Lewis and his world of discourse: "Something, whose truth convinced at sight we find,/ That gives us back the image of our mind." He would remind us that we must choose to be either "Man or Rabbit," either wanting and trying to know or pursuing the carrot of simple efficacy; or that when considering "The Trouble with 'X' . . ." we must consider X's personhood, the charity it requires, and our membership in the same Body as X.

In short, he would continue to act upon the distinction made by the psychotherapist Phillip Rieff, that "religious man was born to be saved; psychological man was born to be pleased." He would, because he knew that "evangelization," as Pope John Paul II writes in *Crossing the Threshold of Hope*, is the "encounter of the Gospel with the culture of each epoch." And so even when "topical" (as in "On Living in an Atomic Age," for example) Lewis is timeless: our "minds claim to be spirit," and "it is part of our spiritual law never to put survival first," so our survival "must be by honourable and merciful means." Finally, like Orual in *Till We Have Faces* we at least consider crossing the greatest gap of all, to that "clearing," as Walker Percy put it, in which Being has been named. Not that which "works" but that which is true -- that which because of its coherence reveals meaning in the apparently meaningless -- ought to win our assent. The establishment of an inter-connected wholeness and a renewed confidence in our ability to apprehend it was the basis of Lewis' own conversion and became the basis of his maieutic, existential appeal.

Paul Holmer, in *C. S. Lewis: The Shape of His Faith and Thought*, writes:

> He shows us repeatedly . . . how a kind of moral certitude is finally achieved. He sends us back to our fathers, mothers, nurses, poets, sages, and lawgivers. The dignity he ascribes to all of us is exceedingly flattering. . . . The tissue of life around us, when taken with seriousness, is already a moral order. We have to become its qualified readers. . . . The world has no single character, and it must be understood in a variety of ways. His books create, almost as Kierkegaard did, the living variety of paradigms. . . . Here the requirements are new capabilities, new capacities altogether. . . . For his works, especially the novels, have a way of creating a kind of longing for innocence, for purity, for humility, candor, and contentment. . . . Only its occasion can be created by another, and that is what Lewis' literature becomes. Wisdom has to be read off the whole shape of his thought and is not one trick within it.

Another of the most thoughtful appraisals of Lewis is this one from Debra Winger, the noted actress who so capably played the role of Joy Davidman in *Shadowlands*. Responding to a question that posited Lewis as a man who gave "easy" answers to "difficult questions" – a charge made promiscuously in the film – Winger (who in preparation had read much Lewis and Joy Davidman and had visited the Wade Center at Wheaton College) demurred. After avowing that she was not a Christian she told me, "he may make difficult *questions* accessible. I don't think he makes the answers 'easy'. I don't think he answers questions. I think he discusses them." She added that "he's in that school of discourse where his statements are not like books that are written by experts"; instead, she concluded, "he's saying 'think about this'. That's why I think he opened [Christianity] to so many people. He wasn't dogmatic." In all its regions Lewis' rhetoric is inseparable from his voice, both reasonable and rhapsodic, doubly inviting.

Thus in his output Lewis comes as close as any to how the philosopher and rhetorician Richard Weaver describes the Complete Man: "The 'lover' added to the scientist; the rhetorician to the dialectician; understanding followed by actualization." Lewis adumbrates precisely this view in yet another poem unpublished during his lifetime, calling more for integration and maturity than for redemption. In the last half of his sonnet "Reason," with Athene representing that faculty and Demeter the Imagination, he writes:

> Tempt not Athene. Wound not in her fertile pains
> Demeter, nor rebel against her mother-right.
> Oh who will reconcile in me both maid and mother,
> Who make in me a concord of the depth and height?
> Who make imagination's dim exploring touch
> Ever report the same as intellectual sight?
> Then could I truly say, and not deceive,
> Then wholly say, that I BELIEVE.

More than merely the Roman rhetor Quintilian's "good man speaking well," this man who so seamlessly combined imagination and reason is a reliable guide to the things that matter most. It is of more than passing interest that "I believe" is (as Lewis would have known) a close translation of 'Peitho', the Greek goddess of rhetoric, usually seen in the company of Aphrodite herself. Lewis was not the apostle from across the sea, as Walker Percy describes him, who puts the message in the bottle; rather, *he was one of us*, shipwrecked. But unlike most people, he worked to make a clearing for the message, knew it when he saw it, and labored his lifelong to interpret it for all who are on the island with him.

Lewis, C. S.
in *American Conservatism: An Encyclopedia*

Culturally conservative and militantly orthodox in his religious beliefs, **Clive Staples Lewis** (1898-1963) is nevertheless difficult to categorize in terms common to political discourse. Precisely to avoid such categorization (he viewed it as polemically inconvenient) he refused an offer of knighthood from Churchill's post-war government. In that light he is best seen as conservatively disposed rather than as a conservative *per se*.

Touchstones of his conservative thought are his: trust in the validity of reason, defense of Natural Law, general reliance upon tradition ("Mere Christianity"), objective view of creation (both natural and supernatural) and the legitimacy of its claims upon us (our moral and aesthetic responses are trainable and ought to be ordinate), distrust of emotion as a guide to truth, refusal to equate progress with innovation or to see it as at all inevitable, and a rejection of egalitarianism as both dangerous and immoral. Wounded in the trenches of World War One, his patriotism compelled him to proclaim the duty of men (pronouncedly not women) possibly to die for their country; but he steadfastly refused "to live for it." He distrusted collectivism (especially mass movements) of any kind, loathed government intrusion into everyday life, and reviled statist presumptuousness (despising, for example, "The Humanitarian Theory of Punishment" on the grounds that whereas the state might very well punish wrongdoers it had no business "curing" them).

Yet he allowed that a genuinely Christian society would somehow be a socialist one. His unvarying orthodoxy notwithstanding, he believed that laws against homosexuality and pornography are not only futile but wrong. His allegiance to scriptural inerrancy did not lead to anything resembling biblical literalism or religious fundamentalism (Bob Jones, Jr., after meeting him, said that although Lewis did drink and smoke he believed that "that man is a Christian"); and he counseled that two lovers would be better off living together outside of marriage rather than violating their sacramental vow of marital fidelity. Somewhat like his great creation, the lion Aslan, Lewis was not tame.

Thus his thought must be read within the considerable context that he provided; not as lessons or, worse, tricks, but as an organic worldview arising from inherited culture and faith in the Risen Lord. In over forty books, 200 essays and sermons, and 80 poems, he was one the very greatest Christian apologists ever to have written in English; a formidable religious thinker, psychologist, and devotional writer; a philosopher and poet; a fiction writer who arguably produced benchmarks in religious allegory, the first-person novel, children's fantasy, and science fiction; and one of the foremost literary historians and critics of the twentieth century. Withal, he is what he famously called himself in his inaugural lecture as the first Professor of Medieval and English Literature at Cambridge University, an Old Western Man, and he would consistently remind us that "anything not eternal is eternally out of date."

In short, his imaginative effusions are as radical as nature itself; his reason as conservative as the multiplication tables; and his spirit as liberal and as liberated as the open arms of the Cross at which he worshipped.

Part 3

PERSONAL VIEWS

23

A Clerke of Oxenforde

Five years ago my wife, Alexandra, and I became lost in the wilds of Staten Island, that marshy, purgatorial province which, doubtless the folly of some ancient cartographer, is said to be part of New York City. Already late, without map, compass nor even star to guide us, we tentatively made our way, from car-ferry to blessedly solid land, thence to inland roads leading from darkness to utter darkness. Forty minutes past the appointed hour, cold, wet, and wind-blown, we arrived; and it is a simple matter of fact that neither of us will ever forget that moment or the evening which followed. We rang, were received, entered, and every man of the assembled company rose; and rising with them were light, warmth, and an intimate, if yet formal, cheer. For a fleeting moment I mused that perhaps we were enacting a Charles Williams novel.

Five years after this founding of the New York C. S. Lewis Society, or some three-and-one-half months ago, we arrived, small son in hand, at Oxford. Here "pilgrimage" or (worse) "five-year pilgrimage" would be inappropriate and inaccurate; a happy coincidence of doctoral dissertation and sabbatical leave made possible our visit. Yet for a Lewis admirer were place and man ever so nearly synonymous as Oxford and CSL? Indeed, for a Christian there are no coincidences.

The attempt to see Oxford as Lewis saw it is, for the foreign admirer, probably inevitable. How would CSL – how could he? – have addressed himself to Woolworth's, Marks and Spencer, vehicular pollution, and Wimpy's, the hamburger palace supreme? All would have to be negotiated in getting from Magdalen College to the "Bird and Baby." And what of Lewis waiting on a long bus-queue, in the rain (shades, rather Shades, of The *Great Divorce*), for a lurching, careening double-decker? Thus proceeds the attempt; but as it proceeds one gradually, almost imperceptibly, comes to notice that there are two Oxfords: Town and Gown. For inside a College, the twentieth century literally disappears; the Deer Park and Addison's Walk of Magdalen, the spaciousness of Christ Church, the manicured gardens of St. John's, the aged complexity of New College – all manage to exclude, to ignore, the very sights, sounds, and smells of modernity. Soon one is struck by the realization that, all along, he has not really been trying to see Oxford as Lewis must have seen it but to see Lewis himself *in* Oxford.

Now the wanderer wanders more purposefully. He turns into Mansfield Road, off Holywell Street, to see the first house on the right, where CSL spent his first night in Oxford, and he continues down to the chapel of Mansfield College, where CSL preached "Transposition." Back on High Street, number 36, is Williams Hairdresser, a visit to which prompted "The Efficacy of Prayer," and further down The High is the University Church of St. Mary the Virgin where, in Oxfordian terms, a multitude heard "The Weight of Glory" and "Learning in War-Time." (In that Church were tried Latimer, Cranmer, and Ridley; John Wesley preached there, and from the very same pulpit used by Lewis Newman and Keble preached, the latter giving his famous Assize sermon which started the Oxford movement.) Still on High Street are the Examination Schools, where Lewis delivered his Prolegomena, University College, which he loved so very much, and, of course, Magdalen College. And then, past Blackwell's and Thornton's (bookstores haunted by Lewis, especially the young Lewis) are the Lamb and Flag and, finally, the Eagle and Child, wherein hangs the plaque (composed by Walter Hooper) commemorating the Inklings.

One cannot actually "wander" to The Kilns, though the route can be leisurely walked (as Lewis often walked it) in well under two hours. The area is much changed since CSL and the Major lived there, and since the latter's death the house has been sold; close by, however, is Trinity Church, the Lewises' parish church. The Vicar, the Reverend R. E. Head, is a friendly man who, if not too busy, is quite willing to talk about "the Professor." He told me, for example, that CSL and the Major always sat in the same pew, on the side and behind a pillar, and that they left immediately upon conclusion of the service; as a matter of fact, a man would wait at the door to open it for them, as the brothers' physical awkwardness would have made for a thundering of bolts and latches.

If the Lewis admirer is also a Lewis scholar, then no place in the world will suit him better than Oxford. The Bodleian Library possesses a complete Lewis collection, including all of the unpublished letters (index vol. 3 – MS Eng. Lett. C220/l); and of course, the Bodleian has resources related to Lewis studies possessed by no other single institution. Wroxton College, a beautiful converted abbey thirty miles north of Oxford, features the Lewis Room, which houses all of CSL's library not in the possession of personal friends. Surely no one ever made a book as much his own as Lewis did, for underlining, marginalia, summaries of contents, and indices abound. Having seen Lewis' books I can no longer be skeptical of this anecdote about his memory. He would tell a friend to choose a number from one to ten, then a number from one to five, then from one to twenty, and finally a number from one to two hundred, with the numbers corresponding, respectively, to case, shelf, book, and page number. The friend, having fetched the book and opened to the appropriate page, would then quote a line – a single line. To this Lewis would add, from memory, the rest of that page.

Finally, there are Lewis' old friends, living in, or not too far from, Oxford. But here a warning. I have heard of the most uncharitable intrusions upon the time and hospitality of these people, whom we may too easily tend to look upon as yet another "resource." The generosity displayed by, say, Mr. Barfield in attending our anniversary meeting is not untypical of what the admirer would find in Oxford, but the excesses of the person who calls unannounced, who demands information, who pesters with silly ("Why didn't Lewis like scientists?") or with irrelevant ("Did Lewis really like the cold?") questions, or who professes expertise without having read two or three of the most important books: these excesses (each an actuality) are, to say the least, trying. On the other hand, a solid preparation, a well-founded enthusiasm, and a rational attention to the common proprieties of social intercourse will almost guarantee an insightful, complete, and authoritative response, either in person or by mail. I know, for example, that Father Hooper, Lewis trustee and editor, sees or answers by mail Lewis admirers numbering in double figures per week.

On the night of November 8th, under the sign of The Eagle and Child, I toasted our Society, allowing myself, for the moment, to indulge the notion that I was, especially for this occasion, its representative in this most appropriate of cities. It occurred to me that during these past five years there has been in the making a genuine "boom" of interest in C. S. Lewis, and that our Society could do no better than to broaden and to deepen that combination of intellectual rigor and joyful enthusiasm which we have thus far, and right from the beginning, manifested. For CSL is much more – more converted, more brilliant – than even we take him to be from his books; and in choosing Lewis we also choose on issues of great moment. Like it or not, we are "behind the enemy's lines."

A Toast

"If I had known before what I know now," runs the old complaint, "I would have done things much differently, or not at all." Happily, I believe we, with regard to our New York C. S. Lewis Society, can proclaim the opposite: if we had known before what we know now, we would have done the same – only sooner! The reason for this jubilation – for such is our esteem and affection for C. S. Lewis, and especially our gratitude to him for having enriched and augmented our Joy (as he has taught us to call it) – the reason for this jubilation winds back to two men, the two preternaturally selfless and devoted people who are the trustees of Lewis' estate: Owen Barfield and Walter Hooper.

Now, by our human standards ten years is not an insignificant chunk of time; and it is not presumptuous to claim that our modest role in promoting an interest in, and an understanding of, the works of C. S. Lewis has not been inconsiderable. Nevertheless, it is not within our provenance to *honor* anyone. Yet just as surely it is appropriate for us – perhaps especially for *us* – to *thank* them. After all, Lewis himself did, or would have. In 1929 he wrote to Arthur Greeves:

> "Yesterday Barfield came to lunch and afterwards took me out for a drive-and-walk – you see you are not the only friend I sponge on. . . . As often happens with the best of friends, we were not in a very good talking mood – only that pleasant sense of security that comes from being with those who understand you."

And there is no question of Lewis' intellectual debt to Owen Barfield, on the nature of language, of myth, of imagination. CSL frequently reminds his reader of that debt. And how could there not be one? Owen Barfield's books and articles throb with an intellectual vitality that can only grow as the years roll on. Yet in spite of the expense of who knows how much time and energy, Barfield has allowed his devotion to his friend to distract him from his own formidable work; and *we* have been the beneficiaries.

Since Lewis' death, Walter Hooper – "the son," said CSL, "I should have had" – has given us ten of the master's works, an effort culminating most recently in his monumental edition of the Lewis-Greeves correspondence, *They Stand Together*, a magnificent and hard-won achievement. In the face, from time to time, of the slings and arrows of outrageous fortune, this generous and graceful man has made it all look so easy. One of C.S. Lewis' very favorite books was James Stephen's *The Crock of Gold*. I offer this passage as a sort of motto – especially, of course, of Lewis and Barfield, and (in another way) of Lewis and us:

> "To them there were only two kinds of sounds anywhere – these were conversation and noise: they liked the first very much indeed, but they spoke of the second with stern disapproval. . . . 'Do you know . . . that a leprechaun came here today? . . . Are you going to listen to what I am telling you about the leprechaun?' said the Tin Woman. 'I am not,' said the Philosopher. . . . 'Will you ever be done talking?' shouted the Thin Woman passionately. 'I will not,' said the Philosopher."

And, I would add, neither will we; and neither, we hope, will C.S. Lewis, by way of the good offices of Owen Barfield and Walter Hooper.

But I think we need not fear. Hooper has thanked Lewis for his "finest legacy to me – my friend Owen Barfield has stood by me all the way." And together they seem to have taken very seriously the belief expressed by Barfield to Lewis, which the latter recorded in a letter to Greeves: "It is rather important that friends should occasionally share together their experience of a third person." Have we not been so fortunate to have been allowed to revel in that dance?

Mr. and Mrs. Barfield, Father Hooper, accept the enduring esteem of your friends, the members of the New York C.S. Lewis Society, and the remembrances of this occasion which we have sent to you.

Join with us in celebration.

25

A Man for Our Season

Nearly forty years ago a young summer intern at a national magazine of opinion and cultural commentary had the job of reading her boss's mail. Among her purposes in doing so was to suggest to him which letters he might find worth printing, usually with a response, in a highly amusing, personal section of the magazine. That is how Linda Bridges, by now a member of the New York C. S. Lewis Society for all of its decades, drew to the attention of William F. Buckley, Jr., editor of *National Review,* the letter from Henry Noel that gave rise to . . . us.

At our annual "from the floor" July meeting, I asked the assembled company whom we might consider successors to C. S. Lewis. N.T. Wright, Peter Kreeft, and Charles Colson were mentioned, and then a member argued for the inclusion of William F. Buckley, who (*mutatis mutandis*, as Mr. Buckley would – and in fact often did –say) turns out to be a more likely candidate than at first meets the eye. As it happened the mention of Buckley was fortuitous, for after establishing that the respondent and I certainly had *not* conspired prior to the meeting I produced a book that I had at the ready.

Strictly Right is both elegant and lively, authoritative and intimate. Of course devoted readers of the magazine and admirers of Buckley (I happily profess to being both) will not be disappointed, but neither will anyone else. Description, biography, anecdote, and the character sketch (truly, characters abound) alternate seamlessly. The result is often gripping, a mix of charm, controversy, goodwill, close calls, tossed-off wit, and downright nobility; that is, there is Buckley in full, a man whose humors seem so well-mixed that his gifts – not least for friendship – are exceeded only by his consequentiality.

By no means incidental to the value of this book are its strokes of intellectual, social and national history: penetrating, and *useful*. As Dr. Johnson said, people need to be reminded more often than instructed. Finally, this note to my portside friends. To paraphrase C. S. Lewis, a person of the Left cannot be too careful of his reading; but, in this case, be not afraid: all you have to lose are your superstitions.

A Faithful Steward:
Walter Hooper

C. S. Lewis' fame and influence have so steadily risen after a fall in the mid-1960s that he is now an established figure, valued well beyond his devoted Christian readership. Many of his works are classics, in Carl Van Doren's sense of not having to be re-written, and he has produced a vital literature, "news" (as Ezra Pound said) "that stays news." Lewis himself is widely esteemed as one of the great Christian apologists of any age – praised by presidents, prime ministers, fundamentalist preachers, and the pope – perhaps worthy in an ecumenical sense of being regarded as a Doctor of the Church. And although we could call his work the work of a lifetime, we would be wrong; it is actually the work of nearly two lifetimes.

In his two-story Oxford home, a fully-attached cottage smaller than some postage stamps, there dwells Walter McGehee Hooper. Nearly 30 years ago—quite earlier than, and apart from, practitioners of the "Lewis Studies" industry—he saw to it that Lewis' works would continue to issue forth, and his care, unflagging effort, and expertise continue to ensure the availability and reliability of Lewis' *oeuvre*. In addition to writing three books and contributing much of his work to other people's books and to journals, he has maintained the Lewis bibliography (a complicated chore requiring both diligence and vigilance) and, above all, has edited more than 15 Lewis works, most of them major. Among these are Lewis' juvenilia *(Boxen)*, *The Dark Tower* (a long, fictional fragment included in a collection of Lewis' short fiction), *Literary Essays*, two poetry collections (the lyric collection being Hooper's personal favorite), and especially *They Stand Together: The Letters of C. S. Lewis to Arthur Greeves* (on a par with, say, some of Frederick Pottle's great work on Boswell's papers). This year he published *All My Road Before Me*, Lewis' only diary, and this January he set to work on a three-volume edition of selected letters. Especially noteworthy are Hooper's major prefaces, introductions, and essays. Together they constitute a thorough and precise history of many of Lewis' works, their composition and the circumstances of their first (and subsequent) appearances, and an informal biography rich in feel and nuance.

On the most important questions – Has his work been done well? Has he failed to do what he ought to have done? Has he done anything better left undone? – the answers, especially for those who know the facts, redound to his credit. Some have said that he intrudes himself excessively into his prefaces; others that he permitted, even if he did not invite, his audience to assume that *he* knew Lewis longer than was actually the case. But these matters are even more subjective than they are trivial. Hooper's use of himself in his prefaces is almost always by way of recounting a useful or amusing anecdote about Lewis. (I have been among the many who, upon hearing Hooper tell a story to a group, have urged him to put it into print.) And whether in print or in person he has been as candid as he is sad about the brevity of the period he spent with Lewis. There are also the complaints (mine among them) that too many editions have been mere recompilations, including several pieces already available joined to only one or two new ones – but irresistibly enticing new ones. Yet these are for the most part collections of essays otherwise out-of-print in Britain or not for sale in the United States, and publishers do have interests that, after all, supersede those of a disinterested editor.

Finally, there are those critics who complain that Hooper has published too much of Lewis or, worse, that he has published matter more appropriately left unpublished altogether. But which works are these? *The Dark Tower*, which lends itself to all manner of disagreeable psychoanalytical interpretation (often telling us more about the analyst than about the author)? Restored passages from the Greeves correspondence that evince a sexually-fantasizing adolescent Lewis? Or the diary, a volume that speaks to Lewis' greatest single biographical *and* autobiographical gap and alone documents the life that Lewis converted from? Lewis readers – students, scholars, admirers, and zealots – have been routinely accused of "cultism," and among these readers there are cultists indeed. But surely people who would care to know even the warts are not cultists. And it is odd that critics who accuse Lewis aficionados of wanting every little relic of the man do not make similar charges with respect to other authors, some of whose very laundry lists (or does it merely seem that way?) are grist for all sorts of academic mills.

In all, Hooper's body of work warrants the assertion that, given the magnitude of his achievement, there is no greater nor more reliable authority on the life and works of C.S. Lewis than Walter Hooper.

Once when I asked him why he assumed such a burden so early in his life with no prospects for his own future, without remuneration or guarantee of success, when Lewis' popularity was at a very low point, he responded, "It's something I asked myself very often over a period of years, and especially when looking after Warnie [Lewis' talented, genial, and devoted, but alcoholic, older brother] occupied me so much. My answer to myself was quite simply that Lewis was a unique and great man who wrote unique and great works which the world needed far more than anything [of my own] I could give it." It was a risky decision that invited jealousy, frustration, and failure, but it has paid off for us as the beneficiaries of his achievement. For 15 years he has been a salaried employee of the Lewis estate (now a company administered by the Curtis Brown Literary Agency), and upon retirement he will receive- a pension. But during the first ten years he received no pay and lived in near-poverty as a part-time teacher and as an Anglican chaplain to an Oxford college. Now he owns a large and valuable collection of Lewis manuscripts which has been donated to a university, to be transferred upon his death.

Yet his most recent and riskiest decision resulted not in another achievement, but rather in Hooper being "achieved." In 1984 he visited Rome and met the pope, who had expressed a desire to "chat" with him, and in the summer of 1988 he *came* to Rome, permanently. Since then, he has been snubbed by some who no longer regard him as a 'gentleman." So he gleefully tells the story of Belloc at Mass, standing when everyone else kneels. "Sir," says the usher, "at this point it is our custom to kneel." When Belloc responds with an obscenity, the usher (without missing a beat) answers, "Oh, excuse me. I didn't realize you *were* a Roman Catholic." After telling the story, Hooper will proclaim himself proud to be a "mackerel snapper." He seems more himself than ever.

He is a sensitive and attentive man, refined in manner. Though by no means fragile, he is perhaps naïve in bestowing so much of his time and attention on strangers who take advantage of his knowledge, his position, and his pre-disposition to be helpful. He has made some enemies over the years, though remarkably few, given how often he has had to refuse requests for rights to reprint, to gain access to, or to publish Lewis' work for projects of dubious merit. (The New York C. S. Lewis Society, for example, had planned some naïve projects that Hooper prudently and gently prevented.) Some have accused him of hero-worship, others of betraying the master. Yet during the 23 years I have known him, I have witnessed nothing but gratitude to, and affection for, Lewis. Nothing to confirm the "worship" charge (though he does have "heroes," two being John Paul II and Mother Teresa). What is called "betrayal" is simply editorial integrity, as when he decided to publish *The Dark Tower,* demanded by Lewis devotees and scholars alike, or when he restored those passages written by the young Lewis to Greeves (the partial cause of a particularly ludicrous and febrile assault: his custom has always been not to respond to attack, distortion, or factual error with respect to himself).

Five other people have edited Lewis, and many have used his work variously. It is worth noting, too, that present American copyright law allows an editor to claim the contents of a book as his own (something that Hooper has promised in writing never to do), that he does not own anything he writes which in any way deals with Lewis or his work, and that Douglas Gresham (one of Lewis' two stepsons and heirs) has absolute power to censor anything Hooper writes about Lewis or his work.

On March 27 Hooper turned 60 and still resembles James Mason or Denholm Eliot or (if a dear lady friend is to be believed) Tyrone Power (Hooper would prefer Charles Bronson). He likes movies (his favorite being *The Good, the Bad, and the Ugly,* even if it does pre-date the rise of Arnold Schwarzenegger, a fellow former bodybuilder), Louis L'Amour, Jane Austen, singer James Taylor, and Mozart. He seems particularly susceptible to the charms of old-fashioned, exotically attractive, yet not unassertive women (South Americans, for example). He leaves no papal encyclical undigested and has just completed a reading of St. Thomas's *Summa*. But his abundant good humor can be both broad and sly, shining best when accompanied by tobacco and bourbon. He inspires loyal and enduring friendships, perhaps the greatest of which is the one he shares with the noted philosopher (and Lewis' lifelong friend) Owen Barfield, whom Hooper calls "Lewis' greatest legacy to me."

His original home is in Reidsville, North Carolina, and nearly every year he travels from Oxford to visit his brothers and sister and their closely-knit families. He has strong loyalties to the University of North Carolina at Chapel Hill where, before a two-year stint in the army and another two as an instructor in medieval English literature at the University of Kentucky, he received both his B.A. and M.A. degrees. In his junior year he became a serious Christian; in basic training he first read Lewis and immediately began a correspondence with him, exchanging some ten letters. When he visited Lewis, it was with contract in hand to write a book for the Twayne series on English authors. Instead, he became for a short time before his death the great man's private secretary and, according to Lewis, "the son I never had."

I could not forget my first meeting with Hooper. During Easter week of 1969 my wife and I were in Oxford, I carrying a letter of introduction from Professor Clyde Kilby, the godfather of Lewis interest in America. When we knocked at the door of the Warden's lodgings at Keble College, a shabby, paint-spackled fellow answered and, very apologetically, assured us that Father Hooper would be down soon: we could wait in the antechamber. We did, for 15 minutes, after which that same fellow – this time in priestly garb and not at all shabby – descended to greet us. We were surprised and looked it; he was greatly amused and showed it. It was three in the afternoon. Would we care to stay for tea at four? This would allow time for my wife, thanks to some pills provided by Father Hooper, to recover from a particularly bad headache. He explained that he was staying at Keble to care for Kay Farrer, widow of Austin Farrer, the noted theologian and great friend of C. S. Lewis (and Hooper).

We had the tea, then wound our way through Oxford to dinner, and finally to a pub for very late drinks. The conversation was wide-ranging and non-stop – invigorating, uproarious, moving – for Hooper is both a great talker and listener. He was clearly over-burdened, tired and stressed by (we supposed) the tasks of caring not only for Mrs. Farrer but for Lewis' brother as well. We parted, fast friends, at two in the morning. My wife and I had chanced to provide a respite, and with what we would come to see as his customary blend of ingenuousness, spontaneity, sincerity, and gusto, Hooper availed himself of it, generously inviting us to do likewise.

In 1974, while on sabbatical and living in Oxford with my wife and son, I saw how good a priest he was, whether saying Mass or preparing for a counseling session. The depth and thoroughness of his empathy was quite extraordinary, as I saw when he alone realized how badly an aging and ill veteran of World War 11 desired to visit his old Army base but was discouraged by its remoteness. Hooper would not allow the man to give up on the idea—ultimately to his great happiness. It is odd, perhaps, but strangely unsurprising, that those who knew Hooper as a priest did not at all know of his international reputation as an editor.

On November 14, 1984, Hooper met the pope. He had been heavily saddened by the efforts of many groups to use Lewis' legacy for their own ends. These efforts and his resistance to them were "like a huge and heavy stone fastened to [his] heart," he later wrote. "As I knelt and kissed the Holy Father's ring, I felt something rush out of me. . . . I felt as light as a feather as I got to my feet and I knew that 'stone' was gone. Then, sorrowfully, I was aware of something that I had never bothered to consider. When I saw the look of shock and pain on the pope's face, I knew he had taken my burden upon himself." Thereafter, the two, to Hooper's surprise, conversed. First the Holy Father asked if Hooper liked *his* apostolate; then, "Do you *miss* your friend Lewis?" Hooper answered that the gift he received from God in knowing Lewis had continued to grow and that the pleasure of the work had now "blossomed fully." He concluded, "meeting you is the culmination of one, single, happy reality." "Our Walter Hooper," the pope replied, "you are doing very good WORK!"

Very early on some of that work was done by quill pen in a flat on Beaumont Street near the center of Oxford. The pen was a comfort, Hooper has said, helping him stall for time as he framed his next thought; the flat was a steal, if you did not mind climbing nearly 70 steps and huddling in the one heated room ("cozy" and "charming" to be sure) when the outside temperature dropped. He went on to fountain pens (he will not use a ballpoint) and a typewriter. Some ten years ago he moved to his cottage on St. Bernard's Road, and within a few years thereafter he was word-processing. Always a Stakhanovite, he now accomplishes an astonishing amount of work, with long spells at the machine or with manuscripts interrupted by trips to the Bodleian, or by correspondence, or by a phone call from (as I once witnessed) a bishop.

He inevitably walks to and about Oxford –he is an impressive walker – or bicycles to its further reaches. He knows Oxford intimately, of course, and loves it dearly, from the Kilns (Lewis' old house) to the "Bird and Baby" (that is, the Eagle and Child, a pub where Lewis and his friends regularly met and where Hooper has installed a plaque of his own composition commemorating the famous Inklings). He routinely greets strangers, either in passing or when, as happens frequently, they simply drop by unannounced to learn about Lewis. And on a short walk (two miles, say, to a tenth century Saxon church) he will be greeted by passersby with warmth and uncommon frequency. In short, he seems at home.

In fact, though, home has never stopped being Reidsville. His earnest hope is that, one day, he may retire there as a Catholic priest and in that sparsely populated parish carry on the work of an old priest who so helped and impressed him many years ago. I do know that, in his eyes, however significant his accomplishments (many lie ahead, and he is resolute) and however much he labors towards them, they can only add to the significance of his meeting with the pope, which itself so thoroughly encompasses the richness and centrality of his Catholic faith. A modest man who has never considered himself a "Lewis scholar" – indefatigable, amusing, and passionate – Hooper has always subordinated his achievements to the goal he has many times identified: Worshipping, and helping others to worship, the only real Hero we could ever have.

A Seeing Eye

About a year and a half ago, when my son was some months past his twenty-first birthday, I put a hand on his shoulder – worried as I was over his apparent lack of direction – and said, "you know, son, when I was your age I already had the job I still hold and the wife I'm still married to." "Gee, dad," he answered, as he put a hand of his own on my shoulder, "I . . . I'm really sorry."

Now, I do know better than to attempt to tease out the many nuances that reside within that exchange; instead, I will add merely – how we here can delight in the coy ingenuousness of that word – I will add "merely" that, when I was the age my son is now, I helped to found this Society. Please note that it is with much deliberateness, gratification, pride and no small dose of humility – since achievement both great and small mature only with Providential care – that I place that founding in the same class as my job and my marriage, not only in that each has made me who I am, but that each is something rare and invaluable when it is authentic: a unique, healthy and abiding community, a "spill," to paraphrase CSL, from that eternal Community into which we are destined to rise one day. It is in that spirit – of rare achievement and genuine community – that I am so pleased to welcome you to this celebration of the twenty-fifth anniversary of the New York C. S. Lewis Society.

There are empty seats, and the missing pull upon us, as though they have left behind great gaps into which we might tumble: Jack Boies, in whose home we first met; Richard Hodgens, who just could not be unenlightening or stale; and John and Hope Kirkpatrick, without whom there simply would be no Society – all founding members, those – Fr. Bill Eddy, one of the most versatile people at the Society and the best priest I have ever known, and Jerry Daniel, who for ten years carried the Bulletin on his back. Is it a sort of self-pity that makes us mourn their going hence?

Then let it be the self-interest of pure delight that occasions our celebration of seeing old friends: Ruth and Walter Ramshaw, who as much as anyone defined the ethos of this community; Bev Arlton, who from a remove of some three thousand miles still keeps the Bulletin circulating; the indefatigable Neil Gussman; and Byron and Phyllis Lambert, founding members who must be regarded as our godparents.

Thanks to the initiative of Henry Noel and to the resourceful intervention of Linda Bridges at *National Review* – she is now its managing editor but was then an intern, I believe, recommending letters for inclusion in William Buckley's "Notes and Asides" – we met that first time on November 1, a Saturday. I have elsewhere described how my wife, Alexandra, and I felt upon finally entering the Boies home; I will add only that the light, warmth and good fellowship were felt all the more for coming as a reward for our trek through the wet and marshy wilds of Staten Island. Until we entered that portal, I was very glum indeed and Alexandra was about as excited as a puddle.

Not only did Byron act as chair for the business portion of that meeting, but, at the second meeting, also held at the Boies home, on December 12 (the algorithmic Second Friday of Each Month), he read the first paper, which treated of the Incarnation in Lewis. Owing to foul weather, our first anniversary celebration was something of a happy misadventure in the back room of a restaurant. Our fifth and tenth anniversaries included histories of the Society, the former by Eugene McGovern and the latter by Richard Hodgens. The twentieth anniversary was celebrated, notes the Bulletin, with "white wine and a huge birthday cake," and is noteworthy, not only for Fr. Ian Boyd's wonderful paper on Chesterton, but for the responses of Maggie Goodman, Richard Hodgens and Bob Merchant to the question, "Why do we come?" I would not steal the thunder of these various past Bulletins – it is among my purposes to entice you into visiting, or re-visiting, these and many other numbers of our journal, as much for the sheer pleasure you will be afforded as for the compelling history lesson – but I cannot forgo citing three of Maggie's seven reasons:

> 4. I enjoyed being with a group of people at least once a month who don't sing, dance, or act...."
>
> 6. I became addicted to Ruth Ramshaw's cakes!
>
> 7. And finally, I guess I really want the answer to the question, Will Jim Como ever be able to change my opinion of *Till We Have Faces*?"

Oh, Maggie, in the intervening five years have you come to see – *what surely everyone else knows* – that this is the master's greatest artistic achievement? If not, I despair . . . at least until our next meeting – I'm ready for it! – on that much misapprehended triumph.

These recollections suggest, in however abbreviated a fashion, what the Society has been, but not, necessarily, what it is, let alone what it might become (a question that we shall raise at our September meeting). Granted what others sometimes assume about us, I am given pause. As corresponding secretary, Clara Sarrocco is often given a sort of risible *agita*. I do not simply mean the many letters and phone calls that assume a vast organization, ready to respond to the most arcane query, as though we had a highly trained staff; you know, like the people at the New York Public Library or, better yet, at Microsoft, ready twenty-four hours a day and lacking only an eight hundred telephone number. I do not mean only those. Rather, I mean letters like the one that asked if Clara could help the writer trace her family roots back to . . . William Butler Yeats. Or the one asking for – was it not more of a demand, Clara? – a few thousand dollars to facilitate travel to Scandinavia for research on a thesis (and one, at that, *un*related to C. S. Lewis). Or (my personal favorite) the one in which the caller told me that she was re-decorating her daughter's room, perhaps to include a Narnia motif, and asked if I had any design suggestions. . . .

On the other hand, could we ever have imagined, twenty-five years ago, when all knowledge about CSL – his life, the writing of his books, and much of the writing itself – was scarce, hard-won when finally gained, and seemed so fresh, had such enormous *moment* – could we have imagined then how very much we would now know and how easily we could come by that knowledge? How many among us knew of Joy Davidman, let alone of Mrs. Moore or of Warren's alcoholism? The degree of new information and our ready access to it surely represent a sea change – as evidenced, for example, by the *Shadowlands* phenomenon, about which the most remarkable thing that can be noted is that it happened at all.

Why, even the Vicar of Holy Trinity parish, Lewis' church in Headington Quarry, has noticed. Fr. Christopher Hewetson recently wrote to his congregation that he "thinks [they] are forced to improve [their] connection with C. S. Lewis." He continues, "when I came here three and a half years ago. . . . [t]here was a certain 'yes but'. I found it difficult to get a well known preacher to preach at the dedication of the Narnia window. Since then his rating has increased. . . . He was a very committed Christian, a man of great prayer. . . . We must be proud of our connection with him and learn from it. Ideas here would be welcome."

Shall we suggest a Headington Quarry C. S. Lewis Society?

After all, are not we – we here in New York, and we there in Oxford and in Toronto, and at Wheaton, and in Southern California, and in many other places – are not we all responsible, in part, for this great epiphany? I am long past defending against the tiresome canard of 'cultism' still leveled against us in some quarters from time to time. There are cultists, of course, as there are those who would expropriate Lewis' legacy, as there are opportunists who make inflated claims, as there are bad scholars, bad journalists, bad manners, and those of transparently bad faith and highly mutable conclusions. We can only lament, for example, the disingenuous, false, and gratuitously *ad hominem* attacks conducted against our friend and fellow-member Walter Hooper. But the cultism, expropriation and the like are quite literally negligible. I would be satisfied if Lewis were judged as he suggests we judge other authors: by what the attentive and serious readers – namely, us, that great republican *Us* – say about him. Mark further: I would be just as happy that *we* be judged by that very same criterion. No. Far from apologizing, we claim credit, for taking seriously these words of Keats and having applied them to C. S. Lewis:

> A Man's life of any worth is a continual allegory – and very few eyes can see the mystery of his life – a life like the Scriptures, figurative – which such [uncurious] people can no more make out than they can the Hebrew Bible.

Amidst the congeniality and joy, the celebration and Enjoyment – "looking along," as Lewis would have it – there is also some "looking at"; and we *and the world* are the better for it.

For we are a *mediating* community, organic not contrived. We mine, explain and assess; we synthesize, analyze, assimilate, and communicate. And we are not done. I, for one, would like to know much more than I do of *Mr.* Moore, of Arthur Greeves, of Warnie (I believe George Sayer is at work on him), and most especially I would like to know – know better – Albert and Flora, particularly the extraordinary, multi-lingual, mathematical Flora. In fact, I would like extended, reliable, and ruminative joint portraits of Flora, Minto, and Joy – but especially, always especially, of Flora. I could even stand to know more than the virtual zero that is now the case of the workings of C. S. Lewis Pte. Ltd. Too far afield, that last one? I will not disagree. We are far from done with Lewis the artist, critic, historian, scholar, apologist, cultural commentator, and philosopher; less done, even, with Lewis the romancer, novelist, parabolist, poet, journalist, lecturer, teacher, preacher, essayist, broadcaster and (among my own favorites) epistolist. Are we done with the touchstones of his thought, like the Laws of Inattention and Undulation, Quiddity, Sacramentalism, or, my goodness, Joy? With techniques and tactics, antagonists and friends, sources, influences and favorites? And are we done with sheer appreciation?

We have been at it a while, you know. We have been at it, collectively, for longer than the period between the two World Wars; the time separating the start of the Korean War from the end of the war in Viet Nam is less than we have so far had. When we began there was neither videotape nor CD player nor touch-tone telephone nor cable television nor home computer; a hand-held calculator could set you back a couple of hundred dollars. There were men on the moon that year, though, and there was plenty of yahooing at Woodstock, along with the twenty-fifth anniversary celebration of D-Day. The Mets won a world championship, the Knicks were on their way to winning one, but the Yankees were still seven long, long years away from theirs. *Hair* was a hit. We were, to say the least, unlikely; and yet we have outlasted . . . we have outlasted the classic Thursday night meetings of the Inklings.

I have called us a *community*, a word that resonates with ancient Christian chimes (for it is more a Christian concept than it is anyone else's). But as a *society* we have me baffled. We are unincorporated, we have no office, and I would bet our *Eldila* have no juridical standing whatsoever. We have not lasted, let alone lasted so well, because of how we are constituted, I think, but because of what we do. Quite unselfconsciously, absent any overt statement (there is a Charter but none of us knows it), much more by way of custom than by a fixed and deliberate plan (we have had no "standing committees") we have partaken of what Lewis called the Seeing Eye.

If you do have an opportunity to look through back-issues of *CSL* – and I fervently hope that you do – you will notice that our formal title, "CSL," appears for the first time on the March, 1971, issue. As an *eldil* when the choice of title was made, I can report how narrowly that decision was taken. It did not, of the nine options, receive the most first-place votes. "CSL" received the highest *total* number of votes, and so it became our title; but "The Seeing Eye" received the greatest number of first-place votes.

Do you remember Lewis' essay by that name? It is the last in the first posthumous collection that Walter edited, *Christian Reflections*, and it is, I think, among Lewis' most useful. In it he ponders the assertion that Russian astronauts have not found God in outer space and goes on to say things which, typically, seem manifestly self-evident – *after* he has said them, of course, but also said them almost peripherally. Note: "If God created the universe, He created space-time" – so far, so obvious. But next comes the *subordinate clause*: "which is to the universe as the metre is to a poem or the key is to music." Well, of course! That *certainly is* space-time. (All along, of course, there is a really small, soft voice, at least in my head, whispering, "so *that's* space-time.") Thus, Lewis continues, "to look for Him as one item within the framework which He Himself invented is nonsensical." After all, he adds, "a fish is no more, and no less, in the sea" – here he will drive the point home – "after it has swum a thousand miles than it was when it set out. . . . To some, God is discoverable everywhere; to others, nowhere. Those who do not find Him on earth are unlikely to find Him in space. . . . Much depends on the seeing eye." He then proceeds, remarkably – unprecedentedly? uniquely? certainly rarely – to tell us *absolutely nothing more about what he means by such an image.*

Now, if I have led you to believe that I shall presume to say what he meant then, well, I apologize, because this I know from Lewis: You do not look *at* the eye but *with* it – an "it," to paraphrase Ramandu, that allows you to see not what something is made of but what it is. You use the eye; you get behind it, or in it, and you peer out, beyond the melody to the key, and beyond that to the composer; beyond the words to the meter, and beyond that to the poet. Most of us, most of the time, do not have such an eye. But Lewis seems to have it always, and so *he has become our Seeing Eye.* His is the eye of which we have partaken. Those who do *that* together constitute a Lewis Society or, as I would have it, a Lewis Community. And that is precisely what we have been doing for these twenty-five years.

In the old joke three clergymen are asked when life begins. "At conception, of course," answers the priest. Says the minister, "we cannot be certain." "But you are both wrong," asserts the rabbi. "Life begins when the dog dies and the children move out." Twenty-five years ago I had no children; now the dog really *is* dead and our youngest is on the verge of leaving. Twenty-five years ago I not only did not have tenure: I did not know there was a thing so wonderful. Now I'm on the cusp of academic fogeyhood. One cannot be too grateful. The profession of teaching and the family – but especially the family, most especially my wife – have been Seeing Eyes, too; literally (so I believe) miraculous. And that is why I am puzzled by something.

Whereas I have rarely been nervous when speaking to students, and only infrequently nervous – well, something like, but actually a bit more than, nervous – when being "spoken to" by my wife, I have frequently been *at least* nervous when addressing our Society. I do not know exactly why that is, but I would guess that it has less to do with the Eye, that is, with Lewis, per se than with those in whose company I have been privileged to see (and for that company one *really* cannot be too grateful) or with what, finally, we have beheld. And what is *that*?

The answer goes well beyond this occasion, and is even much farther beyond me. But James Stephens seems to have known it. He wrote one of Lewis' very favorite books, *The Crock of Gold*. It ends with a description that easily could have served us as a sort of manifesto for these past twenty-five years; indeed, which might serve as one for this very weekend. It is not an *exact* fit, but, since no matter how good the Eye we are still seeing as through a glass darkly, it is mighty close enough:

> They swept through the goat tracks and the little boreens and the curving roads. Down to the city they went dancing and singing; among the streets and the shops telling their sunny tale; not heeding the malignant eyes. . . . And they took the philosopher from his prison, even the Intellect of Man they took from the hands of the doctors and lawyers, from the sly priests, from the professors whose mouths are gorged with sawdust, and the merchants who sell blades of grass . . . and then they returned again, dancing and singing, to the country of the gods.

Tides of Timelessness

This November the Society celebrates its twenty-eighth anniversary, no special landmark but one worthy of this note at least: "Generation X" does not remember a world without the New York C. S. Lewis Society! More importantly, though, is that that generation, this Society, and most of the *knowing* world are dancing out the year leading up to the centenary of the birth of its earthly master. Now, manifestoes have never been our style, but some surveying, for the sake of perspective, couldn't hurt.

1.
Possessed of a highly nuanced (as well as astonishingly well-furnished) intellect, a religious faith devoid of any thing remotely facile, rhetorical gifts arguably unmatched in this century in their adroitness and versatility, inexhaustible powers of invention, and a will to deploy all of these (one of his oldest friends called him a "genius of the will" above all), C. S. Lewis is a far more complex figure and sophisticated writer than the ease of his style and the popularity of his work suggest. The contours of his current reputation are often mischievous, giving scant sign of the rootedness and richness of his stature as a religious thinker. To apprehend the man and his work one hundred years after his birth, we must do what has thus far not been systematically attempted: compass his breadth, describe the traditions to which he rightly claims allegiance (he hated the word 'originality'), place him in his many contexts, account for his appeals, and finally appreciate the scope and magnitude of his achievement. In short, we must search out Lewis' many *geniuses* and explore the landscape (especially the internal landscape) about which they played.

Virtually on the eve of the centenary of his birth, C. S. Lewis is – as he has been for more than sixty years – the Provident Voice. It was sixty years ago that he diagnosed our age as *post-Christian,* and fifty that he warned us about the "Poison of Subjectivism." He predicted a strength so hideous that Value itself would fall before it, allowing the most horrific re-inventions that would lead not only to *The Abolition of Man,* but to a reign of Nonsense, a deconstructed world of relativism. selfism, and unbelief in which "everything has been seen through," even man himself - a world so transparent as to be invisible.

But the prophet and diagnostician also gave the prescription. The only reason to belief anything, he wrote, is because that thing is *true*. And this axiom he turned upon religious belief, from *a priori* questions such as, is reason valid? (it is) and, by way of it, do we gain access to the *Tao,* or Natural Law? (we do), to the tangible probability of the supernatural and visions of a grand design from questions about prayer, the various genres of scripture, and the possibility of miracles, to the psychology of temptation, the dilemma of the unarrived Second Comings and the "transposition" of nature itself. As literary historian and theorist, critic, and reviewer, his brilliance, wit, authority, and clarity make him still the standard against which others in his chosen field are measured and against which those who would take him on are matched. ("Take him on": in many another field, like boxing, trial law, or movie melodrama he would be, simply, The Man – a hope that merits development, but I think not here.)

To apprehend Lewis, therefore, is to a very great measure to recontextualize the thinking of whatever-we-have-become and thus to re-constitute Meaning itself, for Lewis (who never exhorted nor even argued in *direct* support of a single religious tenet) marshaled great learning with seeming effortlessness in order to clear away obstacles to belief, to make questions accessible to reason, and finally – in virtually all that he wrote – to remind us that we, here, are but sojourners. Whether it is Logical Positivism, psychological or historical determinism, the Enlightenment or Postmodernist fads and fancies, "anything not eternal,'" he insisted, "is eternally out of date."

This apprehension does require a view of Lewis that has not been generally posited, and one somewhat at odds even with his view of himself, or at least that view of which he makes such ample use in the preponderance of his work. Is it not odd, for example, that a man in his early fifties, and a famous apologist of the Faith to boot – a man who had written, but not published, an essay titled "On Forgiveness" in the late forties – is it not odd that *this* man believed that *his own* sins (one sin in particular, I would argue) *had not been forgiven?* Would it not be engaging, then, to establish the sources of the spiritual appeal of this man, since that appeal is bound to rise (at the centenary of his birth in 1998 and for long thereafter) and, like any rising tide, to help lift us all above our and all mere *Zeitgeists?*

The antidote, then, to our self-delusional new 'belief about belief' is a sort of restoration. Robert Jastrow, one of our leading astronomers (former head of the Goddard Institute), once wrote that, having scaled the peaks of knowledge, our scientists peered beyond them into the valley below, only to see the theologians patiently waiting for them to catch up. Well, Lewis is waiting. His appeal has grown commensurate with the want of meaning in our lives (even as his reputation has been mown for a Major Motion Picture, a *Love Story,* yet, for the nineties). To see Lewis at once within a great tradition of religious thought as well as its embodiment (to see him as a member of many different *constellations* of writers: MacDonald, Chesterton, and Lewis; Undset, Wilder, Percy, and Lewis; Swift, Johnson, and Lewis; Hooker, Baxter, Bunyan, Law – and Lewis) would be to arrest much of our intellectual drift, on the one hand, and to reclaim some concreteness, some *fixed hope,* on the other. After all, "people" (as Dr. Johnson said) "need to be reminded more often than instructed."

2.

Not only was he a writer of enormous genius, but he was possessed of very many *geniuses,* lending him a versatility and scope of achievement virtually un-paralleled in this tide of times. And what makes him more compelling yet than his greatness and his geniuses, and the question less puzzling and more engaging, is this: *No one – not even his most ardent admirers, those whose lives he has changed and, in some cases, will brook no criticism of their hero (in short, not even the cultists) – have made these claims on his behalf.* The claim wants vindication, of course. But granted that, the claim is only part of the answer, the rest of which lies elsewhere, in those very *geniuses.*

Examining them is no easy task, for that which I had regarded as obvious turns out to have much greater depth and complexity than meets even the favorably disposed eye (one like my own, for example). In other words, it was not so obvious to begin with; rather, it is. . . *intuitively* accessible. The sociology of reputation (which is really what we are discussing) is no simple matter, after all, but once one has reified into Celebrity it assumes a life of its own. Now, a celebrity is "a person" according to Daniel Boorstin, "who is famous for being well-known." (Case in point: If you are reading this essay nearer the millennium, you might consider one Madonna, of whom you may have heard. Not quite a singer, not much of a dancer, but a world-class tramp, she had a" genius for marketing herself" – *her fans,* who did not bother to defend her singing or her dancing but, finally, only her *celebrity.* She was good at being well-known.) That this has happened to Lewis is beyond dispute, as evidenced by the woefully-simplistic-yet-sappily effective *Shadowlands* (the Attenborough version).

Yet, even much earlier than that (1994-95) the Celebrity Syndrome had struck Lewis. On the one hand, he had been denied the larger ambit of reputation which his work so clearly warrants, being widely regarded — or more likely dismissed — as a "lay theologian" or "popularizer"; on the other, his new and growing readership scarcely knows him as a scholar, critic, reviewer, social commentator, philosopher, poet, and elegant essayist. Thus though greatly esteemed Lewis is, nearly one hundred years after his birth and thirty-five after his death, under- and wrongly-estimated. Owing in part to his anti-modern stance as a self-styled "dinosaur," and to his having been hijacked by some of his readers, the most devoted of whom are Christians who feel besieged or whose concentration is salvifically utilitarian, Lewis seems somehow intellectually marginal. Furthermore, when the breadth of his learning, the distinctiveness and acuity of his thinking, and the scope of his intellectual and literary reach are routinely assumed, they are largely unexamined as such even in the very best studies of his work.

It says nothing of his most impressive genius, antecedent to most of the others, his *commitment to a vocation.* Not too long ago, certainly within the lifetime of a good number of readers of this essay, a well-muscled Christian apologetic was a thriving enterprise, as Chesterton, Frank Sheed, Arnold Lunn, Fulton Sheen and many others held the field. But it seems to have fallen out of favor. *Apologetic,* meaning "defense," has come to mean saying sorry. Austin Farrer, a dear friend of Lewis' and a formidable apologist-theologian, thought that a flourishing apologetic indicated a Faith under strong attack. This is undoubtedly true, but the converse is not. A dramatically diminished apologetic does not mean a Faith secure from assault. It may have been relegated to the basement. Expressions of religious faith, like most other expressions, are subject to trends, of course; and since the thirties (when Lewis began his apologetic career), we have had our share.

It is an aspect of Lewis' apologetic genius that he discerned and understood this problem as well as anyone before or since. He noted that we, post-Christians, are to pagans what divorcees are to virgins. We are no longer wedded to our spiritual convictions, since *conviction* seems to matter so little to begin with. Why does this trivializing of conviction matter so much? Lewis provides the answer, and it is among the most important things he ever wrote, self-evident but not therefore obvious. The only reason to believe in Christianity – not one among many but the *only* one – is the same reason for believing in anything: *that it is true.* Not that it makes us feel good, or even "well"; not that "it works for" us; not even that we are "comfortable" with it, but that it is, simply, true. If one does not think a thing true, then why believe it at all? Indeed, what could *believe* mean in such a case?

The Faith is timeless; its interpreters might make it fresh, but not original. This is precisely the distinction Lewis saw in his own apologetic models, people such as St. Athanasius, William Law, George MacDonald, and Chesterton. And not only does the Faith not change. We live in "enemy-occupied territory." The heresies merely seem new, but they never are. They are, though, unceasing. This is why Lewis was, in one sense, relentlessly militant, a "frontiersman" as Austin Farrer described him. And he went on to say,

> There are frontiersman and frontiersman, of course. There is what one might call the Munich school who will always sell the . . . They are too busy learning from their enemies to do much in defense of their friends. The typical apologist is a man whose every dyke is his last ditch. He will carry the war into the enemy's own country; he will not yield an inch of his own.

One of the most potent and dangerous heresies was that led by Arius during the reign of Constantine in the fourth century. Arius denied the divinity of Christ, holding (as Jehovah's Witnesses now do) that he was not of one substance with God but merely the highest of created beings. But for one man, St. Athanasius (c.297-373), Arianism would have triumphed. "It is his glory," Lewis wrote, "that he did not move with the times; it is his reward that he now remains when those times, as all times do, have moved away." That is why Lewis championed "mere Christianity," no "insipid interdenominational transparency" but the same old set of convictions that St. Athanasius would profess. Lewis continues:

> In the days when I still hated Christianity, I learned to recognize, like some all too familiar smell that almost unvarying *something* which met me, now in Puritan Bunyan, now in Anglican Hooker, now in Thomist Dante. It was there (honeyed and floral) in Francois de Sales; . . . it was there (grim but manful) in Pascal and Johnson. . . . It was, of course, varied; and yet not to be evaded, the odour which is death to us until we allow it to become life. . . .

That is, something worth defending and not be sorry over, orthodox Christianity.

As is true of almost every other idea Lewis propounded, this one is old, at least as old as the apologetic tradition itself (starting with the Apostles, especially St. Paul). Lewis certainly saw himself as firmly within that tradition, an explicator and defender of "mere Christianity," a phrase he adopted from Richard Baxter (1615-1691), a Non-conformist clergyman who was persecuted when he left the Church of England. (One of his best-known books is *A Call to the Unconverted*, 1657.) In a paper entitled "Christian Apologetics" Lewis defined the phrase: "the faith preached by the Apostles, attested by the martyrs, embodied in the Creeds, expounded by the Fathers. . . . Each of us has his individual emphasis: each holds, in addition *to* the Faith, many opinions which seem to him to be consistent with it and fine and important. And so perhaps they are. But as apologists it is not our business to defend *them*. We are defending Christianity; not 'my religion.'"

3.

The chronology of Lewis' life and its major *motifs* are well-established; or so it seems. Lewis himself revealed much, distorted some, and concealed some more. I would argue that much of what he revealed was itself "apologetic," revelations representing choices made from the knowledge of himself that he had worked through, which knowledge could not – not even with Lewis – be all the knowledge there was to be had. By its nature, *Surprised by Joy*, Lewis' sole autobiographical attempt directly to discern shape in his life, could not be the entire story. In fact, he undertook a relentless struggle to derive meaning from experience; that is, from life, literature, and thought. Thus he would attempt, not so much to argue for the tenets of Christianity, as to establish its coherence.

Starting from ordinary experience and addressing ordinary people, he used the lessons he learned to equip his readers with their own interpretive instruments, thereby to discover the next world in this one, in short, frankly to *regress*, as though to a place of origin for which they have always longed. Basic to this enterprise is the premise that each of us must "take the road right out of the self" if we are to become, not "creatures of God but sons of God." Lewis was, and would have us be, *fugitives*. Towards this end he would argue, reconcile, sympathize, browbeat, confess, or (ostensibly) withdraw as the particular circumstances warranted. Most at home with a rhetoric of "demonstration," he got behind platitudes by creating out of the ordinary the *conditions* of belief. And to do so he often turned himself into a *datum* by an act of will, distilling from his own hard-fought struggle those qualities most suited to combat and molding them into a posture most likely to be effective. They become elements of an intellectual, emotional, and imaginative world – not the separate world of, say, Narnia or Deep Space, but an all-inclusive world of discourse bounded by a moral and artistic purpose and incarnating a spiritual vision. He invites the audience to participate in that world, to partake of its texture, and they find it fundamentally familiar and Lewis trustworthy. In it, the irrational bases of modern disbelief are cleared away.

I have mentioned that elusive spectre called reputation. Lewis' has gone through many metamorphoses, from a very great height in the thirties, forties, and fifties as a literary scholar, to another, quite separate towering peak in the forties and fifties as an apologist, to some waning of both shortly before his death, and then to inconspicuousness shortly thereafter. The slow re-ascent began, I think, in the mid-seventies (some dozen years after his death), as more of his work appeared and several societies devoted to the study of that work took hold. At this time academic interest began to take hold as well and a veritable Lewis Industry was established. (In the late seventies an editor from Eerdmans, long one of Lewis' publishers, was heard to cry at a convention of the Modem Language Association, "no more books on Lewis, please!" Eerdmans has since changed its mind.) A plateau was then reached, as many Lewis books, and the contents of books, were (and continue to be) juggled about sometimes between publishers. Whole mini-generations had "discovered" this or that part of Lewis as though it were the *only* part. But enough people had discovered enough parts for Lewis to be a recognizable reference in the works of others. Robertson Davies and Tom Wolfe could drop his name in novels secure in the knowledge that audiences would know whom they meant and why they were dropping it; Walker Percy could use one his most prominent ideas, *Sehnsucht* (or Joy), as coin of the realm; and he could be referred to, or quoted by, Pope John II, Margaret Thatcher, Ronald Reagan and George Bush ("a thousand points of light" is from *The Magician's Nephew*). Knowledge of Lewis' life and work that was unknown and virtually unknowable two decades earlier became common. Finally, Lewis' socio-cultural epiphany was official: Hollywood would exploit him in *Shadowlands*.

All along he has been and remains the same C. S. Lewis, an inspirational and devotional writer, as well as apologist (in the technical sense of that word that I have been using): the North Star in yet another great constellation. (See, for example, the excellent *Mission and Ministry*, XLI, for a modem roll call of some members of that dazzling array.) So we should examine the sources of his appeal – the nature of all his geniuses – always in context: historical, literary, intellectual, or biographical. There would be some surprises, as I was surprised when I realized that Lewis did *not* know himself as thoroughly as he seemed to (there is that rhetorical genius again, concealing as well as revealing). And in looking at Lewis whole we would apprehend his greatest accomplishment, the *re-constitution of Meaning*, for meaning at its core is connectedness (including connectedness to current controversies, the ever-satisfying *relevance*).

For when brilliance, intellectual authority, and breadth of achievement; reliability, reason, reasonableness, and the promise of glory all cohere, the allure is irresistible. Surely sanity must follow?

Why Not IN The World?
Preface to the Third Edition
Remembering C. S. Lewis

Never in the late seventies did I suppose I would be writing a third preface to this book, let alone a quarter century hence; thirteen years after that first edition, when I wrote the second preface, I did not suppose there would be a third. Yet here it is, and after another thirteen years. One never knows, as Anthony Flew has learned. In the twenty-six years since the appearance of the first edition there has been at least this much progress: the famous philosopher-atheist – for fifty years an icon for unbelievers – recently allowed that there probably is a God, albeit of the Deistic sort. His reasons for conversion are complex, being based upon some explanatory weaknesses of Evolutionary theory and on the ability of Intelligent Design theory to pick up that slack. But I do not mention Flew because his new view was influenced by Lewis; in fact, there seems to have been no such influence at all. When I first read the Flew story, his name rang a bell more distant than his repute as an atheist, so I looked him up in Walter Hooper's essay on the Socratic Club in this book, and, sure enough, there he is listed on p. 180 as having spoken to the Club, February 23, 1948, on "Plato and Christianity." Of course, much more than Anthony Flew's religious belief has changed during that same twenty-six-year span.

"What would the world think of us if we don't?"

That was the response of an Archbishop of Canterbury when the Church of England was discussing the ordination of women. On another occasion, near Easter, an interviewer asked the archbishop if he believed in the physical resurrection of Our Lord. Carey replied that he did, "personally." When the interviewer said that many Anglican bishops didn't, the archbishop said he didn't care at all, that "what's true for them is true for them. What's true for me is true for me." The interviewer, finding this difficult to understand, stalked further, asking whether "the Church of England as a whole" believed in the Resurrection. The archbishop, vexed by the move of so many Anglicans to Rome because of the Anglican ordination of women, answered, "the Catholic Church is an 'excluding' church because there's only the one belief which all must follow – that Christ rose from the dead. But the Church of England is an 'including' church because you can be a member no matter what you believe." So we must ask: just who defines this "world" that so preoccupied the archbishop? Are they Asians, Latin Americans, and Africans? Apparently not. I give you the archbishop's world. . . .

As I was participating in a panel discussion on Lewis a few years ago in Philadelphia, a certain Christian professor of Christian theology bemoaned the datedness of many of Lewis' ideas, ideas such as his agreement with the recent re-proclamation by John Paul II that only through Christ may we gain Heaven. This was insufficiently "sensitive" and "intolerably arrogant" for the professor to abide. I pointed out that the encyclical was addressing the point ontologically: His Holiness was simply describing reality. "But," said the professor, "the typical reader would not understand that distinction." My colleague in the New York C. S. Lewis Society, Bill McClain, noted that, first, he'd surely like to meet the "typical" reader of a papal encyclical and that, anyway, aren't theology professors *paid* to point out such "distinctions"? Peter Singer, the ethicist at Princeton University, in his *Practical Ethics*, doesn't bother with Lewis or with anyone else. He merely proclaims, " . . . characteristics like rationality, autonomy, and self-consciousness make the difference. Infants lack these . . . killing them, therefore, cannot be equated with killing normal human beings, or any other self-conscious beings . . . . Their species is not relevant to their moral status." Just so Stephen S. Hall, in his *Merchants of Immortality*: "Constricting our biomedical opportunities in the face of speculative and often ideologically inspired fears is timid, reactive, and bad public policy." He means cloning, abortion, genetic engineering and the like, and the constriction he would forbid is, in the end, God and His commandments.

Richard Rorty, he of the Liberal Project, in his landmark *Philosophy and Social Hope*, strikes a relatively benign stance: "[it should] seem bad taste to bring religion into discussions of public policy." Rorty is the leading American philosopher of a creedless religion, proclaiming that it *should* be a sort of democratic, civil poetry (in fact based on Walt Whitman). Neither does Rorty bother to take note of Lewis, who had prospectively addressed Rorty's position in his "Is Theology Poetry?", refuting the claim that religion is *merely* that. Alas, the European Union hierarchy agrees with Rorty. Its Draft Conference on a Constitution for the European Union acknowledges the Enlightenment, along with many other elements of "common European heritage," without any similar reference to Christianity – except for a gaseous nod to the "spiritual patrimony" of Europe. I almost wax nostalgic for the now dated, but candid, B. F. Skinner, who at least bothered to argue his case for the "abolition of man" when he borrowed that phrase and the title of his well-known manifesto, *Beyond Freedom and Dignity*, from Lewis' landmark *Abolition of Man*. I say almost – for Skinner spawned the likes of: Rodney Brooks, who professes, "it [the abolition of man] will allow us a deeper understanding of what we really are"; and Gregory Stock, who is worse: "it will pierce the veneer of inside things, [and] we may reach the naked soul of man"; and J. Hughes, who could stand in for Lewis' nefarious and damned Weston from *Perelandra*: engineering minds (i.e. conditioning man unto abolition) will "permit us to think more profound and intense thoughts."

To an experienced Lewis reader the irony is palpable. The archbishop thought all this a *new* world. Surely he hadn't read *Abolition of Man* (let alone *That Hideous Strength*); nor had he read that, according to Lewis writing nearly sixty years ago, "we live in a post-Christian age" in which the post-Christian differs from the Christian "as much as a divorcee from a virgin." And he certainly had not met himself in *The Great Divorce*, where the world below awaits the epiphanies of the Episcopal Bishop on how great Jesus *might* have been had he not died at the age of thirty-three. No, the archbishop did not know Lewis, but clearly Lewis knew the archbishop.

Yet the archbishop's world is not the whole of the world, and there is hope. In *Our Posthuman Future: Consequences of the Biotechnology Revolution*, Francis Fukuyama invokes Lewis prominently, making *Abolition of Man* the basis of an entire chapter; when his book came out Fukuyama said in an interview, "when science can offer a father or a mother a prenatal examination of the genetic patrimony of their child and the possibility of modifying it, human nature itself and, what is more, the very dignity of our species, will be at stake." In the same vein is Bill McKibben, who in his well- and amply-reviewed *Enough: Staying Human in an Engineered Age*, writes: "and now we seem bent on making our own children into devices." Why, he asks, "engineer minds in the first place?" Steven Pinker, while writing his *The Blank Slate: The Modern Denial of Human Nature*, could easily have had the Appendix to *Abolition of Man* open at his elbow when he declares that we share Cognitive Development, Language Capacity, and an Emotional Calculus. This last has four dimensions: 1/ other-condemning (contempt, anger, disgust), 2/ other-praising (elevation, awe), 3/ other-suffering (sympathy, compassion, empathy), and 4/ self-conscious emotions (guilt, shame, embarrassment). These, you see, all cut across lines of autonomy, community, and divinity.

He then refers the reader to Donald E. Brown's *Human Universals*, to which Pinker devotes his own Appendix. Unlike Fukuyama, neither McKibben, nor Brown, nor Pinker shows any knowledge even of the existence of *Abolition of Man* or its famous Appendix which tabulates Natural Law (or the *Tao*, as Lewis calls it). Like much of humanity they must have discovered it all on their own. Of course, I cannot know whether or not the archbishop has read these. If he has, then he must realize that even his world is more complex than he had supposed.

Lewis has been describing this world for seventy-five years, ever since the publication of *The Pilgrim's Regress*. I use the continuing past tense – "has been describing" – because Lewis continues to speak directly to our condition. By all means, let us welcome as many "new Lewises" as we can muster, but the old one has lost none of his telling timeliness. Permit me to coin two neologisms. First, Lewis is our reigning *Prophetic Realist*. He is not *sui generis*; Chesterton readily comes to mind. But Lewis, as the young say, "rules" in being: 1/ *broadly moral*; 2/ *keenly, even intuitively, attentive, especially to people*; 3/ *intellectually fresh, penetrating, and analytical*; 4/ *anticipatory*; and 5/ *typically admonitory*. You will have noticed the omission of any reference to religion or theology. The reason for that invites my second coining. Lewis is no more a theologian than he is an *Anthropologian* (clearly not to be confused with an anthropologist!), one who studies, knows, and teaches the inherencies of our nature. In fact, I believe he did philosophy more than anything else, and although he was deeply interested in Being and Time and the like, he was even more interested in the modes of consciousness and logic we use to know them, and most interested in who – what manner of creature – is doing the knowing. As concepts, Personhood, I think, interested him as much as God. And why not? After all, a person "is a machine meant to run on God."

This Lewis – the Philosophical Realist-cum-Anthropologian – is the subject of a favorite parlor game of many of his readers. The game is called, "What would Lewis say about . . . ?" I do not mean we would ask about the archbishop or about, say, homosexual marriage. (Lewis would probably begin his discussion with the current abuse of the word *gay* and take it from there). Rather, I wonder what Lewis would say about, for example, the unreliability of "proprioceptive cues." According to research summarized in a recent *National Geographic*, sensory stimuli (especially those related to sensing our own bodies) are primarily mental constructions! Of particular interest in the article is the favorable reference to Bishop Berkeley, who asserted that the world is real only insofar as it is apprehended. I will not list my reasons for asking Lewis his thoughts on "proprioceptive skepticism" except for this one:

I would want to see if he were *un*surprised by the reference to the bishop, since he claimed Berkeley as the biggest post-classical philosophical influence on his conversion. "So," I can almost hear him saying, "the scientists have finally caught up with the philosopher!"

I wonder how Lewis would review Philip Pullman's *His Dark Materials* trilogy, Pullman being a self-appointed antagonist of Lewis'. And would he have much to say about Dan Brown's hoaxy *The da Vinci Code* or instead choose to discuss its pathetically credulous readers? I suspect the latter and that, invoking his distinction between the reading of the Few and of the Many, he would show their similarity to the bigoted zealots who have made a virtual scripture of the LaHay-Jenkins *Left Behind* series. Or maybe not. Instead he might paraphrase his remark on emotions by saying something like, "trends come and go, but mostly they go." Thirteen years from now, will Pullman's, Brown's, and LaHay-Jenkins' work be remembered, let alone resonate, at all? (Do you remember Carlos Castaneda?) On the other hand, is there any doubt that almost all of Lewis' will? His thought will likely remain the template for describing and responding to our post-Christian world. At least that is what I believe the world will think of C. S. Lewis.

Over these last thirteen years, we will have seen what I thought most unlikely twenty-six years ago: wonderful, and productive, centenary celebrations of Lewis' birth; various versions (all successful) of *Shadowlands*; a PBS documentary (*The Question of God*) comparing the worldviews of Freud and Lewis, particularly unlikely in its favorable view of Lewis and his beliefs; at least three biographical television documentaries (to go with the earlier film *Through Joy and Beyond*); and finally a live-action film extravaganza based upon *The Lion, the Witch and the Wardrobe* (all my digits are duly crossed). These, plus so much very fine scholarship, have led me to reconsider two claims I've made in my Introduction and in the previous prefaces for this book. I still believe that those "who know little will assume much"; but what once was true – that he had become *primarily* a Celebrity, "famous for being well-known" – is, I think, no longer the case. And I no longer believe, as I had claimed in the Introduction, that "there was very little about himself [that Lewis] did not know."

I do not mean that we have a different Lewis. We know nothing now that contradicts what the good people herein say about the man, and their richness of recollection, reflection and expression remain a collective benchmark. Their Lewis may have been, so to speak, amplified by what we have learned since they wrote, but not substantively altered. There has been no revisionism. Nor is there likely to be: Lewis' contemporaries, give or take a half-generation, are gone, as are most of the contributors to this book, and the dispositive Collected Letters offer fascinating ramifications to the trunk of the man but do not re-define him.

Perhaps we, his readers and students, might amplify our own thinking about him. I cannot recall when *The Pilgrim's Regress* has last been seriously studied and adduced in argument; if Lewis' thought serves as a template, then that book surely is the *meta*-template. As I've suggested, Lewis the philosopher must take his place alongside the apologist: more than ever (I believe) we should be paying attention to his views of the Masculine and Feminine, which (he reminds us) are not quite the same as male and female. And Lewis the literary scholar and theorist must be re-cultivated: Why do even students of his work neglect *Studies in Words* and, especially, *An Experiment in Criticism*? Ought not literary critics be comparing, say, Orual to Humbert Humbert, since both are unreliable first-person narrators of the two greatest modern novels in English, respectively *Till We have Faces* and *Lolita*? And have I mentioned Lewis the *existentialist*? Nuances and shadings, each with its own questions, remain abounding.

There is, however, one question I've had enough of for the time being, and that is the question of Lewis' relation to the One True Faith. Other than that he had a pronouncedly Protestant cast of mind, exactly why Lewis never became a Catholic we will never know, in light of which my own opinion is that we Catholics should not too quickly lament his "Obstinacy in Belief" (the title of a Lewis essay defending a similar obstinacy). Browsing *Josef Pieper: an Anthology* – a compendium of Catholic thought by a brilliant and devoted Catholic –one finds *Joy* as a by-product of love, lust as *desire* in despair, *reason* not as mere logic but as man's power to grasp reality, the emptiness of a theology without sacramental faith, Purgatory – can one *not* think of Lewis? Surely (I imagine) these ideas and their expression must have arisen from an actual conversation between these two like-minded men? Lewis was catholic enough not only to become the most artful, popular, and effective English-speaking explicator of and apologist for Christianity in the history of the language, but Catholic enough to have catalyzed a torrent of conversions to Catholicism and to have resided in the heart of our late Holy Father as a favorite.

Elsewhere I have described what I believe to be Lewis' various geniuses, their sources and workings, and the indisputable greatness of the man, of his labor, and of his achievements. Always when I lecture on the master the question that inevitably arises concerns that last. Frequently people want to know what I would have asked Lewis had I met him, or what book I would recommend to a beginning reader. But *always* they ask this: What is Lewis' greatest achievement? My answer, foreshadowed near the beginning of this essay, is, I think, the same that any experienced Lewis reader would give: *Hope*. Gather together all of us who have been deeply, permanently, changed by Lewis – maybe rent Yellowstone Park – and ask each of us to consult our indwelling vital Spirit on the question. Surely our answer would be – *Hope*. Lewis' exaltation and exploration of Desire was not new, but it remains as fresh as our first childhood Joy, always bringing

Hope. And, as variegated as he is, it is everywhere in each of his many aspects. When Walter Hooper met the Holy Father and John Paul II said to him "your friend knew his apostolate – and *did* it" surely *that* is what he meant?

Neo-Narnia?
A Guest Editorial

The events reported recently in the press here and in England and by Bob Trexler in this issue of *CSL* are of a new sort and require an adjusted understanding among casual and devoted Lewis readers alike. That adjustment is a simple distinction. On the one band there is the C. S. Lewis Company: not "The Estate," governed by devoted and knowledgeable Trustees, with a Trust; nor even C. S. Lewis Pte Ltd, advised (if not always influenced) by a most capable, experienced and faithful steward and an experienced publishing agency of Lewis' own choosing, but a corporation designed to market a product for a profit. On the other hand there are the life, and achievements of C. S. Lewis. The Company would now scavenge within the latter so as to exploit a vast, "potterized" market.

Scavenge? The Company has already argued that by publishing new Narnia tales (which are, they say, somehow *not* new Narnia Chronicles) it hopes to "steal past those watchful dragons" of . . . of what? It seems the books (like their author) *are too Christian*. But given the utter absence of any explicit reference to Christianity in the Chronicles, Lewis' own warning against allegorical interpretations of them (*he* taught us about those dragons), and their popularity among readers of all religions and none (as we are reading in letters to editors), we must ask, "hadn't Lewis already seen to that?"

Yet the vectors of neo-Narnia change are all towards homogenization and trendiness. Do we suppose that change toward "diversity" gender-neutral language, and "cultural sensitivity" are out of the question? The cigarette in a famous Lewis photo has already disappeared, and a letter to an English newspaper has called for the elimination of Calormen – too bigoted. Carol Hatcher may have discovered that to portray Lewis' Christianity acceptably requires a "warts and all" documentary with Christianity as one of the warts.

No contortion of logic or of imagination is required to see how the Company and its publisher might believe that stultifying and demeaning devices would, these days, enhance public receptivity and sales. Why not, for example, re-invent the Pevensie siblings multi-ethnically? Or have Uncle Screwtape as a misunderstood victim of narrow-minded stereotyping who is actually combating a vast and hegemonic right-wing conspiracy? (This really *can* be fun, and I would recommend a new contest for the Society if I didn't fear The Company would steal our ideas.)

Lewis certainly feared distortions, and worse: "I am sure you know that Aslan is a divine figure," he wrote to Jane Douglass on June 19, 1954, "and anything remotely approaching the comic (above all anything in the Disney line) would be to me simply blasphemy." But the story is still unfolding. We know very little of the Company, of the remaining estate, or of the relationship between the two (but do see the current *World Magazine);* and without context there can be much confusion. Moreover, especially with the possibility of benevolent motives – more readers for Lewis, and thus more Christians - - in the mix, we are mindful that damage is largely prospective. The purpose now is to get the Company's attention: Mr. Adley should know that "anything goes" is not to be.

He should know it especially from Douglas Gresham, both the avatar of the remaining estate and the Company's most visible and powerful spokesman and gatekeeper: after all, "game, fame and blame," as they used to say in my old neighborhood. "are a matching set." Mr. Gresham's veto power, and veto power it has been, from time to time allows him to keep that gate not only mightily but well – as when, in fact, he forbade a movie company from multi-ethnicising the Pevensies.

And the powers that be must hear it from us. As stewardship mutates into ownership, and a common heritage into a mere product, then surrogate stewards – various Lewis foundations, institutes, study centers, societies, and individuals – must remain vigilant and vocal, at the very least reminding readers, reviewers, critics and scholars of the distinction between Company and Lewis and, with continuous commentary, helping to establish the boundaries of legitimate marketing.

To the Editor

The events reported by Doreen Carvajal ("Marketing 'Narnia' Without a Christian Lion," June 3) have been long in developing and require that all disinterested readers now understand a simple distinction. On the one hand there is the C. S. Lewis Company, a corporation marketing a product for a profit (notwithstanding C. S. Lewis' intent or questions such as artistic vision and authenticity); on the other hand are the life, work and achievement of C. S. Lewis, not merely a Christian apologist and seminal scholar, but a religious thinker of considerable probity, and one of our great English prose stylists.

The Company will exploit a vast and innocent market, arguing (as it seems with respect to Narnia) that it is attempting, in Lewis' words, to "sneak past those Watchful Dragons" of self-conscious and deliberate religiosity. Well, given the utter absence of any explicit reference to Christianity in the Chronicles and their compelling popularity amongst readers of all religions and none, we must ask, "Hadn't Lewis already seen to that?" Surely the era of even speaking of an Estate, of Trustees, and so especially of trust, has ended, no matter the face put upon it by profiteers and frontmen, whereas the era of caveat emptor respecting "Lewis" books is now, finally, upon us.

> *Addendum*: Since this controversy arose and I wrote what you see above, the Company has not desisted. With the pending release of the second Narnia movie, *Prince Caspian*, three more pseudo-Narnia books have been published. These vary widely in quality when judged on their own, but all remain parasitic, deceptive, and (like the worst of the movie merchandise) treacly.

Why I Believe in Narnia

"It is as absurd to argue men, as it is to torture them, into believing" – Cardinal Newman

There once was a little boy who believed that most animals could speak but chose not to and that hovering above him was a cozy world presided over by a panda-like king whose favorite toy was the moon and whose greatest joy was to share it, especially with the boy as he lay a-bed in the dark. He could not explain these beliefs and didn't care to. His imagination had spoken. On the other hand he was not irrational. For example, his father, in response to the son's unrelenting pleas, told the story of Jack and the beanstalk over and over. Finally the boy asked what had happened to Jack and his mother after the giant fell. "Well," said the father, "that giant made a very big hole. So after they dug him out, the mother and Jack made the hole into a swimming pool and built a motel around it. They lived happily ever after." The boy spent long hours trying to figure out where that motel might be and also planning a visit once he had. After all, he had already been to a motel or two and so his imagination, not entirely untethered to reality, had been informed by both reason and experience.

In short, though he was persistent in his beliefs he was not unduly credulous. Even his Russian grandmother learned this. Truly she seemed on too-intimate terms with enchanted forests, children both hungry and lost, and witches who prey upon such children; she was convincing. But he did not for a nanosecond buy a gingerbread house large enough to live in – he had never seen or known of one and it made no sense. He loved his grandmother's telling of "Hansel and Gretel" (there would be none better) only slightly less than he loved his grandmother, which was boundlessly, but he did not for an instant believe it. Moreover, just as his doubt did not swoon at personal persuasiveness, neither did it whither at authority as such. Even though his high school geometry teacher had told the class that no proof for the trisection of an angle did, or could, exist, he worked hard and long to devise just such a proof: the impossibility seemed both unimaginative and unreasonable. Finally, when he satisfied himself that she was right he told her so – but to this day he remains vexed by that impossibility, and wonders. . . .

Then, as a young graduate student, he read *The Chronicles of Narnia*. Needless to say he has believed them (for nearly forty years) ever since.

The question is, How – as an adult – could I? Given the nature of the believer in question, there are some likely explanations: prolonged juvenilism (a kind of fixed sentimental affection coupled with a too-lively imagination), a not unrelated stubbornness (the Trisection Syndrome), rationality-cum-rationalizing (i.e. wish-fulfillment), and an anarchic streak (fairy tales by their nature are subversive). As motives for belief none of these is entirely false. Yet even in combination they do not come close to accounting for my actual assent, as opposed to a pre-disposition to assent. Rather, I believe *The Chronicles* because I regard them as *true*, the only reason (as C. S. Lewis has said) to believe anything. Of course, a claim like this is not geometrically demonstrable and only imperfectly defensible, especially to the skeptic; but, in light of an opportunity to do so, the time has come to try. So after a pass at the preliminaries of What? and How? I will sketch a Why, which though essentially personal *and* private is not uncommon.

1.

What sort of thing are *The Chronicles*? Does this type – do these examples of type – invite belief? As fairy tales their features are typical. Among them: *1/* right and wrong (and often Good and Evil) are concrete (though perhaps not explicit); events show the world to be neither a pinball machine, nor even a plant, even less a tic of Touret's, but the issuance of a Moral Intelligence; *2/* spatial (and less often temporal) dimensions are small; for example, a kingdom might be walkable in two or three days; *3/* marvels (talking animals, visual spectacles) abound, although these may *not* be wondrous within the tale and they are never random; *4/* prohibitions, usually one very pronounced, are prominent; *5/* very often the wonderworld is marked by order and hierarchy; i.e., they are *medieval*; *6/* aspects of everyday life are comfortably, even cozily, rendered; *7/* the protagonists (and perhaps others) often undergo some transformation of social station, marriage, or family; *8/* a character's identity, either stolen, mistaken or forgotten, is often at issue; *9/* portentous signs, often subtle, are central to the plot; *10/* a sense of "remote proximity" is common: long ago perhaps, and maybe far away, but certainly not inaccessible to visitors from outside the wonderworld.

There are other traits, although among scholars there is no unanimity respecting even these ten. But aren't they enough to invite – skepticism? Where is the plausibility, the quotidian recognizability, that would compel belief here and now? Nearly absent, that's where, though not entirely. *The Chronicles* do offer a sibling dynamic, the enervating dread of looming maternal death, Mrs. Beaver being sure to take along her sewing machine on her flight from the White Witch, and other recognizably this-worldly elements. Still: these elements are not enough to elicit a general plausibility or a common recognizability.

So then what might give us a foot (if not a whole leg) up towards belief? In "Education in Fairy Tales," the great Chesterton as usual sees the big picture and suggests a big answer:

> Civilization changes; but fairy-tales never change. Some of the details of the fairy-tale may seem odd to us; but its spirit is the spirit of folk-lore; and folk-lore is, in the strict translation, the German for common-sense. . . . Fairy-tales are the oldest and gravest and most universal kind of human literature. . . . A seven-headed dragon is perhaps a very terrifying monster. But a child who has never heard about him is a much more terrifying monster than he is. The maddest griffin or chimera is not so wild a supposition as a school without fairy-tales. . . . The human race that we see walking about anywhere is a race mentally fed on fairy-tales as certainly as it is a race physically fed on milk.

Common-sense and milk are hard to resist: but surely figures of speech alone won't satisfy our skeptic, at least not initially? On the other hand – initially – *The Chronicles* do make belief appetizing even for the skeptic, in an artistic way, by way of literary features.

Most good tales can overcome bad tellings, until one signature telling (like my grandmother's of "Hansel and Gretel") prevails. In *A Dish of Orts*, George MacDonald writes that the meaning of a fairy tale, unlike that of an allegory, may be different for each reader, but that it "cannot help having some meaning; if it have proportion and harmony it has vitality, and vitality is truth." In the case of *The Chronicles* there are no prior bad tellings: they *are* the signature telling and it invites belief – or at least the initial stage of belief, precisely because of its proportion and harmony, its vitality. In this mere sketch there is no room for acute, extended literary criticism. Instead, I invite the reader to do his own analysis in light of his reading of *The Chronicles*, keeping the following in mind.

In his seminal *The Rhetoric of Fiction* Wayne Booth identifies three narrative features that draw us through a story: *intellectual* fulfillment, cognitive recreation marked by curiosity; *qualitative* allure, the desire for a completion of a pattern; and *practical* concern, our need to witness success or failure with respect to a difficulty encountered by the protagonist. A postulate from Lewis' own neglected *An Experiment in Criticism* sums up the three:

> The exercise of our faculties is in itself a pleasure. Successful obedience to what seems worth obeying and is not quite easily obeyed is a pleasure. And if the . . . exercises or the dance is devised by a master, the rest and movements, the quickenings and slowing, the easier and more arduous passages, will come exactly as we need them. . . . looking back on the whole performance, we shall feel that we have been led through a pattern or arrangement of activities which our nature cried out for.

Now, the appeal of design, the pleasure of purposeful variety, and the promise of resolution, along with "realism of presentation" (not of content, a distinction which Lewis also amplifies upon in *An Experiment in Criticism*), are all palpable in *The Chronicles*. They *engage*, and engagement *is* that initial stage of belief. Common-sense, milk, *and a willing participation by the reader* in the heavy-lifting of persuasion are hard to resist, even for the skeptic.

Among the ingredients in this recipe, however, there is one that is more salient than any other, perhaps more so than all the others combined, and that one is the element of design. *Meaning is connectedness*: that's it. Maybe it's deep, long-lasting, happy, consequential; meaning might be "meaningful." But even if it isn't, it's still meaning. And we are meaning machines. We live for it and off of it. Virtually all we do is a way of seeking it: patterns in find-a-word, clues in a crossword puzzle or *Law and Order* episodes, a cloud that isn't cumulous but is the spitting profile of Aunt Mabel. It's the Word, the great switchboard *Logos, the ground of all connectedness*, there at the beginning, at work in us and through us. Sometimes, when human nature has its way with our teleology, we seek to maximize meaning, and we ask, What's it all about? That's why Ultimate Meaning is connectedness to some Ultimate. Near the beginning of his wonderful autobiography, *The Golden String*, Dom Bede Griffiths (first Lewis' pupil, then friend, and finally a co-convert, though, unlike Lewis, to Roman Catholicism), writes that people "will not be converted by words or arguments, for God . . . is the very ground of existence. We have to encounter him as a fact of our existence before we can really be persuaded to believe in him. To discover God," he continues, "is not to discover an idea but to discover oneself. It is to awaken to that part of one's existence which has been hidden from sight and which one has refused to recognize.... It is the one thing that makes life worth living." Of course, we may not know this, or be aware of it as it happens – to all of us, whether we know it or not. For anyone over the age of sixteen must agree with the poet Keats: "A man's life of any worth is a continual allegory," he wrote, "and very few eyes can see the mystery of his life – a life like the Scriptures, figurative – which . . . people can no more make out than they can the Hebrew Bible."

In short, virtually any design, any design that compels reader-participation, any design that compels reader-participation and promises an Answer as its resolution – *that* design goes beyond mere engagement and becomes a set of Signs, road signs for any pilgrim making this quizzical journey. As Walker Percy has put it, we either *possess* /a *clear* /*problem* or we *participate*/in a *rich*/ *mystery*. Thus do *The Chronicles* compel: they leave no choice, placing the engaged reader in the midst of Mystery.

2.

Here is piece of common reader's sense that picks up where MacDonald leaves off. It is from Kenneth Grahame, the author of one of Lewis' favorites, *The Wind in the Willows*, and a writer who ought to know:

> Vitality, that is the test; and whatever its components mere fact is not necessary. A dragon, for instance, is a more enduring animal than a pterodactyl. I have never yet met anyone who really believed in a pterodactyl; but every honest person believes in dragons – down in the back kitchen of his consciousness.

This idea of belief *in*, not belief *that*, makes all the difference – the difference between the What and How I've mentioned earlier. I am not being coy. If there were space enough I would eagerly undertake a gleeful butchering of the sacred cow of empirically verifiable fact as the *sine qua non* of belief, a genuinely childish premise if there ever was one. Instead, stenographically, I ask the materialist skeptic: If you think your five senses are the only conduits of reality, then wherefore your own *belief in* the inerrant supremacy of feeble sensation?

Like so many other readers I do *believe that*, if Narnia exists, then it and its history are as Lewis says. Masterfully has he pulled off his literary supposal – the What of a fairy tale of a certain kind. And like so many other readers I have been both engaged and compelled by his How. More to the point, even before I make it through some wardrobe of my own my *belief in* Narnia will persist, rather like the reformed Eustace's. In *The Voyage of the 'Dawn Treader'* Eustace believed *that* stars are balls of flaming gas, but he did not believe *in* them – until he met Ramandu, a retired star. What have I met? Do I posses any *believing that* at all? And, when I *believe in* the tales what am I believing? In other words, is there a deeper How and a deeper What than I've sketched so far? Briefly and directly, I believe 1/ *that* Lewis' particular How of a "mediating illusion" – nothing less than an analogous gospel – is vastly instructive and cogent; and I believe 2/ *in* the Sacramentalism that *The Chronicles* thereby impute to the world.

Lewis writes fairy tales because, as he puts it, sometimes they "say best what's to be said." They deal with a spiritual universe. This is why Lewis, who believed that "a book no longer worth reading by an adult was never worth reading in the first place," wrote with children in mind; fairy stories do what's best to be done, which is to lead forth all – every one of us – who would flee as little children. For those who would not may Susan serve as a warning. At Aslan's rising from the Stone Table she asks "How?" *She* would be grown-up and understand. Finally, like some of the dwarfs at the end of *The Last Battle*, she remembers her Self, only herself, and elects not to be fooled, not to "play silly games." From within Narnia, however, where he belongs, a reader sees things differently from Susan. He stands slightly above the children as they encounter the Narnian creator face-to-face and discovers along with them many of the supernatural workings of that world. From this point-of-view he reads *theogony*, how the gods begin. Now, if that reader shifts his perspective to that of many of the Narnian creatures, yet another form emerges: The appearance of gods and of God in the everyday world and their participation in that world is the stuff of *theophany*. What else – for a Narnian, that is – do these stories chronicle? This combination of elements – wonder tale, theogony, theophany – add up to a sacred scripture, the analogue of Judeo-Christian scriptures that I mentioned above.

I use the word 'wonder' advisedly. Lewis: ". . . the *plot*, as we call it, is only really a net whereby to catch something else. The real theme may be . . . something that has no sequence in it, something other than a process and much more like a state or quality," something ineffable – really a *mode of perception*. "Man loves as he sees," wrote Angela of Foligno, a mystic, and "the vision of this world," continues Carolly Erickson in *The Medieval Vision*, is "linked to the vision of the next," ours being a "graphic model of the continuous act of creation" and "conceived as embracing the geographical locus of unseen truths." The difference between Narnia and our world, and between the historical medieval vision and our own, is in precisely this view of the here-and-now. We have forgotten that it points to, compels us towards, and derives from then-and-elsewhere, that this world *figures* the next. The function of *The Chronicles* – their highest merit – is to figure that very process of figuring. *The Chronicles* compel us to see and to know by way of mediation. Such is the "state or quality" of Narnia, and as such should we believe *in* it. One of the ends of the *Chronicles*, then, is to fix our attention on a *means* of surpassing importance: the symbolical principle that invites us to see the next world in this.

The worthy tale casts a spell. In *The Allegory of Love* Lewis suggests the right sort of spell, drawing a perduring distinction. Allegory results when we invent *visibilia* to represent immaterial facts, such as passions. "But," Lewis continues,

> there is another way of using the equivalence, which is almost the opposite of allegory, and which I would call sacramentalism or symbolism. If our passions, being immaterial, can be copied by material inventions, then it is possible that our material world in its turn is the copy of an invisible world. . . . The allegorist leaves the given -- his own passions -- to talk of that which is confessedly less real, which is a fiction. The symbolist leaves the given to find that which is more real. To put the difference in another way, for the symbolist it is we who are the allegory.

Sacramentalism carries the real power. Lewis concludes, "it is for most poets and in most poems by far the best method of writing poetry which is religious without being devotional." In "Is Theology Poetry?" he suggests how sacramentalism beckons here and now:

> The waking world is judged more real because it can thus contain the dreaming worlds the dreaming world: is judged less real because it cannot contain the waking one. For the same reason I am certain that in passing from the scientific point of view [*savoir?*] to the theological, I have passed from dream to waking. . . . I believe in Christianity as I believe the sun has risen not only because I see it but because by it I see everything else.

The children in *Prince Caspian* perfectly exemplify the sacramental importance of the fantasy surrogate-protagonist. Upon arriving in Narnia they are confused, even lost. Before remembering who and what they are, they must know where they are; this knowledge, though, is preceded by a dawning consciousness, a recognition of an altered state of being. Even their stature and physical prowess are enhanced. They are gods, or angels, who once again know themselves as such. The children, and we by way of them, see "theogonically," as god newly arrived. If Narnia may be so visited, may we not be as well? There opens before us a suggestion that there is indeed nothing arbitrary about our world. *The Chronicles* figure forth a world on the brink, a theatrical set (to paraphrase Lewis and Chesterton) about to become the real thing -- a transposition in which our children-surrogates (that is, we) might have a hand.

This linking of worlds, and our ability to discern the next one in this, is at the heart of the Narnian drama, from the ringing of the bell in Charn to the triumphant gallop following the last battle. As some of the voyagers from the ship Dawn Treader move through "drinkable light" they realize that they are approaching the end of the world and the beginning of another. It requires Lucy – who else could it be? – to know that such an end is an end of obliqueness only. The hieroglyphs, signs, symbols and sacraments are a means by which *The Chronicles* direct us. "'It isn't Narnia, you know,' sobbed Lucy. 'It's you. We shan't meet you" back in our world. "'And how can we live, never meeting you?'" Aslan reassures Lucy, and then sends us all back, out of the world figured forth by C. S. Lewis and into a world – our very own quotidian mediating illusion –figured forth by our Creator: "'This was the very reason why you were brought to Narnia, that by knowing me here for a little, you may know me better there'." This (with no apology to Alexander Pope) seems to me to be "a thing whose truth convinc'd at sight we find,/That gives us back the image of our mind." Dom Bede would not be surprised.

Very well: so much for preliminaries.

3.

Rudolph Otto's *The Idea of the Holy* comes to the point of this affirmation. What do we come to know, however obliquely? What is it that works the wonder of baptism upon the imagination? Lewis' answer is holiness, or (as Otto puts it) the *mysterium tremendum*, the *mysterium fascinosum*, and the *numinous:* the fathomless mystery attaching to the sacred being, the deep enchantment of the worshipper as he contemplates that being, and his accompanying awe and fear before the sacred, respectively. The imagination, when kindled by a beam of sacramental longing, encounters holiness. That is its baptism. Then the result is a feeling, an authoritative response that

Lewis called Joy. But there is a catch. "Only when your whole attention and desire are fixed on something else," continues Lewis, "whether a distant mountain, or the past, or the gods of Asgard" – or the creatures and events of Narnia – "does the 'thrill' arise. It" – Joy, of course – "is a by-product." The phenomenon is central to Lewis' experience, thought, and belief, and he has described it amply, not least in his spiritual autobiography *Surprised by Joy*. Joy is Desire, and it is brings us – finally – to the Why. Why do I believe *The Chronicles*?

At its simplest: *I believe them because they re-affirm my desire*. This is certainly not wish-fulfillment; I do *not* desire to believe. Rather, I desire something far beyond a state of my own mind. I desire that Ultimate Connection; I desire Reality; I desire holiness Himself.

Here is how Samuel Alexander argues it in *Space, Time and Deity*, a book which greatly influenced Lewis: "The religious emotion is as unique and self-sufficient as hungry appetite or love. . . . There is in fact no duty to be religious anymore than there is a duty to be hungry. . . . It is in our constitution." St. Thomas Aquinas, in the *Summa Contra Gentiles* (XLVIII) made the point generally:

> Man's last end is the term of his natural appetite, so that when he has obtained it, he desires nothing more. . . . Natural desire cannot be empty, since 'nature does nothing in vain'. Therefore man's natural desire can be fulfilled. But not in this life, as we have shown. Therefore it must be fulfilled after this life. Therefore man's ultimate happiness is after this life.

The actor (and Catholic convert) Alec Guinness, in *My Name Escapes Me* (Journals, Vol. I), makes it more particularly – and most elegantly:

> I think most . . . human beings have the grace [of desire] once in their lives. . . . And of course it is . . . God giving each man and woman, according to their capacity, a glimpse of His promise to them, an impression of what eternity could mean, a glimpse of their *adoption* as Sons of God. . . . We are all left with a feeling of exhilaration, and yet at the same time, hand in hand with its happiness, a sadness that we are unlikely to encounter it again in this life.

And Socrates, as coy as ever in Plato's *The Symposium* (trans. Gordon) takes it one step further, and that without having heard Aslan's reassurance of Lucy: "Now such a person, and every other person who feels longing, long for what is not at hand, for what . . . he lacks, and [this] is the [sort] of thing that desire is of, and Love?" Well, yes. What else? *Who* else, but Love?

St. Augustine *begins* his *Confessions* (I.1) with that Final Cause: "You have made us for yourself, O God, and our hearts cannot find rest until they rest in you."

I had promised a reason both personal and private but not therefore uncommon. Like uncounted billions of people, I have always desired – without realizing it, of course. Realization came only after learning, from Lewis and Plato and Newman, from Sts. Augustine and Thomas, that what I've felt is Joy, and that how it has come to me has been primarily through my imagination, with my own wonderings (those animals who could speak but wouldn't, that panda-like king) and the wonderings of others, above all *The Chronicles*, which never fail to break my heart.

But uncounted *billions*? Yes. If you are tempted to deny the feeling, remember Keats; he means you. If you are, or know anyone, like the materialist skeptic I've mentioned above, then ponder the atheist I recently debated. We had both appeared (separately) in the PBS documentary *The Question of God*, which compared the worldviews of Sigmund Freud and Lewis. At one point he described his conversion to "the scientific point-of-view," which occurred as he watched Carl Sagan's *Cosmos*; specifically, he remembers the "awe and wonder" that cosmic images aroused in him. At that moment he knew: understanding the cosmos, seeing into it, seeing through it, is what he desired most. Online the next day I asked him why he had felt "awe and wonder" in the first place. After all, if we are talking about molecules randomly arranged, then what is the achievement that merits such a response – such a fundamentally religious response, as though he had beheld the . . . *numinous*? He answered by reporting having felt similarly when he had gazed upon Michelangelo's Sistine Chapel. "Sure," I responded, "that Michelangelo was quite an artist, his Chapel quite a design." And then, "but surely neither measures up to the cosmos and its designer?" He protested, but I drove my point home. You've had feelings. Instead of devoting your life to understanding only their Efficient Cause why not inquire into their Final Cause? In other words, "awe and wonder" *mean* something; they are not quite Joy, but they are certainly roadsigns on the way. And billions have known awe and wonder. As Chesterton might have said, it's only common sense.

Some five thousand words ago I (like my hero Socrates) was being coy. By the time I read *The Chronicles* I already believed that being in the presence of the Blessed Sacrament is as real as being at the foot of the Cross during the Crucifixion; and pre-disposition to assent certainly makes a difference to the assent itself. I trust, however, that my preliminaries of Whats and Hows have helped distinguish legitimate pre-disposition from wish-fulfillment. Insofar as desire is a pre-disposition to belief, then I confess that what I claimed at the start to be irrelevant to belief turns out to be its linchpin. Cardinal Newman, in his *Essay in Aid to a Grammar of Assent*, explains:

> We arrive at our most important conclusions not by scientific necessity independent of our own selves, but by the action of our own minds, by our own individual perception of the truth in question under a sense of duty to those conclusions and with an intellectual consciousness.

While discussing the features of the fairy tale I posed as a skeptic, challenging their plausibility and recognizability (especially recognition of a certain similitude), what philosophers call "truth models" of *coherence* and of *correspondence*. But as the submissive reader I am invited by the mediation of *The Chronicles* to think, "so that's how the Old Testament and, more importantly, the Gospels work," and I read them afresh, as the greatest wonder tales ever written; and I think further, "so that's how the world and I are made, respectively to point to and to be called by the next, where, like Lucy, I belong.

The dynamic is straightforward; Desire summons the cardinal virtue of Hope. Like Lewis' own conversion, *The Chronicles* and so much else that he wrote is, more than anything else, about Hope – *the exalted and continual conveyance of which* (not its inspiration; that is from the Holy Spirit) *is C. S. Lewis' greatest achievement*. Yet he is no sentimentalist. With severe honesty (Lewis is a severe thinker and writer), and along with Plato and the others, Lewis reports the results of his own "dialectic of desire," his hunt for the object of his desire: We can never have it here and now. In *The Problem of Pain* he puts it this way:

> All the things that have ever deeply possessed your soul have been but hints of it – tantalising glimpses, promises never quite fulfilled, echoes that died away just as they caught your ear. But if it should really become manifest – if there ever came an echo that did not die away but swelled into the sound itself – you would know it. Beyond all possibility of doubt you would say 'Here at last is the thing I was made for.'

That is what *The Chronicles* are about; that is what they do; and that is why I believe them.

32

An Apologia along the Way

I first discovered CSL by way of an appreciative article from Jeffrey Hart (blessings upon him) in *National Review*. A junior in college and besieged (it seemed to me) for my belief, I thought when reading it, Can this be? A professing, rational, polemically successful, *academic* Christian who, withal, was the commanding figure in his field? I would see for myself. Now in my sixty-first year I look back on some forty-five continuous years of reading C. S. Lewis with delight and gratitude and I pray for the repose of his soul.

Lewis' literary criticism came first – the neglected *An Experiment in Criticism* – and I was undone. Its clarity, cogency, explanatory power, and, especially, its generosity of spirit pre-figured what would recur again and again: Lewis is always fresh. I went on immediately to *The Great Divorce*, having no idea of its subject: it remains among my favorites. Within weeks my wife-to-be was giving me Lewis books, which, as hard now as it is to believe, were not easy to find in the mid-sixties. Alexandra had discovered the Morehouse-Barlow bookstore, now long-gone, on Forty-First Street just east of Fifth Avenue in Manhattan.

Reading Lewis, reading, thinking and talking *about* Lewis, was like breathing pure oxygen, or rather like emerging from some depth into fresh air: Lewis was *my* discovery. So I was astonished to learn that there were many others like me and always had been. (Sometimes one discovers someone and really thinks that he has *discovered* that someone.) Thus did fourteen discoverers begin the New York C. S. Lewis Society in 1969, the oldest of such groups and still the largest and still going strong. These good people, who over the years have come and gone but who mostly have come and stayed (and sometimes have been sneeringly, and falsely, derided as "cultists"), have been collective lab partners and would change my life, not least because among them are my dearest friends. As Lewis puts it, all along a secret Master of Ceremonies has indeed been at work.

I decided to write a master's thesis on *Perelandra* (and eventually a doctoral dissertation on Lewis); I traveled to what was then the Lewis Collection at Wheaton College (an aisle between two library bookshelves which, with its grated door at one end and wall at the other, resembled a monk's cell); I met Clyde Kilby, to whom we all owe so much; I traveled to Oxford (Lewis' cozy, quirky, fitting world, already quite faded forty years ago but even now, distantly, retaining great imaginative appeal); I met and became a lifelong friend of Walter Hooper, to whom we all owe so much; I taught Lewis to many students who have become lifelong readers; I wrote and lectured and opined on radio and television; I became someone regarded as knowing a deal about Lewis; and now I am invited to write this essay. Who knew?

The progression seems to me at once both surprising and inevitable, in fact, Providential. Now, of the many things I may assert of this experience, this one is enduringly true: it has been very great fun – always satisfying, frequently exhilarating, and often downright joyful. And I am certainly more capacious than I would have been without Lewis; like a great *magister* he enacted what the Greeks called *psychagogia*, "leading me forth" and enlarging my soul.

But here I must acknowledge a *caveat*. Lewis is far from my only master, although he is the most influential one. Could this be because he was my first? As a lifelong Catholic I might have encountered Chesterton before Lewis instead of by way of him. Had that been the case, would the great GKC, now a strong second, have been what Lewis became? And I do know that Lewis' influence is itself limited. I already craved argument before reading Lewis (though he certainly feeds that craving better than anyone else). Nor did he influence my love of Spanish or of rhetoric; in fact, I've been having a forty-year argument with CSL precisely about that oldest of liberal arts. He failed in his attempt to teach me to value William Morris, E. R. Eddison, and Sir Walter Scott, just as he was not among those who taught me to cherish, say, Thornton Wilder (who has enriched me in ways quite other than has Lewis), Walker Percy, Sigrid Undset, Robertson Davies, Bishop Sheen, Chaucer (whom Lewis vastly undervalues, I think), Dr. Johnson, fairy tales, beast fables, the Middle Ages, allegory . . .

And yet, as Lewis was teaching me very much about many things (especially those touchstones of his thought, so memorably phrased), I have watched his *habits* of mind and imagination. Lewis the journalist, essayist, and critic; the philosopher and historian; the diarist, letter-writer, and teacher; and Lewis the public figure of public houses, walking tours and devoted friendships; the lover of nature and of conversation with all sorts of folk

– these Lewises have taught me *as a matter of habit* to make distinctions, to see through prejudices, to value things-as-they-are, to track down and to test the unexamined assumptions that underlie received opinion, neither taking the world for granted nor entirely trusting it, and . . . but better I allow Paul Holmer to say it, as he does so well in *C. S. Lewis: the Shape of His Faith and Thought* (my favorite interpretive book on CSL): "his own paragraphs are a sort of splendid conversation. . . . His books create, almost as Kierkegaard did, the living variety of paradigms. . . . Wisdom has to be read off the whole shape of his thought and is not one trick within it."

Towards the end of *The Allegory of Love*, Lewis said of one of his own favorites, Edmund Spenser, that "his work is one, like a growing thing, a tree . . . with branches reaching to heaven and roots to hell. . . . And between these two extremes comes all the multiplicity of human life. . . . To read him is to grow in mental health." In that light I believe I can claim for Lewis what I cannot say of any of the writers I mentioned above: there really is a Lewis for everyone. The Christian thinker, polemicist and devotional writer (in all his various modes, especially the fictional one) – that is, Lewis the Apologist, whose vast influence and popularity certainly have mitigated the influence of those other Lewises – seems to teach his readers what each of us needs most to learn. The particular lesson I needed most to learn was of Hope, and only the late John Paul II even approaches Lewis' achievement in that respect, nor, I believe, could one or many together have taught me to Hope as Lewis has, even had Lewis been my one-hundredth master.

Finally, throughout his work we see Lewis satisfying Alexander Pope's criterion for great poetry: "Something, whose truth convinced at sight we find,/ That gives us back the image of our mind." That . . . *regression* . . . has come by way of *Sehnsucht* – Lewis' conception of, emphasis upon, and evocation of our longing for Heaven. Because of this Joy (as Lewis calls it), I know that I belong Home, from time to time have recognized its call, and above all else desire to be there.

Mere Lewis

Thirty years after his death, C. S. Lewis remains a Celebrity Author: the complacent professor who churned out winsome children's fiction and quotable religious apologetics. That image, confirmed by the recent celluloid treatment, Shadowlands, trivializes the weight and worth of Lewis' achievement, as well as the struggle behind it.

It was the practice of Clive Staples Lewis, while at Magdalen College, Oxford, during the 1940s, to have friends, students, and colleagues to dinner parties. Amid much drinking and even more revelry, Lewis would sometimes perform an astonishing parlor trick. Upon being told how terrible it was to remember nothing, he would reply that it was worse to forget nothing, as was the case with everything he read. Of course, this declaration would be met with incredulity and demands that he put up or shut up. And so he would solicit a series of numbers from the most skeptical guest, which he then would apply to a bookcase, a shelf within that case, and a book upon that shell. The guest would then fetch the specified volume (which could be in anyone of several languages), open to a page of his own choosing, read aloud from that page, and stop where he pleased. Lewis would then quote the rest of that page from memory. Like some supremely gifted performer – a DiMaggio, or a Spencer Tracy – he made it all look easy.

In its astonishing ease, this feat of memory is emblematic of the facility that many people have come to associate with Lewis' life, work, and even his religious convictions. Precisely because of this facility, he has come to be seen as a trivializing Pollyanna, tremendously gifted but of little ultimate consequence as a writer and thinker. The hit movie *Shadowlands* (about Lewis' late marriage to Joy Davidman Gresham) seems perfectly to have captured this celebrity image by presenting him as a sort of "human tea cozy," as one reviewer aptly put it.

To be sure, as icon and phrasemaker Lewis has had considerable appeal. He has been cited by churchmen of the utmost authority (John Paul II and Billy Graham) and by powerful political leaders (Ronald Reagan, Margaret Thatcher, and George Bush, who borrowed "a thousand points of light" directly from *The Magician's Nephew*). Writers from highbrow critic Wayne Booth to children's author Madeleine L'Engle imitate him. Others use his motifs in their work (the notion of "longing" appears in Walker Percy's *The*

Second Coming) or make allusions to him (Robertson Davies in *The Manticore*, Tom Wolfe in *Bonfire of the Vanities*). Most of his 50-odd books have been continuously in print since first publication, the Narnia series alone selling in the millions-per-year range in several different languages worldwide. A patently uneven industry of anecdotal memoirs, biographies (three in the last seven years, the best being *Jack: CS. Lewis and His Times,* by George Sayer, who knew Lewis well), and especially commentary continues to flourish. And a number of societies devoted to the study of his life and the appreciation of his work thrive both in the United States and in England.

For all his popularity – or, more likely, because of it – Lewis has been vastly underestimated. One reason for this may be that he produced no Grand Theories or intricate methodologies. He never wrote what is formally known as systematic theology. In fact, he claimed to be no theologian at all, and he explicitly disavowed – indeed, shuddered at – the notion that his thought might be construed as "original" Far more significant, though, was his rhetorical opportunism. No venue was too modest, no reader too unlearned, no idea too unremarkable to be spared his gifts, if those gifts, however deployed, might profit the reader. Ironically, though this desire and ability to be accessible and adaptive was integral to Lewis' genius, it is also what has so often elicited charges of triviality and shallowness.

This scholar, storyteller, and philosopher deserves a more discerning appraisal. His output to begin with, was huge and various – so much so that it beggars the capacity of most readers. In addition to his books, he saw to print more than 200 short pieces and nearly 80 poems, excluding those in the cycle *Spirits in Bondage* (1919). His essays range from critical, historical, and theoretical to religious, philosophical, and cultural. Devoted readers of his Narnia chronicles for children may not have read, or even know of, *The Screwtape Letters* (1942), surely Lewis' second best-known work and the one that earned him a place on the cover of *Time* in 1947. Lewis the scholar is likely unknown to the readers of his Ransom trilogy of space fantasies. Those who know *Mere Christianity* (1952), based on the wartime BBC radio talks that made his voice the second most recognized in Britain (after Churchill's), probably will not have read either the subtle *Problem of Pain* (1940) or the short analytical essays and the sermons. Still fewer will have read Lewis' lyrical poetry. And almost no one is aware of his long narrative poems.

As it is known conventionally, Lewis' biography seems simple enough. He was born in Belfast in 1898; his mother, Flora, died nearly ten years later. When he was not yet 19 he arrived at University College, Oxford, fluent in Greek, Latin, and French, only to find himself in the trenches of World War I soon thereafter. In 1919, wounded but not disabled (he would carry shrapnel in his chest all his life), and having distinguished himself by capturing a few dozen German soldiers, he returned to the university and took a rare triple first in classics, philosophy, and English literature. He won a permanent fellowship at Magdalen College, Oxford, in 1925, by which time he had been, in his words, "a blaspheming atheist" for nearly 15 years. Although his journey toward conversion began in these years, it did not gain momentum until the death of his father, Albert, in 1928. But even then, this "most reluctant convert in England" became simply a believer in God. Two years later he became a Christian and remained a professing Anglican for the rest of his life.

For the next 15 years Lewis would be more active as author (18 books) and speaker – from broadcasting over the BBC to presiding at the Oxford Socratic Club (which he helped to found) to giving talks at bases all around England for the Royal Air Force – than at any other period in his life. His many great friendships, above all those nurtured within the small circle known as the Inklings, flourished, as did his worldwide reputation and burdensome correspondence (2,000 letters per week at its crest). In 1952, he met and would later court and marry Joy Davidman. In the meantime Lewis moved to Magdalene College, Cambridge, as its first professor of Medieval and Renaissance English Literature. After the publication of still other books and Joy's death in 1960, and now virtually alone with his beloved older brother and dearest friend, Warren ("Warnie"), he began a slow physical decline. Even so, he completed five more books during this period, including the supremely readable *An Experiment in Criticism* and *A Grief Observed* (both 1961). In 1963 ill health forced his retirement; his death on November 22 of that year went virtually unnoticed throughout most of the world, at least until the shock of John F. Kennedy's assassination subsided.

Now, for all its striking achievements and some unlikely spikes, this life is not complicated – nothing to justify the curious observation of the philosopher Owen Barfield, Lewis' lifelong friend, solicitor, and eventual trustee, that Lewis had yet another genius beside the intellectual and the imaginative ones. According to Barfield, in the 1930s Lewis began demonstrating "a genius of the will," a genius crucial to a religious conversion that required an absolute denial of the self. Such a denial in the case of Lewis would be especially difficult in light of his inclination toward self-indulgence. "What I think is true," Barfield wrote in the introduction to *Light on C.S. Lewis* (1965), "is that at a certain stage in his life [Lewis] deliberately ceased to take any interest in himself except as a kind of spiritual alumnus taking his moral finals." This stage also marks the beginning of what must be called his public ministry, for within a year of his conversion he would publish his first Christian work, *The Pilgrim's Regress* (1933), an allegorical autobiography so severe and unsparing in its assault on 20th-century idols that he would later regret its "uncharitable temper." Only a second, and closer, look at his early life can suggest what he converted from.

Flora Lewis, a loyal communicant in the Church of Ireland, must have been a remarkable woman. She witnessed what might have been a miracle at age 12 when, while visiting a Catholic church in Florence, she saw the eyes of a waxen female saint slowly open and gaze at her; later she earned a bachelor of arts from Queen's College, Belfast, in mathematics and logic. (Her son, incidentally, would prove mathematically useless, failing a simple algebra test required for entrance to Oxford; only because he had volunteered for service in the war was the requirement waived and Lewis admitted.) In *Surprised by Joy* (1955), his spiritual autobiography, Lewis described his mother's indulgent ways and likened her death in his 10th year to a continent's sinking into the sea. Alienation from his father, a solicitor, followed, and Lewis lost his Christian faith.

The university years that followed represented a great gap in what was the published autobiographical record. But Lewis' recently issued diary, *All My Road Before Me* (1991), shows a young man out of sync, working to hold a house yet too young and immature to head it, or even to know what he had gotten into. This strange set of affairs resulted from something that few people knew anything about: The house was presided over by the mother of Lewis' slain army buddy, Paddy Moore. Married but separated, Janie King Moore was an attractive 45-year-old woman when Lewis took up with her in 1919, when he was 20. In its early stages their liaison almost certainly included a sexual dimension. (This was neither the first nor final incidence of Lewis' curious sexual interests. As an adolescent writing about women, he signed some letters "Philomastix" – "lover of the switch." During his university days he read much Freud and Havelock Ellis; later he would dream of seductive "brown girls" – a purely symbolic, not racial, coloration – and finally allow that he had greatly underestimated the ease of overcoming the sin of lust.) This unusual household would end only with the death of Mrs. Moore at age 78, when Lewis himself was 52.

During this long ménage, Lewis eagerly undertook an endless round of menial chores, which warranted Mrs. Moore's observation that he was as good "as having an extra servant." Christopher Derrick, a pupil of Lewis' and a philosopher and Catholic apologist in his own right, has remarked on this episode and on Lewis' later marriage that they represent in his friend a sort of self-indenturing to certain women. Lewis' great friend J. R. R.Tolkien, as well as his brother and father, took Derrick's notion a step further and argued that Lewis was unable to resist anyone – especially a woman – in need. (During his life, he gave two-thirds of his income to charity.)

Perhaps the conversion was "no sudden plunge into a new life, but rather a slow steady convalescence from a deep-seated spiritual illness of long-standing," as his brother Warren described it, a sort of recovery from neurotic atheism. Lewis might have admitted as much. But he would have insisted that both simple maturation (as Barfield claimed) and convalescence helped occasion the self-abnegation that was the key to his conversion. Thus, for example, he could marry an obnoxious American divorcée without regard to the loss of offended friends, and he could achieve great commercial success as a Christian apologist with no concern for the academic ostracism that inevitably followed. The point is that Lewis chose to surrender to all the self-sacrificing and unself-regarding ironies of Christian belief, no matter the consequences to his self or to the dues he had to pay. He did not even believe in the rewards of an afterlife when he first became a Christian; it was not until his fifties that he finally believed his own sins were forgiven. With this willful disregard for – and crucial inattention to – himself, he could seem to those around him a curious mix of enthusiastic affection and quite sheer reticence, while all along he was spiritually "regressing," becoming the innocent "little child" that Jesus counsels his followers to be.

As for the charge of "wish fulfillment" traditionally leveled against Christianity and against Lewis in particular: if, to paraphrase Lewis, his purpose had been to fulfill wishes or to live as Polyanna, even a dull man could have thought up something easier than Christianity. And, I would add, Lewis could have contrived a far more convenient life. Pain and grief, like disbelief and doubt, were old acquaintances. In writing about the diabolical Screwtape he said as much:

> Some have paid me an undeserved compliment by supposing that my *Letters* were the ripe fruit of many years' study in moral and ascetic theology. They forgot that there is an equally reliable, though less creditable, way of learning how temptation works. "My heart" – I need no other's – "sheweth me the wickedness of the ungodly."

His best genius used his pain, grief, doubt, and sin, demonstrating not some shallow facility but a triumph of charity. And the fact that he – not the scavenged, half-understood, misrepresented celebrity – could make it look easy allows it to seem possible for the rest of us. In his famous 1954 inaugural lecture at Cambridge, Lewis called himself "Old Western Man" – one who could read old texts as a native and see newer ones from the vantage of a long perspective. His learning and critical skills were so prodigious that, in this case I think, facility must be conceded. Consider this mere inventory:

He introduced the phrase "personal heresy" into our critical lexicon, arguing that we are wrong to read a book in order to find out about its author, or to study an author's life in order to understand his book; to do either is to abort the strictly literary experience, which is what we are after in the first place. He described the medieval foundations of romantic love and charted its literary genealogy, breathing life into a calcified notion of allegory. He defined *Paradise Lost* for a generation, debunking the Satan-as-hero error along the way. ("From hero to general, from general to politician, from politician to secret service agent then to a thing that peers in at bedroom or bathroom windows, and thence to a toad, and finally to a snake.") He revised our understanding of English literature in the 16th century, believably claiming that there was no Renaissance in England and that, if there was, it did not matter. He explained the medieval worldview, so that we can never again consider those ancestors as specially ignorant, superstitious, or irrational. He described precisely those dozen or so concepts (*wit, free,* and *simple,* among others) that so ensnare us when we take them for granted, especially when reading old books. And, by the pure force of his enthusiasm, he got more unlikely people to read more old books than ever before. He taught us (in *An Experiment in Criticism,* much before its time in 1961 and now too unassuming for our Age of Methodology) what we do, should do, and must not do when we read. Finally, he "rehabilitated" dozens of authors and shot out of the air as many literary fallacies as there are critical schools. And all of it is resplendently, improbably readable. In *An Experiment in Criticism* he wrote:

> Literary experience heals the wound, without undermining the privilege, of individuality. There are mass emotions which heal the wound; but they undermine the privilege. In them our separate selves are pooled and we sink back into sub-individuality. But in reading great literature I become a thousand men and yet remain myself. Like the night sky in the Greek poem, I see with a myriad eyes, but it is still I who see. Here, as in worship, in love, in moral action, and in knowing, I transcend myself; and am never more myself than when I do.

This same commitment to making his ideas accessible motivated the direction taken by his storytelling career. "Any amount of Christianity can now be smuggled in under the guise of fiction," wrote Lewis to his friend Sister Penelope. All of Lewis' fictions are allegorical (or "indirect communications," as Søren Kierkegaard would have called them): *The Great Divorce* (1946), about a bus trip to heaven from what is either hell or purgatory; *The Screwtape Letters,* a correspondence from Uncle Screwtape, a chief devil, to his nephew, Wormwood, an apprentice at work on an earthly "patient"; *The Pilgrim's Regress,* the tale of John the Pilgrim's perilous search for the "landlord" and his return home; even his early short story, "The Man Born Blind," about a man whose sight is restored but who dies in an attempt to "see light." These and other fictional works have us encounter God as we do in reality. Or, as Lewis put it, "God is everywhere but is everywhere *incognito.*"

The most striking manifestation of Lewis' obliqueness is his use of a first-person narrator – a queen, no less – in the masterpiece *Till We Have Faces* (1956). A retelling (or rather a setting right) of the Cupid and Psyche myth, it is an ostensibly simple study of a brilliant, resentful and belligerent mind as it comes to confront its own self-serving, bigoted, militantly anti-divine delusions. The book's themes and motifs are pure Lewis – the poison of possessive love, the dangers of an inflated and unrestrained self, and the concrete immanence of the supernatural, among others. The flavor, however, is new in Lewis: the purpose is broadly moral but not explicitly didactic, the structure (especially its concentrically arranged time frames) is far more intricate than that of anything else he wrote, and the psychology of the protagonist is not only uncharacteristically ugly but ambiguous, too. Queen Orual is in despair, does not know it, but is on the brink of finding it out. In the end, it is she who will *be* found out, along with the rest of us for whom she is a surrogate.

Even in his children's books, Lewis was able to adumbrate the most complicated Christian themes and make them appealing to his reader. Consider Lewis' most remarkable speech, from *The Silver Chair* (1953), a Narnia book. Puddleglum the Marshwiggle has accompanied two children on a search for a lost prince who has been held captive by the Queen of Underland. The four are finally free, thanks to Puddleglum's heroic action, though still deep in the queen's cave, when she comes upon them and begins casting a spell to convince them that there are no real trees and stars, nor even a real Asian, the great lion who sang Narnia into creation. At the point of psychological and spiritual collapse, Puddleglum speaks:

Suppose we have only dreamed, or made up, all those things – trees and grass and sun and moon and stars and Aslan himself. Suppose we have. Then all I can say is that, in that case, the made-up things seem a good deal more important than the real ones. Suppose this black pit of a kingdom of yours is the only world. Well, it strikes me as a pretty poor one. And that's a funny thing, when you come to think of it. We're just babies making up a game, if you're right. But four babies playing a game can make a play-world which licks your real world hollow. That's why I'm going to stand by the play-world. I'm on Asian's side even if there isn't any Asian to lead it. I'm going to live as like a Narnian as I can even if there isn't any Narnia.

There is a textbook here on the Christian notion of faith (as well as on a number of other more esoteric concepts). Trusting in what you once knew to be true, what your reason and even senses showed you to be true, is crucial when that reason and those senses are clouded – by passion, or by the dismal spell cast, say, by the loss of a spouse – crucial if we are to live as God intended. Lewis realized, as Paul Holmer put it in C. S. *Lewis: The Shape of His Faith and Thought* (1976), that how we live "determines what [we] love and finally even know . . . [a] frame of life and mind within which some things become accessible to us."

Lewis' polemical genius worked as unrelentingly as, but even more single-mindedly than, the scholar and the storyteller to make a great variety of ideas comprehensible to the general reader. Moreover, his essays – from "The Humanitarian Theory of Punishment" to "Dangers of National Repentance" to "The Poison of Subjectivism" to "The Necessity of Chivalry" – could not only shed light upon, but virtually settle, any number of current debates. He would make short work for example, of an oxymoron such as "the politics of meaning." But like Aslan, Lewis was not tame. There are in his work improbable opinions that surprise even his most devoted readers: that young lovers should live together without marriage if the alternative is infidelity; that anti-obscenity and -sodomy laws are useless at best; that a truly Christian economic order would have more than a small bit of socialism in it; that Darwin is useful even if he mistook a metaphor that was already in the air (Keats used a version of evolution in *Hyperion*); and that Freud has much to teach us (though a good deal less than he thought). No one has offered a more astute, trenchant, or profoundly Christian critique of the impact of European civilization upon the New World than Lewis:

> The English . . . conceived [colonization] chiefly as a social sewage system, a vent for 'needy' people who now trouble the commonwealth and are daily consumed with the gallows. . . . Nor was the failure [of English exploration] relieved by any high ideal motives. Missionary designs are sometimes paraded in the prospectus of a new venture: but the actual record of early Protestantism in this field seems to be "blank as death'."

In an essay entitled "Religion and Rocketry" he expands upon the theme, claiming that "the missionary's holy desire to save souls has not always been kept quite distinct from the arrogant desire, the busybody's itch, to (as he calls it) 'civilize' the (as he calls them) 'natives.'" And in "The Seeing Eye" he contemplates the possibility of humanity meeting an alien rational species:

> I observe how the white man has hitherto treated the black, and how, even among civilized men, the stronger have treated the weaker... .I do not doubt that the same story will be repeated. We shall enslave, deceive, exploit or exterminate.

After his conversion, Lewis explicitly committed his will and his rhetorical genius to his apologetic vocation. In "Christian Apologetics" he defined the scope of that task: "modern man is to a pagan what a *divorcée* is to a virgin"; that is, "we live in a post-Christian world": "a century ago our task was to edify those who had been brought up in the Faith: our present task is chiefly to convert and instruct infidels. Great Britain is as much a part of the mission field as China." Among our contemporary biases is the tendency to reverse the ancient attitude and to approach God as the accused; "if God should have a reasonable defense. . . . the trial may even end in God's acquittal. But the important thing is that Man is on the Bench and God is in the Dock." In the final analysis, says Lewis, "Christianity is a statement which, if false, is of *no* importance, and, if true, of infinite importance."

The territory that most engaged Lewis was the concept of personhood. "You can't study people," he said, "you can only get to know them." Personality and our view of it was of particular concern. Recall for a moment Barfield's observation that Lewis willed his own self-disregard, and then consider this declaration of purpose:

> I have wanted to . . . expel that quite unchristian worship of the human individual as such which is so rampant. . . . I mean the pestilent notion . . . that each of us starts with a treasure called 'Personality'. . . and that to expand and express this . . . is the main end of life.

This theme of self-centeredness, its dangers and (of course) its antidotes, lies at the center of Lewis' philosophy of human nature. One of his works that is better known than read is *The Abolition of Man* (1943), ostensibly "Reflections on Education with Special Reference to the Teaching of English in the Upper Forms of Schools," or so its subtitle would have us think. In fact it is a diagnosis and a prophecy: when subjectivism is rampantly triumphant and natural law has been, not refuted, but "seen through," we begin to "innovate," first on nature (Lewis was environmentally alert long before the cant began), then on animals (he was also a vehement anti-vivisectionist), and finally on our favorite subject, the Self, which we will "condition" unto extinction. Any eugenicist or "harvester" of human fetal tissue should take note, if not of this book then of its horrifying fictional correlative, *That Hideous Strength: A Modern Fairy Tale for Grown-Ups* (1946), the last book of the space fantasy (or Ransom) trilogy. In it Lewis both raises to glorious heights and lowers to terrifying depths the idea of geniuses as tutelary spirits, especially the particular "genius" of our century, a totalitarian death wish.

Not shy about depicting evil or its motive, he would have agreed with Edmund Crispin's detective Gervase Pen, who remarked, "1 always think that psychology is wrong in imagining that when it has analyzed evil it has somehow disposed of it." But he nowhere uses upon his reader the stick of eternal punishment in any way remotely resembling the enervating horror of, say, Jonathan Edwards, the 18th-century New England philosopher and divine, whose "Angry God" has his arrows of vengeance poised at our hearts, ready to be made "drunk with our blood" for nothing more than "His mere pleasure." Instead, Lewis tells us (in his 1941 sermon "The Weight of Glory") that "all the leaves of the New Testament are rustling with the rumor" that we will not always be on the wrong side of the door. "Some day, God willing, we shall get in." Lewis thought that nothing could be more pleasurable than salvation. The final page of Lewis' final book, *Letters to Malcolm: Chiefly on Prayer* (1964), contains a typically delectable image of just that:

> Then the new earth and sky, the same yet not the same as these, will rise in us as we have risen in Christ. And once again, after who knows what aeons of silence and the dark, the birds will sing and the waters flow, and lights and shadows move across the hill, and the faces of our friends laugh upon us with amazed recognition.

"Joy," he says, "is the serious business of heaven."

But Lewis understood the limits of volubility and of argument, the dangers of verbal facility and intellectual smugness. I believe they frightened him. In *The Great Divorce* (1946), the only passenger on the bus to heaven who stays all the way to the end is the man who does not utter great rhetorical pronouncements. At the end of *Till We Have Faces* the queen writes, in what is her lucid and convincing complaint, "only words, words; to be led out to battle with other words." And in *The Silver Chair,* Puddleglum's great affirmation follows upon his determining action: with his naked webbed foot he stamped on the fire that is part of the witch's verbal spell. Lewis said he never understood a doctrine less than when he was just done defending it.

Such humility seems ironic coming from "a genius of the will," much the same way his obsession with accessibility seems ironic. But the humility, the will, and the accessibility are all of a piece. Lewis' will was the instrument of his Christian conversion, which occasioned the denial of self. Only then could Lewis be at the disposal of those for whom – owing to his great intellectual, imaginative, and literary gifts – he could do great good. Thus his astounding ability to bring Christianity to so many (precisely what invites the dismissive charge of superficiality) is the product of one of the more complex emotional and intellectual processes. What he said about his beloved Edmund Spenser and *The Faerie Queene* can be applied to the scholar, storyteller, and philosopher-apologist:

> His work is one, like a growing thing, a tree . . . with branches reaching to heaven and roots to hell. . . . And between these two extremes comes all the multiplicity of human life. . . .To read him is to grow in mental health.

His former pupil Peter Bayley was among the few to attend his funeral. He has since written that "there was one candle on the coffin as it was carried out into the churchyard. It seemed not only appropriate but almost a symbol of the man and his integrity and his absoluteness and his faith that the flame burned so steadily, even in the open air, and seemed so bright, even in the bright sun."

Name and Title Index

(Excluded are fictional characters' names, names and titles in illustrative lists (esp. 19), and names and titles from the notes and bibliographies for ch. 14, 15, 17, 18, and 20)

Adams, Father Walter, 63
American Conservatism: An Encyclopedia, 179
Amory, Mark, 67
Anthroposophy, 5, 81
Alexander, Samuel, 55, 71, 74, 235
  Space, Time and Deity, 55, 74, 235
Aristotle, 31, 118, 147, 152, 159
  Poetics, 139
  Rhetoric, 169, 170;
  Metaphysics, 169
Arius, 211
Arnold, Matthew, 91
Askin, Dr. John ("Doc"), 5
As One Devil to Another, 120
Atkins, J.W.H., 150
  English Literary Criticism, 150
Atlantic, 47
Attenborough, Richard, ii, 19, 20, 22, 26, 28, 35, 209
  (dir.) *Shadowlands*, 19-30, 35, 177, 209, 219
Auden, W. H., 11, 94
Aunt Twiggy, v
Bacon, Leonard, 120, 130
Baker, Leo, 5, 59
Barfield, Owen, 5, 6, 22, 52, 61, 110, 145, 173, 185, 187, 194, 245, 247, 251
Barfield, Mrs., 5
Bate, Walter Jackson, 144
Baxter, Richard, 41, 212
  A Call to the Unconverted, 212
Bayley, John, 50
Bayley, Peter, 27, 253
Beevor, Anthony, 88

The Fall of Berlin, 1945, 88
Belloc, Hillaire, 88, 193
Berg Collection, New York Public Library, 120
Berkeley, George (bishop), 218
Bettleheim, Bruno, 76
  The Uses of Enchantment, 76
Bloom, Harold, 147
  The Visionary Company, 147
The Bodleian Library, viii, 184, 196
Boehme, Jacob, 74
Boies, Jack, viii, 199, 200
Book News and Reviews, 95
The Book of Common Prayer, 67
Boorstin, Daniel, 209
Booth, Wayne, vii, 104, 122, 230, 243
  The Rhetoric of Fiction, 104, 230
Borges, Jorge Luis, 103
Boswell, James, 5
Boyd, Father Ian, 200
Branches to Heaven, vii, 117
Brando, Marlon, 28
Brett, Jeremy, 24
Bridges, Linda, 84, 189, 200
  Strictly Right, 189
British Broadcasting Corporation (BBC), 19-23, 39-41, 64-65, 118-119, 244, 245
Brooks, Rodney, 217
Brown, Dan, 219
  The daVinci Code, 219
Brown, Donald E., 82, 218
  Human Universals, 82, 218
Browne, Sir Thomas, 174
  Religio Medici, 174

Buckley, Wm. F., Jr., 87, 189, 200
Buddha of Kamakura, 15
Bultitude, Mr., 15
Bush, George (H.W.), 213
Bush, Douglas, 145, 148-149
  English Literature in the earlier Seventeenth Century, 148;
  'Paradise Lost' in Our Times, 148
  The Renaissance and English Humanism, 149
Calabria, St. Giovanni, 61, 63, 65
Carvajal, Doreen, 224
Castaneda, Carlos, 219
Catholics United for the Faith, 64
Cary, John, 49
Cecil, Lord David, 146
  The Oxford Book of Christian Verse, 146
Chaucer, Geoffrey, iii, 5, 150, 171, 240
Chesterton, G. K., 7, 11, 44, 73, 75, 78, 88, 89, 200, 210, 218, 229, 234, 236, 240;
  "Education in Fairy Tales," 229;
  The Everlasting Man, 7;
  "Morality and Philosophy," 74
Christian Science Monitor, 47
Christie, Agatha, 52
Churchill, Winston, 244
Clarke, Arthur C., 145
  Childhood's End, 145
Coghill, Neville, 156
Collins (pub.), 47
Colson, Charles, 189
Commonweal magazine, 47
Como, Alexandra (author's wife), i, v, vii, 183, 195, 200, 239
Como, James (author), 1-iii
Como, Jim (author's son), 20, 124, 199
Constantine, Emperor, 211
Coogan, Daniel, 166
Crispin, Edmund, 251
C. S. Lewis: A Companion & Guide, 53-56
C. S. Lewis at the BBC, 39-41
C. S. Lewis at the Breakfast Table, 71, 72, 87
C. S. Lewis Pte Ltd., 33, 55, 202, 223
Cuneo, Andrew, 57
Cunningham, Richard, 96
  C. S. Lewis: Defender of the Faith, 96
Curtis Brown (literary agent), 55, 193
Daiches, David, 140
  Milton, 140
Daily Telegraph, 50
Daniel, Jerry, 199
Dante, 150, 172, 211
Darwin, Charles, 250
Davidman (Gresham Lewis), Joy, ii, 13, 20-29, 51, 52, 55, 62, 66, 67, 145, 174, 178, 201, 243, 245
Davies, Robertson, 54, 213, 240, 244
  The Manticore, 244
de la Mare, Walter, 11
de Meun, Jean, 154
De Mille, Cecil B., 21
De Niro, Robert, 19
  (dir. and acted) *A Bronx Tale*, 19
de Rais, Gilles, 148
de Rougement, Denis, 95, 149, 150, 151
  Passion and Society (Love in the Western World), 95, 149
Derrick, Christopher, 50, 51, 77, 246

Name & Title Index

Desiree, 28
Dewey, John, 88, 91
DiMaggio, Joe, viii, 243
Donne, John, 109, 110
Dorset, Lyle, 36
Dougherty, Jude B., 88
  John Dewey and the Decline of American Education, 89
Douglass, Jane, 224
Dryden, John, 158
  The Conquest of Granada, 158
Dunbar, Nan, 66
Dyer, Wayne, 76
Dyson, Hugo, 33, 63
Eastman, Brian, 22
Eddison, E.R., 142
  The Worm Ouroboros, 142; *The Mezentian Gate*, 142
Eddy, Father William, 199
Edwards, Jonathan, 252
Eerdmans Publishing, 72, 213
Eliot, T. S., 11, 63, 79, 164
Ellis, Havelock, 5, 246
Empson, William, 87, 140, 145, 157
  Milton's God, 140
Erickson, Carolly, 232
  The Medieval Vision, 232
Eternity, 48
European Union, 81
Every, Brother George, 147
Farrer, Austin, 27, 195, 210, 211
Farrer, Kay, 195
Fenn, Eric, 40
Ferrara, Abel, 28
  (dir.) *The Bad Lieutenant*, 28
Fifth Avenue Presbyterian Church, ii
Fitzgerald, Robert, 153
  (trans.) *The Odyssey*, 153
Flew, Anthony, 215

Frankl, Viktor, 111
Fraser, Lady Antonia, 49
Frazee, Harry, 79, 84
Frazer, Sir James George, vi, 131, 132
  The Golden Bough, vi, 131
Freud, Ernest, 67
Freud, Sigmund, 5, 43, 44, 67, 219, 236, 246, 250
Fukuyama, Francis, 82, 217
  Our Posthuman Future, 82, 217
Garcia Marquez, Gabriel, 102
Gehringer, Mary, viii
Geoffrey of Vinsauf, 171
  Nove Poetria, 171
Gibb, Jocelyn, 66
Gielgud, Val, 39
Godfather, The, 28
Gollancz Memorial Prize, 156
Goodell, Henry, 85
Goodman, Maggie, viii, 200, 201
Gorgias, 65
Gould, Stephen Jay, 44
Grahame, Kenneth, 231
  The Wind in the Willows, 231
"Great War, The," 6, 61
Green, Roger Lancelyn, 14, 46-52
  C. S. Lewis, A Biography, 14, 46-52
Greeves, Arthur, 4, 7, 15, 61, 62, 187, 194
Greeves, Mrs., 4
Gresham, David, 23, 55
Gresham, Douglas, 20, 23, 29, 32, 55, 194
Gresham, William, 21
  Nightmare Alley, 21
Griffiths, Alan Bede (Dom), i, 22, 107, 112, 150, 230, 234
  The Golden String, 107, 230
Guardian, 120

The Guardian, 50
Guinness, Alec, 24, 235
  My Name Escapes Me, 235
Gunn, Alan M.F., 154
  The Mirror of Love, 154
Gussman, Neil, 200
Habakkuk, 111
Habermas, Jurgen, 98
Hall, Stephen S., 81, 216
  Merchants of Immortality, 81, 216
Hamilton-Jenkin, A. K., 5
Hart, Jeffrey, 156
Hatcher, Carol, 223
Harvard Medical School, 43
Havard, Robert, 64
Hawthorne, Nigel, 19, 21
Hamlet, 16
Harcourt Brace Jovanovich, 47
Hardie, Christian, 55
Hardie, Colin, 55
Hardwicke, Edward (and Sir Cedric [father]), 24
HarperCollins (publisher), 55
Hart-Davis, Rupert, 67
Hart, Jeffrey, 239
Head, R. E., 184
Hen, T. R., 95
  Longinus and English Criticism, 95
Hewetson, Father Christopher, 201
Hill, Forbes I., v
Hillegas, Mark, 49
  (ed.) *Shadows of Imagination*, 49
Hitler, 59, 64, 88, 119
Hoare, Dorothy M., 151
  The Works of Morris and Yeats in Relation to Early Saga Literature, 151
Hodgens, Richard, viii, 200
Holmer, Paul, 176, 241, 250
  C. S. Lewis: the Shape of His Faith and Thought, 177, 241, 250

Hook, Mrs., 163
Hooper, Madge, v
Hooper, Walter, ii, v, vii, 3, 14, 26, 36, 39, 47-52, 53-56, 57, 61, 64, 75, 95, 144, 175, 184, 185, 187, 188, 191-97, 202, 203, 215, 221, 240;
  C. S. Lewis, A Biography, 14, 46-52;
  Through Joy and Beyond, 219
Hopkins, Anthony, ii, 20, 23, 24, 26
Horace, 160
Howard, Thomas, 73, 155
  The Achievement of C. S. Lewis, 73
  C. S. Lewis: Man of Letters, 106
Hughes, J., 217
Hume, David, 89
Hynes, Samuel, 71, 72, 76
Inkling, The, 11, 13, 196
James, Henry, 102
Jarret-Ker, Martin, 50
Jastrow, Robert, 76, 208
  God and the Astronomers, 76
John Paul II, Pope, 36, 194, 195, 196, 216, 221;
  Crossing the Threshold of Hope, 176
Johnson, Dr. Samuel, 144, 189, 209
Jones, Dorothy, v, viii
Jones, Ernest, 49
Jones, John, 152
  On Aristotle and Greek Tragedy, 152
Joseph Pieper: an Anthology, 220
Jung, C. G., vi, 74, 131, 133, 134, 161
Keats, John, 107, 147, 202, 231, 236, 250
Ker, W. P., 95, 152, 154
  Form and Style in Poetry, 95, 152
Kierkegaard, Søren, 174, 241

Name & Title Index

Kilby, Clyde S., viii, 11, 12, 14, 15, 73, 195, 240; *Images of Salvation*, 73; *A Mind Awake*, 14
Kilns, the (Oxford home), 24, 35, 184
Kingsley, Ben, 36
Kingsmill, Hugh, 153
  Matthew Arnold, 153
Kipling, Rudyard, 74
Kirkpatrick, Hope, viii, 199
Kirkpatrick, John, viii, 199
Kirkpatrick, William T. ("The Great Knock"), 18, 87, , 128, 146
Knox, Ronald, 153
  Ronald Arbuthnot Knox, 153
Kolbitars, 5
Kreeft, Peter, 189
Lambert, Byron, viii, 200
Lambert, Phyllis, viii, 200
Lasch, Christopher, 79
  The Culture of Narcissism, 79
Law, William, 211
Leavis, F. R., 11, 49, 80 , 91, 147
LeHay and Jenkins, 219
  Left Behind, 219
L'Engle, Madeleine, 243
Lepenies, Wolf, 88
  The Seduction of Culture in German History, 88
Lewis, Albert (Pappy), 3, 4, 6, 17, 18, 22, 23, 59, 61, 245
Lewis, C. S. (works only):
The Abolition of Man, 76, 79, 81-83, 90, 208, 217, 218, 251;
The Allegory of Love, 62, 144, 156, 157, 164, 165, 233, 241;
All My Road Before Me, 3-8, 22, 191, 246;
"The Anthropological Approach," 163;
"The Apologist's Evening Prayer," 112, 119, 174;
"As the Ruin Falls," 173;
"Bluspels and Flalansferes," 161;
Book reviews (several titles, in varying venues), 143-54;
Boxen, 191;
"Bulverism," 91;
"Christian Apologetics," 251;
"Christianity and Culture," 150, 161;
"Christianity and Literature," 175;
Christian Reflections, 83, 175, 203;
The Chronicles of Narnia, I, 31, 52, 66, 72, 124, 129, 223, 227-37;
Collected Letters, Vol. II, 57-59;
Collected Letter, Vols. I-III, 61-67;
C. S. Lewis' Letters to Children, 61;
"The Dangers of National Repentance," 250;
The Dark Tower, 54, 191, 192;
"De Descriptione Temporum," 55, 84, 152;
"Delinquents in the Snow," 92;
"Democratic Education," 91;
The Discarded Image, 119, 157, 171;
Dymer, 5, 7, 8, 77;
"The Efficacy of Prayer," 184;
English Literature in the Sixteenth Century, Excluding Drama, 62, 144, 149, 157, 171;
"Equality," 94;
An Experiment in Criticism, 71, 75, 80-84, 97, 102, 151, 158, 164, 165, 220, 230, 239, 245, 248;
"Forms of Things Unknown," 102;
The Four Loves, 11, 24, 103, 107, 151;
God in the Dock, 83;

The Great Divorce, 18, 102, 103, 118, 161, 173, 183, 217, 239, 249, 252;
A Grief Observed, 55, 62, 118, 173, 175;
"The Hegemony of Moral Values," 5;
"The Humanitarian Theory of Punishment," 92, 179, 250;
"Is English Doomed," 90;
"Is History Bunk?", 90;
"Is Theology Poetry?", 216, 233;
The Last Battle, 18, 71, 72, 103, 164, 232;
The Latin Letters of C. S. Lewis, 61;
"Learning in War-Time," 91, 170, 184;
The Letters of C. S. Lewis, 61;
Letters to an American Lady, 61;
Letters to Malcolm, 108, 118, 173, 252;
The Lion, the Witch and the Wardrobe, 24, 32, 66, 127, 219;
Literary Essays, 83, 191;
The Magician's Nephew, 20, 173;
"The Man Born Blind," 248
"Man or Rabbit?", 176;
Mere Christianity, 41, 77, 110, 113, 114, 173, 244;
"Modern Man and His Categories of Thought," 90;
Miracles, 78, 83, 89, 103, 163;
Narrative Poems, 54;
"The Necessity of Chivalry," 91, 250
Notebooks, 172;
Notes on the Way, 91;
"Obstinacy in Belief," 220;
"On Forgiveness," 65, 208;
"On Living in an Atomic Age," 90, 177;

"On the Reading of Old Books," 90;
Out of the Silent Planet, 118, 129;
"The Parthenon and the Portative," 91;
"The Poison of Subjectivism," 208, 250
Perelandra, vi, viii, 5, 16, 102, 119, 124, 127-38, 162, 163, 217, 240; as *Voyage to Venus,* 127 ;
The Personal Heresy, 43, 140, 144, 157, 163;
The Pilgrim's Regress, vii, 62, 90, 118, 164, 165, 218, 220, 245, 248;
Prince Caspian, 225, 233
Poems, 54;
"The Poison of Subjectivism," 207
Preface to 'Paradise Lost', 119, 139-41, 144, 163, 171;
Present Concerns, 64, 83, 175;
"Priestesses in the Church," 91;
"Private Bates," 93;
The Problem of Pain, 25, 62, 78, 83, 237, 244;
"Prudery and Philology," 93;
"Psychoanalysis and Literary Criticism," 163;
Queen of Drum, 119;
"Reason," 178;
Reflections on the Psalms, 164;
'Rehabilitations' and Other Essays, 157;
"Religion and Rocketry," 251
"Revival or Decay?", 98;
The Screwtape Letters, 59, 62, 65, 95, 117-26, 172, 244, 249;
"The Seeing Eye," 175, 203, 251;
"Sex in Literature," 92;
"Shelley, Dryden, and Mr. Eliot," 163, 164;

The Silver Chair, 119, 173, 249, 253;
Spirits in Bondage, 7, 244;
Studies in Medieval and Renaissance Literature, 144;
Studies in Words, 157, 220;
Surprised by Joy, 3, 6, 22, 28, 51, 52, 55, 65, 128, 212, 235, 246;
That Hideous Strength, 15, 76, 89, 110, 124, 217, 252;
They Stand Together, 15, 61, 77, 188, 191;
Till We Have Faces, vii, 55, 66,75, 83, 101-116, 119, 156, 170, 173. 177, 220, 249, 252;
"Transposition," 170, 184;
"The Trouble with 'X'," 176;
"Vivisection," 92;
The Voyage of the 'Dawn Treader', 232;
"The Weight of Glory," 170, 184, 251;
"Willing Slaves of the Welfare State," 94;
Lewis, Flora Hamilton (Mammy), 12, 17, 18, 20, 22, 23, 26, 61, 65, 67, 244, 245
Lewis, Warren ("Warnie"), vi, 4, 5, 8, 22, 23, 24, 35, 54-55, 58, 59, 62, 63, 66, 184, 193, 201;
Brothers and Friends, 11-18; *Letters of C. S. Lewis* (ed.), 13; Lewis Family Papers, 12; *The Splendid Century*, 13
Light on C. S. Lewis, 245
Linden, Bill, viii
Lindskoog, Kathryn, 65
Little Lea (Lewis Irish home), 12
Lolita, vii, 66, 220
London Times, 156, 157
Loth, David, 95, 148

The Erotic in Literature, 95, 148
Louis, Joe, 124
L. Russ Bush Center for Faith and Culture, vi
Louis XIV, 13
Love Story, 209
Luther, Martin, 126
MacDonald, George, 73, 108, 210, 229
Diary of an Old Soul, 108; *A Dish of Orts*, 229
Macmillan, Harold, 158
Madonna (performer), 88, 209
Magdalen College (Oxford), 20, 28, 183, 243, 245
The Magic Never Ends (doc.), 35-36
Maisie (young woman helped by Lewis), 5
Manchester Guardian, 128
Manlove, Colin, 36
Martlets, 5
Maritain, Jacques, 73
Creative Intuition in Art and Poetry, 73
Martin, Thomas L., 83
(ed.) *Reading the Classics with C. S.Lewis*, 83
Massachusetts General Hospital, 43
Mathew, Father Gervase, 50
Maurois, Andre, 49
Mazzello, Joey, 20, 24
McClain, Bill, 216
McGovern, Eugene, viii, 27, 200
McKibben, Bill, 82, 217
Enough, 82, 217
Mead, Marjorie Lamp, 11, 12, 14, 15
Michelangelo, 236
Medium Aevum, 145
Meileander, Gilbert, 74

The Taste for the Other, 74
Mendieta, Eduardo, 98
　(ed.) *Religions and Rationality*, 98
Menninger, Karl, 76
　Whatever Happened to Sin?, 76
Merchant, Bob, viii, 200
Milton, 5, 138-41
　Paradise Lost, 139-41, 248
Mitchell, Christopher, 36
Mission and Ministry, 213
The Modern Language Association, 213
The Monastic Realm, 85
Moore, Janie King ("D," "Minto"), 3, 4, 5, 6, 7, 12, 13, 15, 16, 17, 23, 35, 40, 51, 59, 61, 62, 63, 65, 66, 67, 77, 121, 201, 246
Moore, Maureen, 3, 4, 17
Moore, Paddy, 3, 15, 246
More, Paul Elmer, 58,63
　The Sceptical Approach to Religion, 58, 63
More, St. Thomas, 126
Morehouse-Barlow bookstore, 239
Morris, William (trans. *Odyssey*), 17, 151
　The Death of Jason, 151
Muggeridge, Malcolm, 11, 49, 50
Nathan, George Jean, 158
　The House of Satan, 158
National Anti-vivisection Society, 92
National Geographic magazine, 218
National Review magazine, i, 20,189, 200, 239
New Blackfriars, 50
New Catholic Encyclopedia, 169
New England Anti-vivisection Society, The, 92
Newman, John Henry, Cardinal, 176, 227, 236;
　An essay in the Aid of a Grammar of Assent, 176, 236
New Statesman magazine, 49
New York C. S. Lewis Society, i-iii, v-viii, 188, 189, 193, 199, 205, 207, 239
　CSL: The Bulletin of the New York C. S. Lewis Society, v, 200
New York Times, 47, 71, 76, 155
New York Times Book Review, 90
Neylan, Mary, 66
Nicholi, Armand, ii, 43, 44
　The Question of God, ii, 43, 219, 236
Nicholson, William, 22, 23, 26, 28
Noel, Henry, I, 200
Observer, 49, 94
Observer Weekend Review, 95
O'Connor, Flannery, 102
Olivier, Lawrence, 24
Otto, Rudoph, 74, 234
　The Idea of the Holy, 74, 234
The Oxford English Dictionary, 73, 75, 97
Oxford Magazine, 95, 145
Oxford Socratic Club, 43, 245
Papworth, Mr. (Household dog), 17, 24, 29
Paradise Lost, 139, 140, 248
Parkin (Warrens' army buddy), 13
Pascal, Blaise, 125
　Pensees, 125
Patrick, James, 83
　The Magdalen Metaphysicals, 87
Paxford, Fred, 17
Payne, Leanne, 73
　Real Presence, 73
Peake, Mervyn, 145
　Titus Alone, 145

Name & Title Index

Pellican, Conrad, 153
Penelope, Sister, 66, 75
Pepys, Samuel, 5
Percy, Walker, 76, 102, 113, 175, 177, 178, 231; "The Message in the Bottle," 175; *The Second Coming*, 76
Petrarch, 150
Phillips, Justin, 39
Philosophical Society, 5
Picasso, Pablo, 158
Pidcoke, Faith Sand, 48, 49, 50
Pinker, Steven, 82, 217
The Blank Slate, 82, 217
Pitter, Ruth, 29, 55, 66
Plato, 50, 65, 235, 236
Gorgias, 119; *Symposium*, 235
Pollack, Sidney, 23
Pope, Alexander, 155, 176, 241
An Essay on Criticism, 155, 176
Pottle, Frederick, 57
Pound, Ezra, 191
The Prelude, 16
Pullman, Philip K., 32, 33, 219
His Dark Materials, 219
Punch, 98
Queens College, Belfast, 22, 246
Queens College (CUNY), v
Quintilian, 178
Ramshaw, Ruth, 200
Ramshaw, Walter, 200
Reagan, Ronald, 213
Republic (Plato), 5
Reynolds, Barbara, 57
Richards, I. A., 49
Rieff, Phillip, 176
The Rise of the Medieval Church, 85
Robinson, Sugar Ray, 118
Rogers, Merril, vi
The Romance of the Rose, 144, 156

Rorty, Richard, 81, 216
Philosophy and Social Hope, 81, 216
Royal Air Force, 245
Rudolph Steiner School, ii
Russell, Bertrand, 44
Ruth, Babe, 79, 84
Sagan, Carl, 44, 76
St. Augustine, 169, 174
Confessions, 235;
De Doctrina Christiana, 169
St. Athanasius, 75, 211
St. John-Stevas, Norman, 50
St. Paul, 107
St. Thomas Aquinas (*Summa*), 5, 73, 194
Summa contra gentiles, 235
Sagan, Carl, 236
Cosmos, 236
Sammons, Martha C., 72
A Guide Through Narnia, 72
Sarrocco, Clara, viii, 201
Saturday Review of Literature, 47, 120, 129
Saurat, Denis, 139
Sayer, George, 29, 202, 244
Jack: C. S. Lewis and His Times, 244
Sayers, Dorothy L., ii, 14, 40, 66, 144
The Man Born to Be King, ii
The Poetry of Search and the Poetry of Statement, 144
Schakel, Peter, 106
Reason and Imagination, 106
Schmelling, Max, 124
Schwarz, W., 152
Principles and Problems of Biblical Translations, 152
Shelburne, Mary Willis, 63
Sibley, Brian, 23

Singer, Peter, 81, 219
  Practical Ethics, 81, 216
Simmons, Jean, 28
Skinner, B. F., 81, 217
  Beyond Freedom and Dignity, 81, 217
Smith, Logan Pearsall, 147
  Milton and His Modern Critics, 147
Solzhenitsyn, Alexander, 73
Song of Bernadette, The, 21
Spectator, 50, 93, 94
Southeastern Baptist Seminary and College, vi
Spenser, Edmund, 241, 253
  The Faerie Queene, 253
Staten Island, New York City, 183
Stebbins, Lyman, 59, 64
Steiner, George, 75, 152
  The Death of Tragedy, 75, 152
Steiner, Rudolph, 61
Stephens, James, 8, 188, 205
  The Crock of Gold, 8, 188, 205
Stock, Gregory, 217
Stone, Irving, 49
Sunday Telegraph, 92
Sunday Times, 49
The Tablet (U.K.), 57
Tauran, Jean-Louis, 81
Teresa, Mother, 194
Thackery, Wm. Makepeace, 54
Thatcher, Margaret, 213, 243
Theology magazine, 95
Thomas, Mary, 29
Tillyard, E.M.W., 140, 157
  Milton, 140; *The Personal Heresy*, 140;
  Studies in Milton, 140
Tim (family dog), 62
Time magazine, 19, 21, 244
Time and Tide, 91

Times Literary Supplement, 50, 57, 145
Tolkien, J. R. R., 13, 14, 22, 33, 52, 63, 66, 247;
  The Hobbit, 144; T
  The Lord of the Rings, 144
Tolstoy, Leo, 14
The Three Musketeers, 17
Tracy, Spencer, 243
Travers, Michael, 85
Treneer, Laura, 39
Trexler, Bob, viii, 223
Triumph magazine, 50, 76
20th Century: An Australian Quarterly Review, 92
Undset, Sigrid, 102
  Kristin Lavransdatter, 102
Van Doren, Carl, 191
Van Rooy, Bev Arlton, vii, 200
Wade Center, Wheaton College, viii, 14, 25, 144, 177, as Lewis Collection, 240
Waugh, Evelyn, 67
Wain, John, 14, 22, 52
Waldock, A.J.A., 140
  'Paradise Lost' and Its Critics, 140
Walmsley, Lesley, 90
  (ed.) *Essay Collection*, 90
Walsh, Chad, 49, 71
  The Literary Legacy of C. S. Lewis, 71, 74, 106
Ward, Michael, 57
Waugh, Evelyn, 144
  Rossetti, 144
Weaver, Richard, 75, 169, 178
  "The Cultural Role of Rhetoric,"169; *Ideas Have Consequences*, 75
Webb, Alison, 20
Welch, James, 40

Weston, Gordon, viii
Whichcote, Benjamin, 149
Whitman, Walt, 216
Wilde, Oscar, 67
Wilder, Amos, 76
  Thornton Wilder and His Public, 76
Wilder, Thornton, 75, 78
  The Angel That Troubled the Waters, 75;
  The Alcestiad, 75;
  The Eighth Day 76
Williams, Charles, 64
Wilson, A. N., 57, 59
Wilson, Edmund, 11
Winger, Debra, ii, 20, 24, 25, 26, 36, 177
Wolfe, Tom, 213, 243
  Bonfire of the Vanities, 243
Wolfson, Harry, 111
Woods, Thomas E., 85
  How the Catholic Church Built Western Civilization, 85
Wright, N. T., 189
Wroxton College, 184
Yeats, William Butler, 201
Ziman, H. D., 50

Related Titles from Zossima Press

C.S. LEWIS & PHILOSOPHY AS A WAY OF LIFE

A Comprehensive Historical Examination of his Philosophical Thoughts

ADAM BARKMAN

C.S. LEWIS
VIEWS FROM
WAKE  FOREST

Walter Hooper　　　　Michael Travers
James Como　　　　　　Editor
& many Others

www.ingramcontent.com/pod-product-compliance
Lightning Source LLC
Chambersburg PA
CBHW031237290426
44109CB00012B/328